Seasonal Living
with
Splendid Poetry

By Crystal Tai | 盧琪綺 著

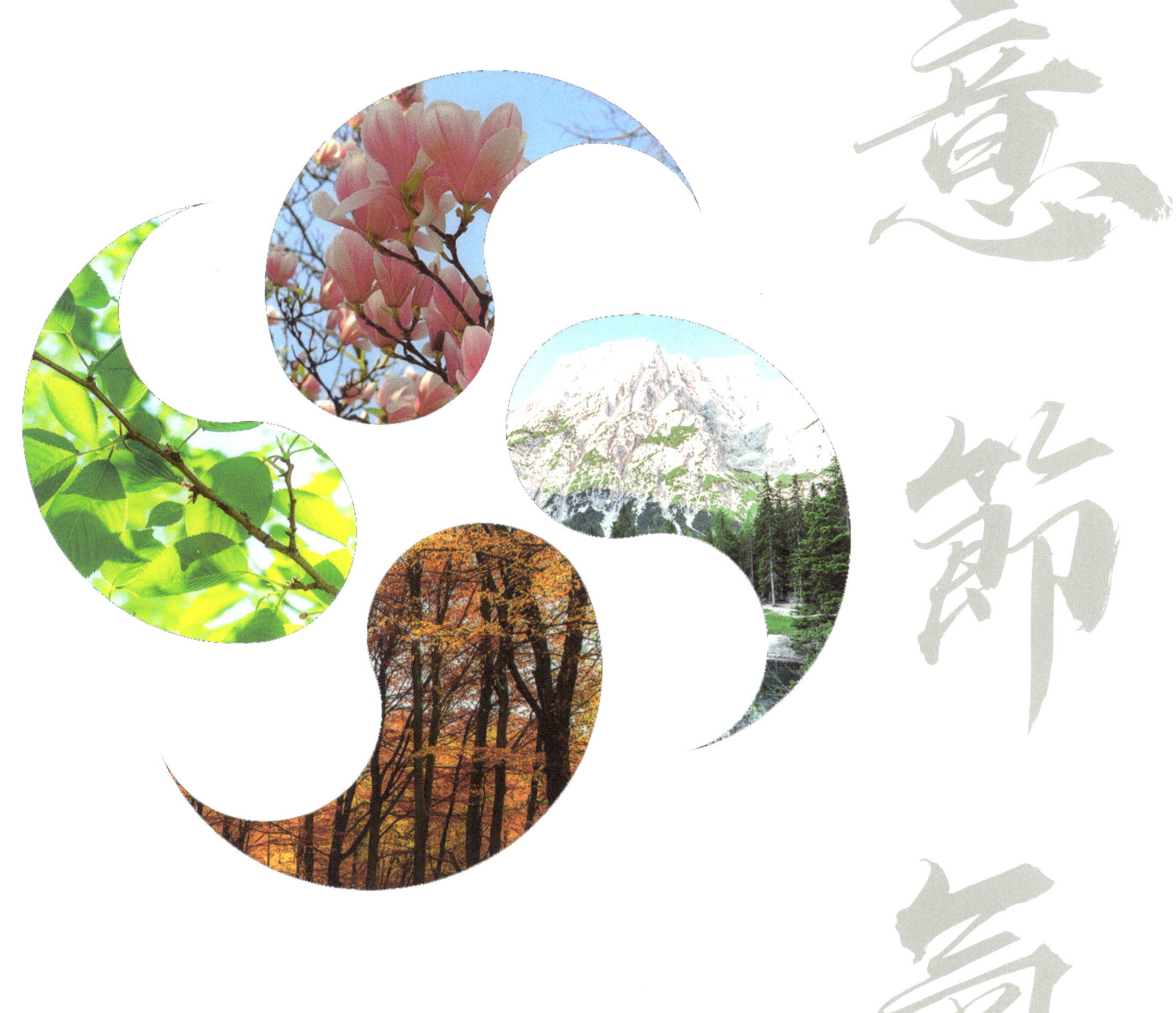

iCultures Publications | 美國文化橋出版社

Author: Crystal Tai 盧琪綺
Translator: Crystal Tai 盧琪綺
Calligrapher: Lillian Don 董楊麗蓉
Editor: Qi Li
Design and Production: Qi Li
ISBN: 9798868964046
LCCN: 2023921313
Size: 8.25 x 11 inch (280x210mm)

Publisher: iCultures Publications | 美國文化橋出版社
Developmental Editor: Phoenix Huan
Address: 3769 Peralta Blvd. Ste I , Fremont, CA 94536
Website: www.eastwestart.org / www.icultures.org
First edition published in the US, Feb 4, 2024
Email : info@eastwestart.org

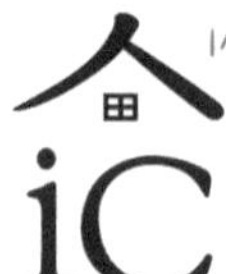

To My Husband Andy Li-Cheng Tai,
who supports all my creative pursuits through the seasons
獻給時時相伴相助的夫君戴立崢

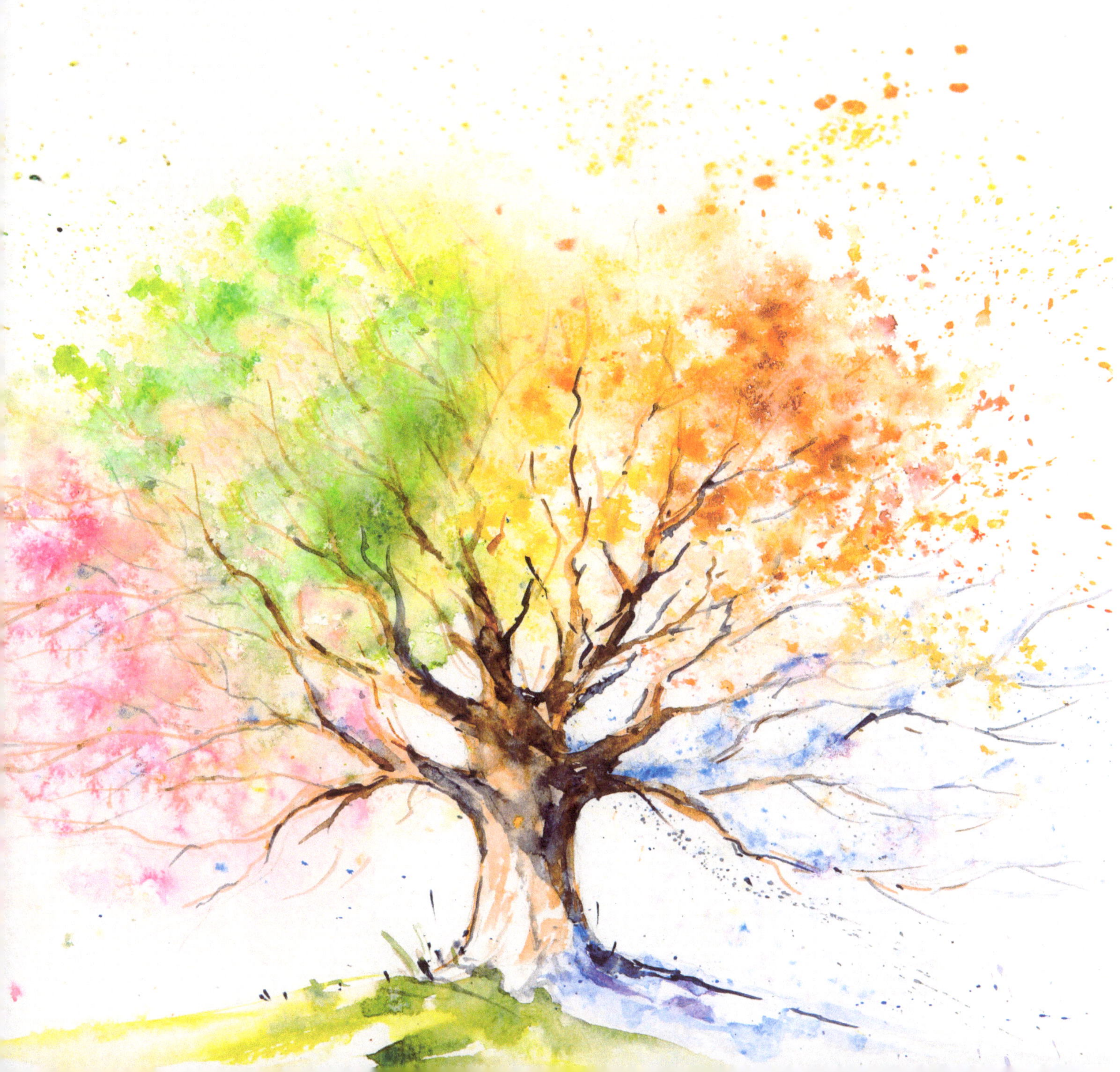

目 録 Table of Contents

- 秋 -

- 冬 -

Introduction
Time-tested Wisdom for Seasonal Living

In the 21st century, sustainability is an increasingly pressing issue, making it more and more desirable to live in tune with nature for the sake of energy conservation. In addition, scientists have found seasonal living to have health benefits.

According to a scientific paper published in the Proceedings of the Royal Society B on Oct 22, 2015, "seasonal human morbidity is observed in non-infectious diseases, including heart disease, cerebrovascular disease, and lung cancer."[1] The same article points out seasonal changes in immunity and in the occurrence of infectious diseases as well.

It is not exaggerating to say that humans are seasonal beings. There is no doubt that seasonal living is worth embracing. The only question is how.

There are many guidebooks that teach how to live in harmony with the changing seasons. What distinguishes this book, however, is the wisdom it brings from one of the world's oldest cultures.

Seasonal living was already a way of life in ancient China, based on a lunisolar calendar invented in 104 BC.[2] The solar section of the lunisolar calendar divides the year into 24 periods, each with weather conditions and natural phenomena that set it apart from the other 23.

These 15-or-16-day-long periods are called the solar terms in English. The United Nations Educational, Scientific and Cultural Organization inscribed the 24 solar terms on the Representative List of the Intangible Cultural Heritage of Humanity in 2016.[3]

Although the 24 solar terms have gained international recognition since 2016, they are still unfamiliar to the vast majority of the world's population. They need to be introduced to English speakers worldwide through a book like this one.

This book consists of bilingual chapters to target not only English speakers but also Chinese speakers. Better yet, each chapter contains a classical Chinese poem with a seasonal theme and an elegant English translation to make the

---

1   Stevenson, T. J. et al. "Disrupted seasonal biology impacts health, food security and ecosystems." Proceedings of the Royal Society B, Oct 22, 2015. https://royalsocietypublishing.org/doi/10.1098/rspb.2015.1453

2   Cheng, Rongjing. Everything about the Taichu Calendar (漢太初曆考). Shanghai: Shanghai Bookstore Publishing House, 1994.

3   "The Twenty-Four Solar Terms, Knowledge in China of Time and Practices Developed through the Sun's Annual Motion." United Nations Educational, Scientific, and Cultural Organization. https://ich.unesco.org/en/RL/the-twenty-foursolar-terms-knowledge-in-china-of-time-and-practices-developed-through-observation-of-the-sun-s-annual-motion-00647

reading experience more enjoyable.

Prior to the 24 chapters, here is a diagram of the 24 solar terms.

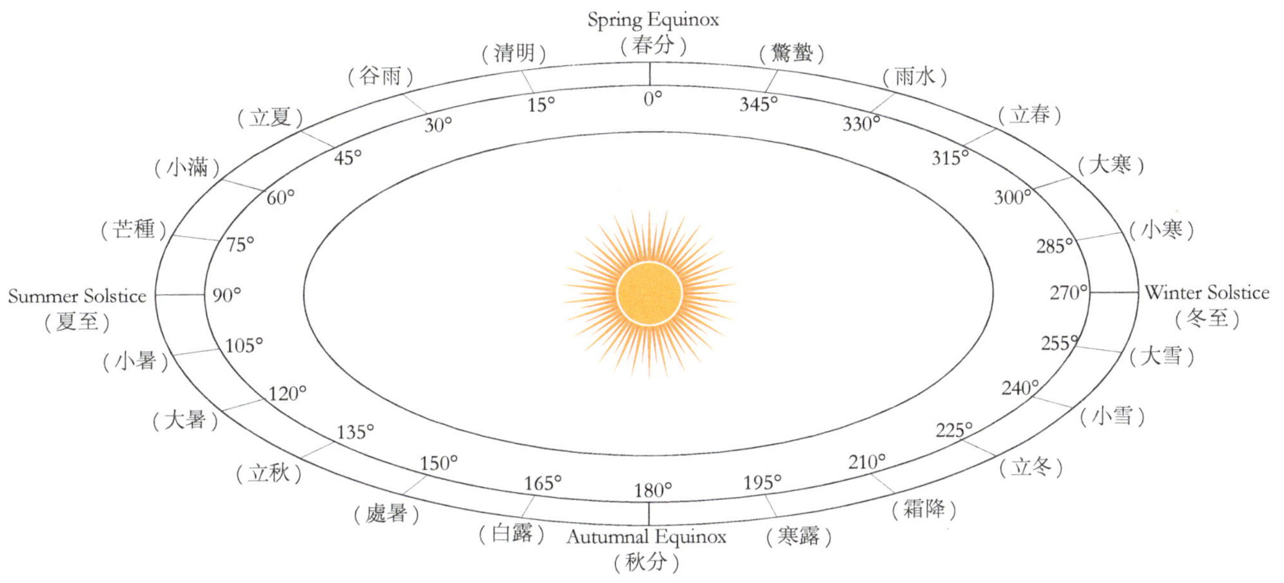

This diagram depicts Earth's orbit around the sun. Ancient Chinese astronomers once drew something similar, but from their viewpoint, it was the apparent path of the sun's motion on the celestial sphere in the course of a year. Although they didn't know Earth was moving, they observed the relative positions of the Earth and the sun accurately.

Based on the fact that Earth revolves around the sun, the modern drawing of the solar term orbit places the sun at the center. It starts with the spring equinox, coincidentally as the Western zodiac does, though the latter is divided by 12 instead of 24. The spring equinox in the Northern Hemisphere is marked as zero degree on both.

However, the spring equinox was not considered the beginning of spring in ancient Chinese culture. This may surprise today's Westerners, but would not have confounded Europeans prior to 1780. Why?

Please read on! The answer is in Chapter 1...

Chapter 1
First Signs of Spring

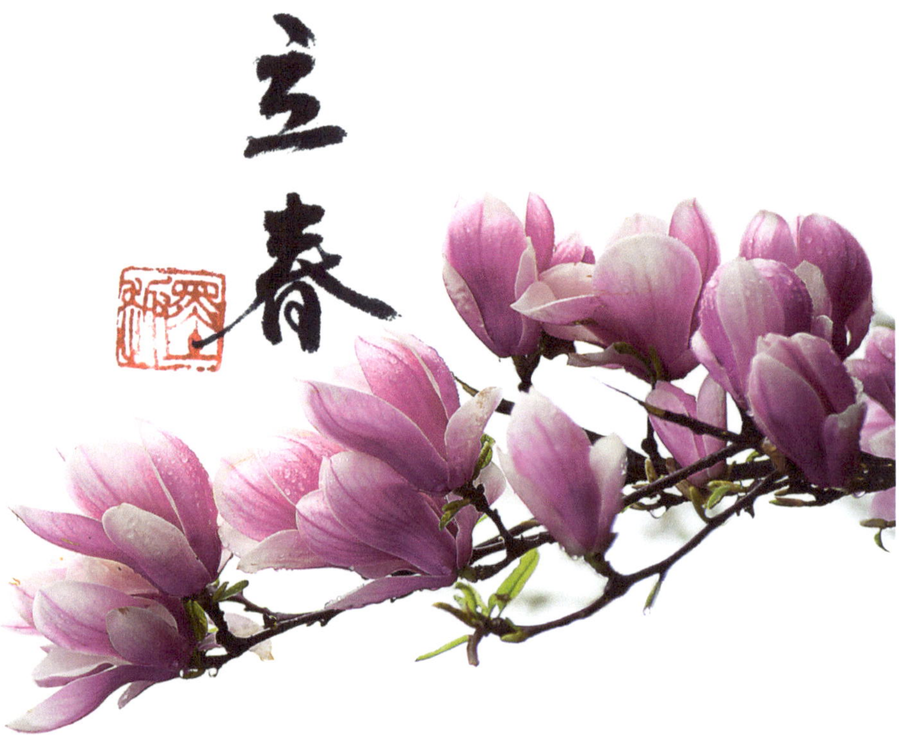

In early February, the weather is still chilly in the temperate zone of the Northern Hemisphere, but magnolias, primroses, and violets seem to announce the arrival of spring.

在陽曆二月上旬，北半球溫帶氣候依然寒冷，但到處綻放的玉蘭花、報春花，以及紫羅蘭似乎已帶來了春天的氣息。

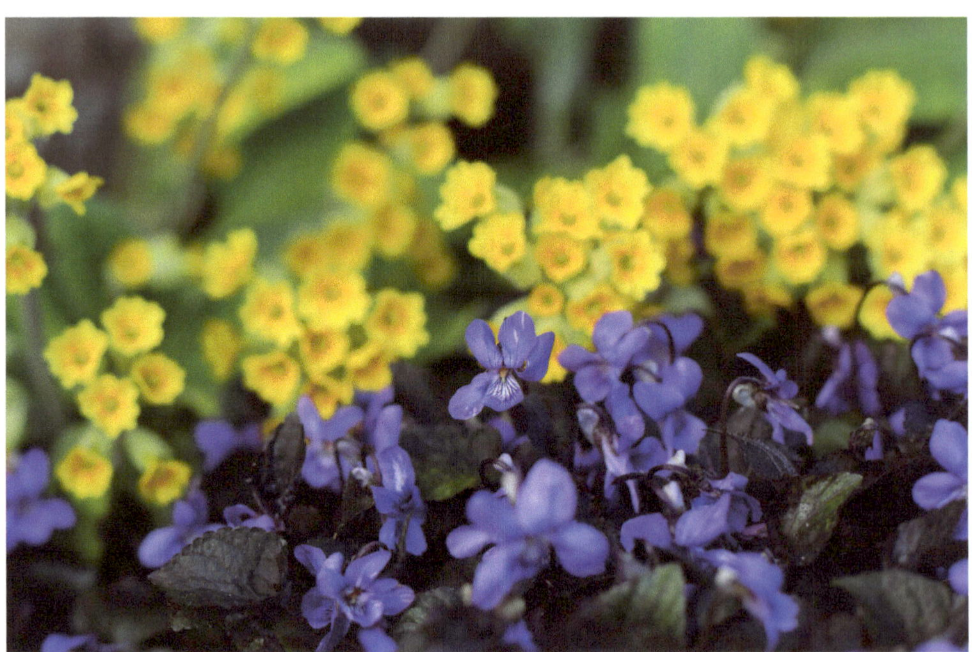

In fact, it was not until 1780 when an international organization for meteorology defined spring as the months of March, April, and May.[1] Prior to that, Europeans generally associated February with early spring. For instance, 14th-century writer Geoffrey Chaucer described birds mating on Valentine's Day in a popular poem.[2] The traditional concept remains in today's Ireland, where the Gaelic calendar marks the beginning of spring in February.[3]

其實，過去直到西元 1780 年，才有一個國際氣象組織定義陽曆三、四、五月為春天。在那之前，歐洲人一般認為陽曆二月是初春。例如，十四世紀作家喬叟在一首名詩中描寫鳥類於情人節求偶。這種傳統觀點尚存於今日的愛爾蘭。愛爾蘭曆法是以陽曆二月為春天的開端。

There was a similar definition of spring in ancient China. The solar section of a Chinese lunisolar calendar marks the beginning of spring in early February. It may be Feb 3, Feb 4, or Feb 5, depending on when the sun reaches 315 degrees of the ecliptic drawn by ancient Chinese astronomers, or when the Earth arrives at 315 degrees of the celestial orbit redrawn by modern Chinese scientists to present the 24 solar terms.

中國古代的春天定義亦然。原來，中國古代曆法不止是陰曆，也包括陽曆，其中所設定春天初始日期在現代陽曆的二月上旬，日期可能是二月三日、二月四日，或二月五日，取決於古人所謂太陽到達黃經三百一十五度的日子，亦即現代科學家按照地球繞太陽軌道所重畫的橢圓形二十四節氣圖表上，地球運轉到第三百一十五度之時。

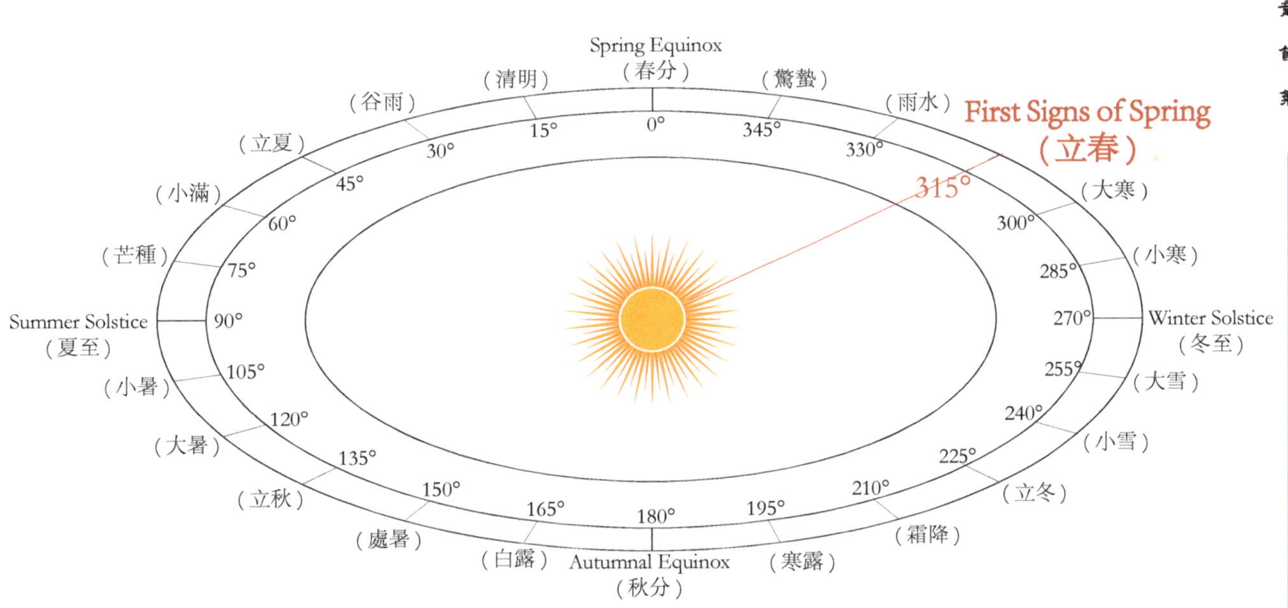

1   Wikipedia. "Season." Wikipedia Foundation.
 https://en.wikipedia.org/wiki/Season#:~:text=In%201780%20the%20Societas%20Meteorologica,world%20have%20used%20this%20definition.

2   Chaucer, Geoffrey. "The Parliament of Fowls." Translated by A.S. Kline. Poetry in Translation, 2007.
https://www.poetryintranslation.com/PITBR/English/Fowls.php

3   O'Connor, Rachael. "Today Marks the First Day of Spring on the Gaelic Calendar." Irish Times, Feb 1, 2021.
https://www.irishpost.com/news/today-marks-the-first-day-of-spring-on-the-gaelic-calendar-202700

On the ancient-Chinese-defined first day of spring (on or around Feb 4), the emperor had to plow a field in front of his subjects. He was putting on a show to encourage farmers to work hard during the time of year farmers were about to return to work after their winter break.
在古中國定義的春天首日（陽曆二月四日當天或前後），皇帝必須在臣民面前親耕。那是皇帝表演來鼓勵農民努力工作，因為每年此時，農民都在過冬之後重新開始耕田。

In the meantime, Chinese people would eat spring rolls, with colorful shredded vegetables wrapped inside, to symbolize biting into spring, but this tradition is no longer a must-do. Nowadays spring rolls are available all year round.
同時，含有各種彩色蔬菜的春捲是必吃的食物，以象徵咬春。不過，此一傳統已經不再為大眾所奉行。春捲在現代是整年都有的食品。

Interestingly, spring rolls evolved from a dish called five spices on a plate, which comprises garlic, green onions or sand leeks, chives, rapeseed, and cilantro. All of these five pungent vegetables were meant to boost immunity by clearing the respiratory and digestive systems in the capricious weather of early spring.

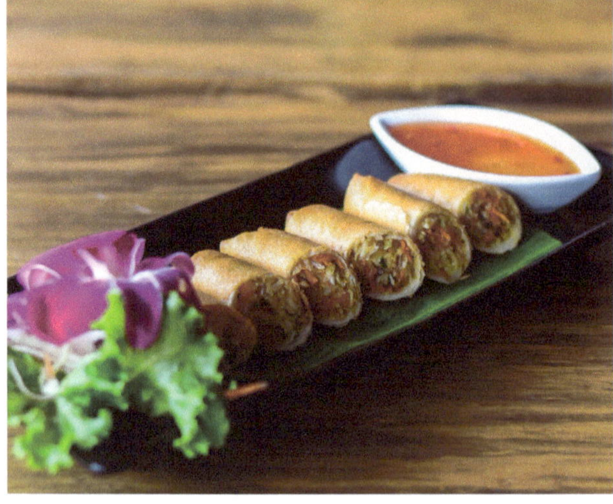

有趣的是，春捲最初是由五辛盤演化而來。五辛盤是冷盤，在盤子上鋪着大蒜、青蔥或小蒜、韭菜、蕓薹（油菜），以及胡荽（香菜）。這五種具有辛味的蔬菜都是為了在初春多變的天氣之下疏通呼吸系統和消化系統，以提高免疫力。

Later on, the five spices were wrapped as spring rolls, which kept evolving. Various vegetables in different colors gradually replaced the original five as the fillings. Multicolored vegetables not only represent the colors of spring, but they will enhance health as well. Modern science has found plant pigments to be phytonutrients, with antioxidant properties that can help prevent damage to cells throughout the body. In other words, vegetarian spring rolls have health benefits, especially when they are not deep-fried.

後來，這五種辛味蔬菜被包成了春捲。隨着春捲的演變，其中內餡逐漸變成了多種顏色的蔬菜。多彩蔬菜不僅更能代表春天的色調，也有增進健康的效用。現代科學已經發現植物天然色素是營養素，有抗氧化功能，可以預防身體細胞受損。那就表示素春捲有益健康，尤其是未經油炸的素春捲。

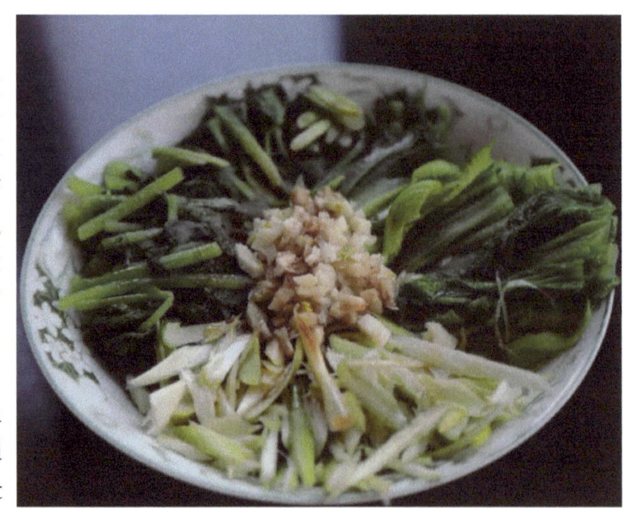

Even though the 21st century's spring rolls can be consumed in all seasons, it may be a good idea to have more of them during the first solar term of spring, which is the 15-or-16-day period starting with the ancient-Chinese-defined first day of spring. This day and the solar term are both called Lichun in Chinese, which literally means "the beginning of spring" but can be translated as "the first signs of spring" to make it easier for Westerners to accept, because today's Westerners generally think spring starts in March.

儘管二十一世紀的春捲整年都吃得到，但在古中國定義的春天首日以及春天第一個節氣，則不妨享用更多春捲。春天首日以及春天第一個節氣皆稱為立春。立春的含意雖是春天的開端，但是英譯為“春意初露的跡象”會比較能讓西方人接受，因為立春在陽曆二月，而現代西方人一般認為春天始於陽曆三月。

The first solar term of spring in February always overlaps with the 15-day celebration of Lunar New Year, which starts with the new moon between Jan 21 and Feb 20. Even when Lunar New Year's Day falls in late January, the last few days of the 15-day celebration will coincide with the first solar term of spring. That explains why Lunar New Year is also known as the Spring Festival.

立春節氣總會遇上為時十五天的陰曆新年，因為陰曆大年初一是在陽曆一月二十一日到二月二十日之間的新月之日。即使某些年份的大年初一在陽曆一月下旬，陰曆新年十五天的最後幾天也會在立春節氣範圍之內。於是，陰曆新年又稱春節。

Of course, the weather is still very cold during the first solar term of spring, namely Lichun, in the Yellow River region of northern China, where the solar terms were invented. However, ancient Chinese meteorologists found ice starting to melt during this time of year, and they stated, "East winds begin to unfreeze everything during the first five-day period of Lichun."

當然，立春之於古人發明節氣所在的黃河流域，還是很冷的時節。然而，古代氣象學家發現，每年此時冰雪初融。因此，他們寫下了“立春一候東風解凍。”

Ancient Chinese meteorologists divided each solar term into three parts. Each part is five or six days long. According to their observations, the second part of Lichun is when a small number of hibernating insects wake up. The last part of Lichun is when fish swim under floating ice sheets.

古代氣象學家劃分每個節氣為三候，每一候五或六天。依照他們的說法，立春二候蟄蟲始振。立春三候魚陟負冰。

Obviously, ancient Chinese meteorologists had enough evidence to call this time of year the beginning of spring.

顯然，中國古代氣象學家有足夠的證據，可以顯示立春名符其實。

February looks more like spring in the Yangtze River region of eastern central China thanks to blooming flowers, including those called winter jasmine in English, or *yingchunhua* in Chinese, which means "spring welcoming flowers." They burst into bloom in early February in the Yangtze River region as the first of the three flower species blooming during the first solar term of spring.

陽曆二月在中國長江流域看來更像春天，因為有春花開放，其中包括英文名稱是冬日茉莉的迎春花。在長江流域，迎春花初開於陽曆二月上旬，乃是立春一候之花。

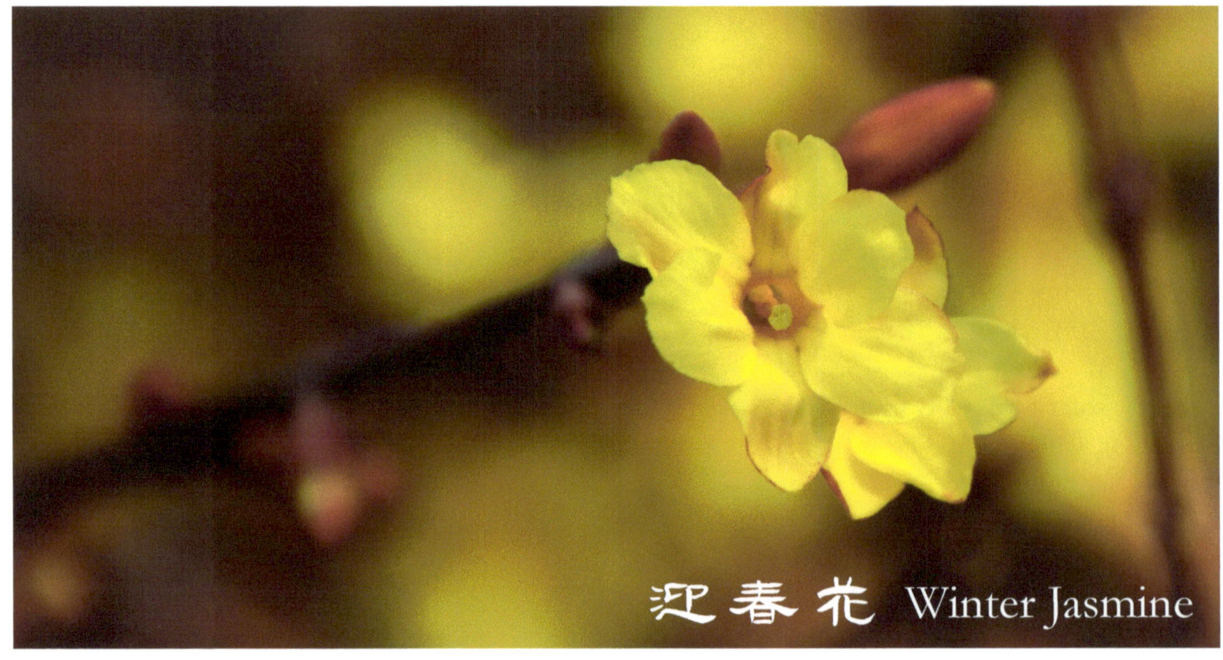

Next are cherry blossoms on trees that will bear edible cherries. These cherry trees become flower-laden in early to mid February in eastern central China, about a month or two earlier than those ornamental cherry trees.

立春二候之花是櫻桃花。櫻桃花會結出可供食用的櫻桃。在華中，櫻桃樹在陽曆二月上旬到中旬之間開花，比櫻花樹的花期早一兩個月。

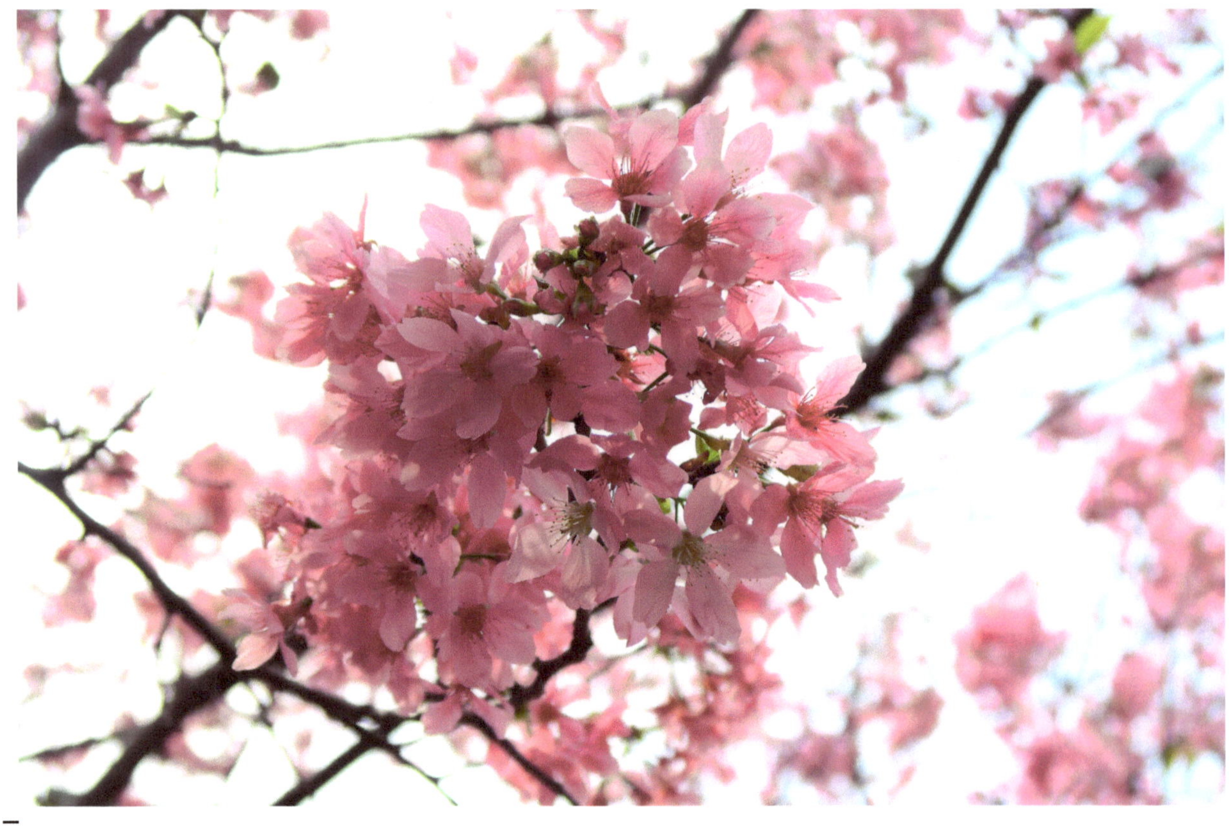

The third flower species that embellishes the first solar term of spring is Yulan magnolia, which generally begins blooming in mid February in eastern central China. Some Yulan magnolia flowers have ombre pink petals. They all look absolutely adorable.

立春三候之花是玉蘭花，又名望春花。玉蘭樹在華中的花期通常始於陽曆二月中旬，有些花瓣呈現宛如渲染的粉紅色，令人賞心悅目至極。

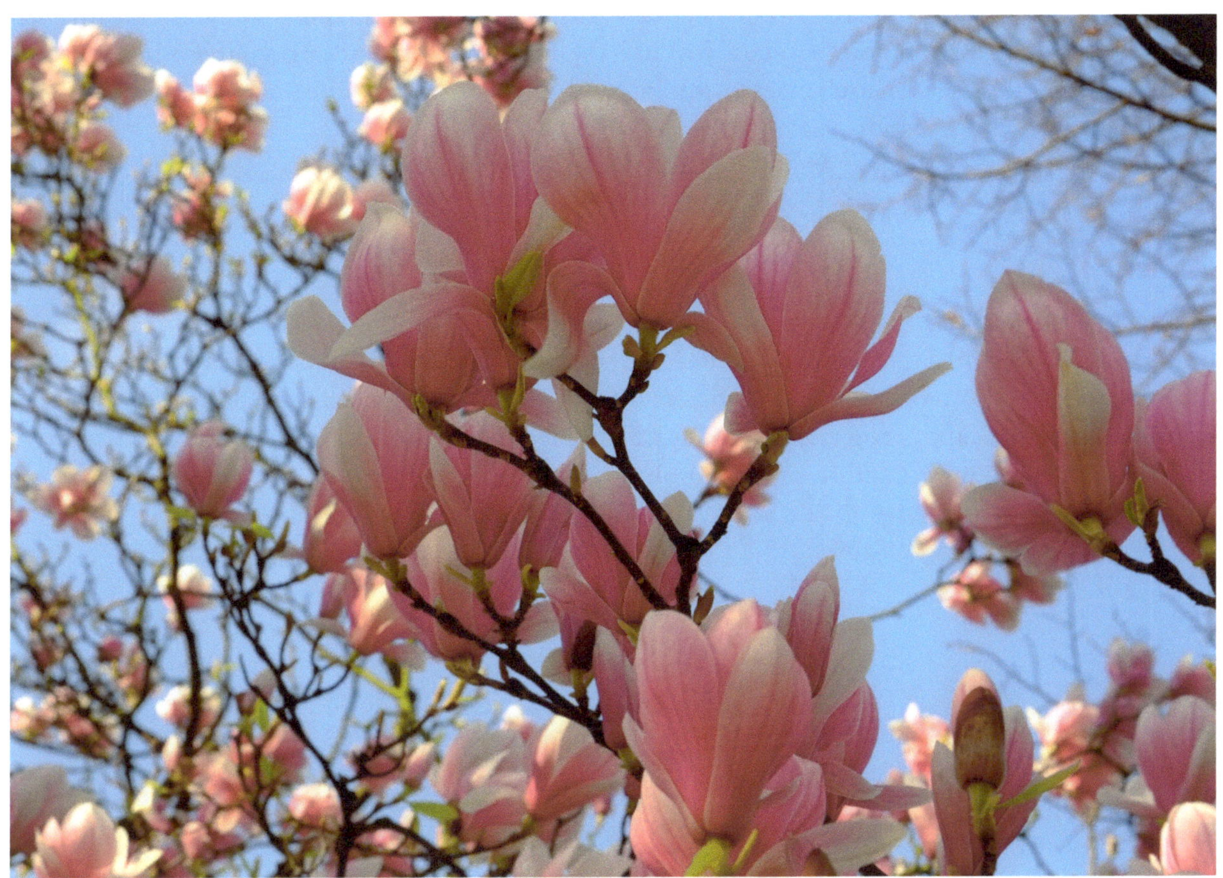

Coincidentally, magnolia trees in California also come into bloom in February, but normally in early February. Evidently, the Chinese solar terms can be roughly applied to other places in the temperate zone of the Northern Hemisphere. Those who live in the Southern Hemisphere may find out how the 24 solar terms match seasonal changes by placing the first solar term of spring in August.

湊巧的是，美國加州的玉蘭樹也在陽曆二月份繁花滿枝，但花期稍早，二月上旬就開花了。顯然，中國的節氣能夠大致適用於別國的北半球溫帶地區。南半球居民則不妨將立春放在陽曆八月份，來看二十四節氣如何配合當地物候變化。

Whether it is February in the Northern Hemisphere or August in the Southern Hemisphere, the weather still tends to be wintry, but other creatures sense the arrival of spring earlier than humans do. Humans used to be humbler, so they called February early spring despite how cold they felt. That was based on a nature-centered viewpoint, whereas the meteorological definition of the four seasons is all about how humans feel. The human-centered approach also applies to the way modern astronomy makes spring start with the vernal equinox.

無論在北半球的陽曆二月或南半球的陽曆八月，天氣都還像冬天，但別的生物比人類早一些感應到春天的降臨。古人比較謙卑，他們不顧本身寒冷的感覺，稱呼陽曆二月份為早春。那是以大自然為中心的觀點。至於現代氣象學的四季定義，以及現代天文學將春分定為春季之始的做法，則都基於人類自我中心的態度。

Now, for sustainability, humans need to relearn respect for nature, and understanding the 24 solar terms can be a good point to start. Just like the first solar term of spring, the other 23 solar terms also manifest seasonal changes often ignored in modern life, all of which will be vividly portrayed through the rest of this book…

如今為了永續，人類必須重新學習尊重大自然，而了解二十四節氣就會是良好的起點。正如立春，其餘二十三個節氣也都代表着現代生活中經常讓人忽略的時令變化，將在本書中精彩呈現 …

To make each solar term even more impressive, each chapter of this book ends with a timeless poem about certain natural phenomena only occurring during the solar term featured in the chapter. On the next page is the classical Chinese poem that will conclude this chapter, presented through captivating calligraphy by a famous calligrapher, along with a carefully crafted English translation by the author of this book.

為了讓每個節氣留給讀者更深的印象，本書每一章都在正文後面引用一首亙古常新的應景詩篇，透過引人入勝的名家書法來呈現詩句，並附有本書作者精心作成的英譯。
下一頁就在展示對應立春的絕句《立春偶成》。

立春偶成　Inspired by the First Signs of Spring

Author： Zhang, Shi 張栻 (1133-1180)
Translator: Crystal Tai

律回歲晚冰霜少　At the end of the lunar year, ice and frost dwindle.
春到人間草木知　Grasses and trees become aware of spring's arrival.
頓覺眼前生意滿　All at once, revival is everywhere in front of my eyes!
東風吹水綠參差　An east wind urges the green water surface to ripple.

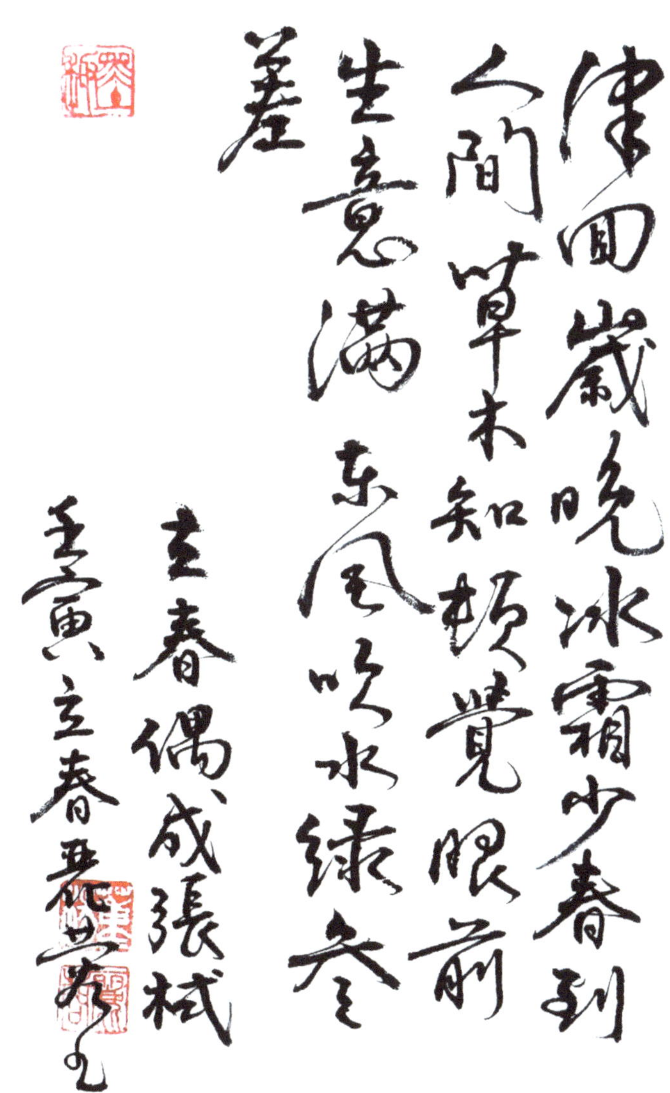

Chapter 2
Transition from Snow to Rain

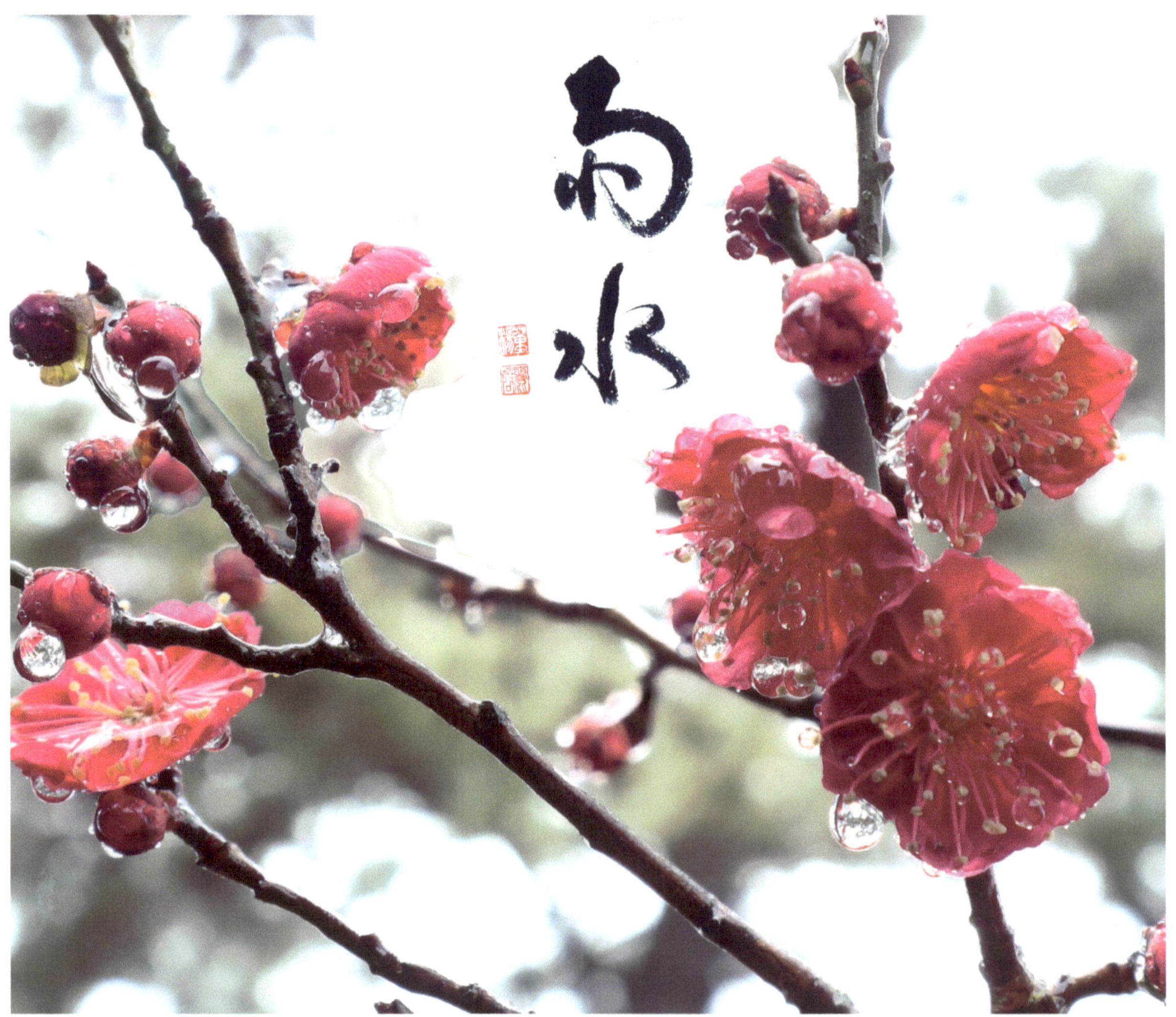

Among those who live in a place where it snows, how many have ever noticed when snowfall is shifting to rainfall every year?

在冬天會下雪的地區，有多少人注意過每年何時冬雪開始變成春雨？

According to a Chinese almanac, which can be applied to other places in the temperate zone of the Northern Hemisphere, the transition starts to take place on Feb 18, Feb 19, or Feb 20, depending on when the sun reaches 330 degrees of the ecliptic drawn by ancient Chinese astronomers, or when the Earth arrives at 330 degrees of the celestial orbit redrawn by modern Chinese scientists to present the 24 solar terms.

根據可適用於北半球溫帶所有地區的黃曆，從冬雪到春雨的轉變始於陽曆二月十八、十九，或二十日，取決於古人所謂太陽到達黃經三百三十度的日子，亦即現代科學家按照地球繞太陽軌道所重畫的橢圓形二十四節氣圖表上，地球運轉到三百三十度之時。

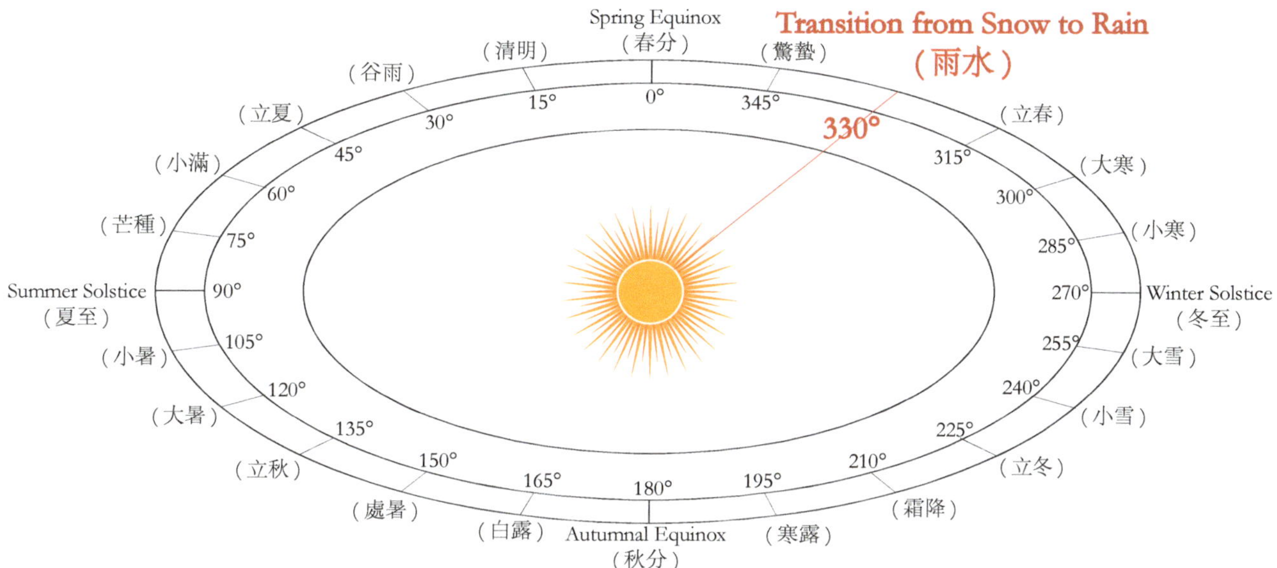

The solar term that marks the transition from snow to rain is called Yushui in Chinese, which literally means "rainwater." Ancient Chinese meteorologists divided this solar term into three parts. Each part is five or six days long.
此一節氣稱為雨水。中國古代氣象學家將雨水分為三候，每一候五或六天。

The first part of this solar term is when otters come out to eat fish. The second part is when wild swans and wild geese migrate north. The third part is when trees and seeds are sprouting. No wonder this is when many Chinese farmers pick a sprouting wild vegetable named *jicai* in Chinese and shepherd's purse in English.
雨水一候獺祭魚，二候鴻雁來，三候草木萌動。難怪在雨水時節，中國農民收割如同野生草葉的薺菜。

Shepherd's purse is often shredded as an ingredient for dim sum items, such as buns, dumplings, and wonton. Many Shanghai-style restaurants, including those in America, serve these dim sum items.
薺菜常用於包子、餃子、餛飩等點心。上海館子總會有這些薺菜點心。美國的一些上海餐廳也不例外。

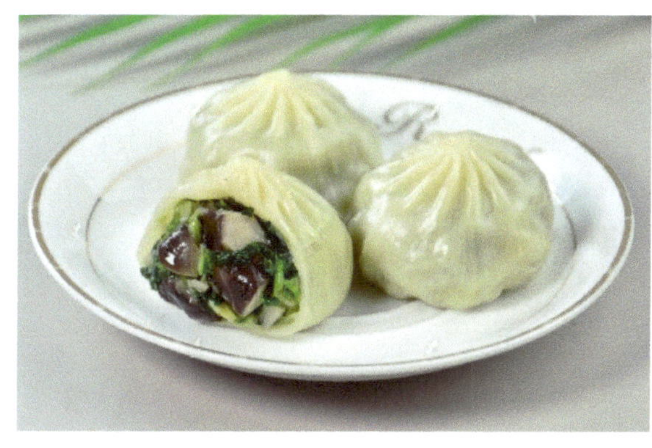

Shepherd's purse is high in vitamin C, carotenoids, a number of other nutrients, and fiber. It can help improve vision, lower blood pressure, increase bowel movements, and boost the immune system. Chinese medicine practitioners sometimes use it as a medicinal herb to treat minor illnesses.[1]
薺菜富含維生素 C、胡蘿蔔素，還有其他營養素，以及纖維。薺菜可以明目、降血壓、促進大腸蠕動、加強免疫系統。中醫有時候會用薺菜入藥來治小病。

1   Chinese Medicine News. "Shepherd's Purse Is a Good Vegetable with Healing Properties" (Chinese edition). Lingnan Chinese Medicine Net. http://www.lngygy.com/2015/0317/1856.html

Chinese medicine practitioners always encourage the consumption of green vegetables during the three months from around Feb 4 to around May 3. These three months are traditionally defined as spring, the season during which the liver works extra hard and needs more care, based on Chinese medicinal classics. Chinese medicine practitioners believe the nutrients of green vegetables will enter the liver meridian and improve liver function. [1]

中醫總是提倡在陽曆二月初到五月初這三個月多吃綠色蔬菜，因為這三個月是傳統定義的春天，而根據中醫典籍記載，春天肝臟特別辛苦，需要養肝。中醫相信，綠色蔬菜的養份能入肝經而改善肝功能。

This Chinese medical theory has been proven true. Modern science has discovered that leafy greens can reduce the risk of non-alcoholic fatty liver disease by half.[2] Shepherd's purse certainly belongs to the category of leafy greens.

這項中醫理論已獲證明屬實。現代科學也發現綠葉蔬菜有助於減半非酒精導致的脂肪肝罹患率，而薺菜當然屬於護肝的綠葉蔬菜類。

Shepherd's purse is a flowering plant, but it comes into bloom about a month later than rapeseed, which starts blooming in late February in the Yangtze River region of eastern central China. Those who go to a village near Shanghai in late February or March will see a sea of golden yellow flowers carpeting farm fields. This is the first of the three flower species that embellish the solar term from late February to early March.

薺菜會開花，但花期要再過一個多月才到，不像油菜花期已至。在長江流域，油菜花初開於陽曆二月下旬。上海外圍的農村到了陽曆二月底三月初，總會有大片金黃色油菜花海。油菜花是雨水節氣第一候之花。

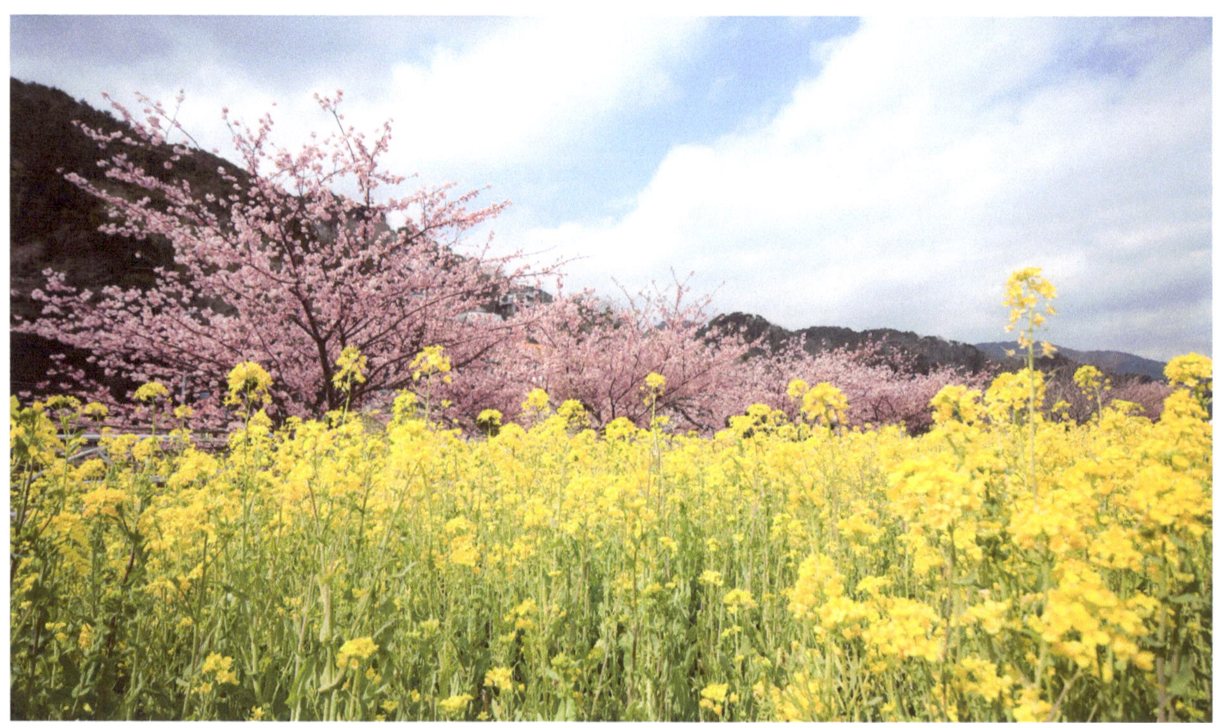

1 Yang, Shu-Mei. "What to Eat in Spring" (Chinese edition). China Medical University, March 1, 2011.

2 Harvard School of Public Health. "Green Mediterranean diet may reduce risk of fatty liver disease." https://www.hsph.harvard.edu/news/hsph-in-the-news/green-mediterranean-diet-fatty-liver-disease/

The second flower species blooming during this solar term is apricot blossoms.
雨水第二候之花是杏花。

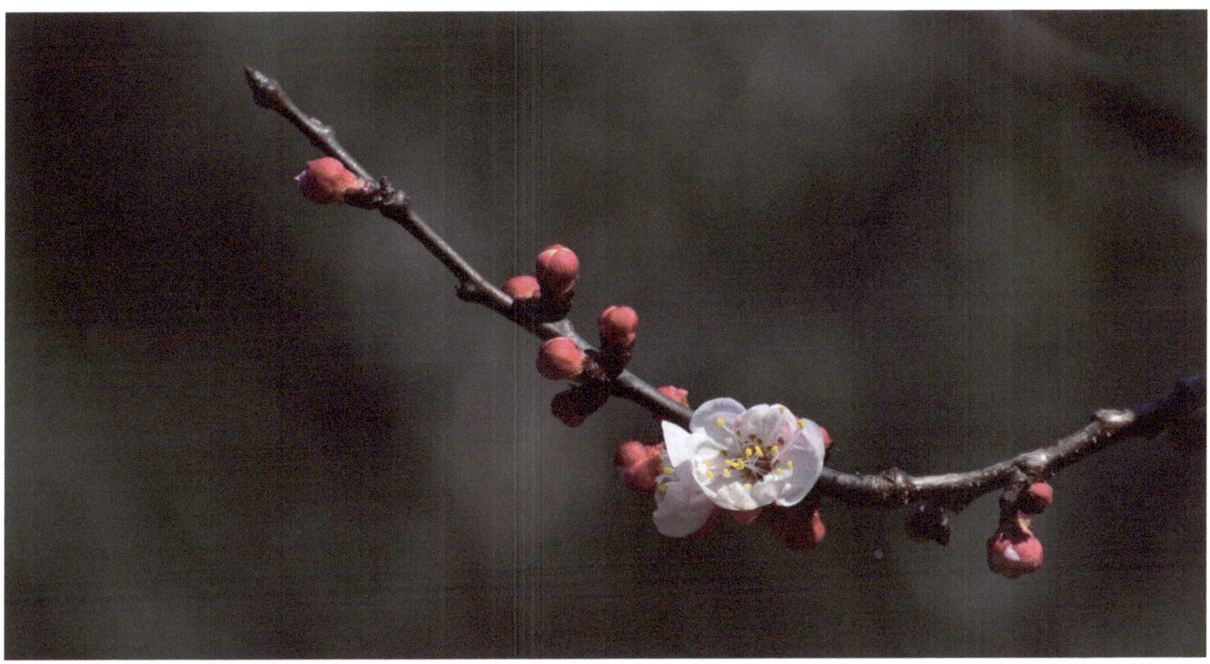

The third is Chinese plum blossoms.
雨水第三候之花是李花。

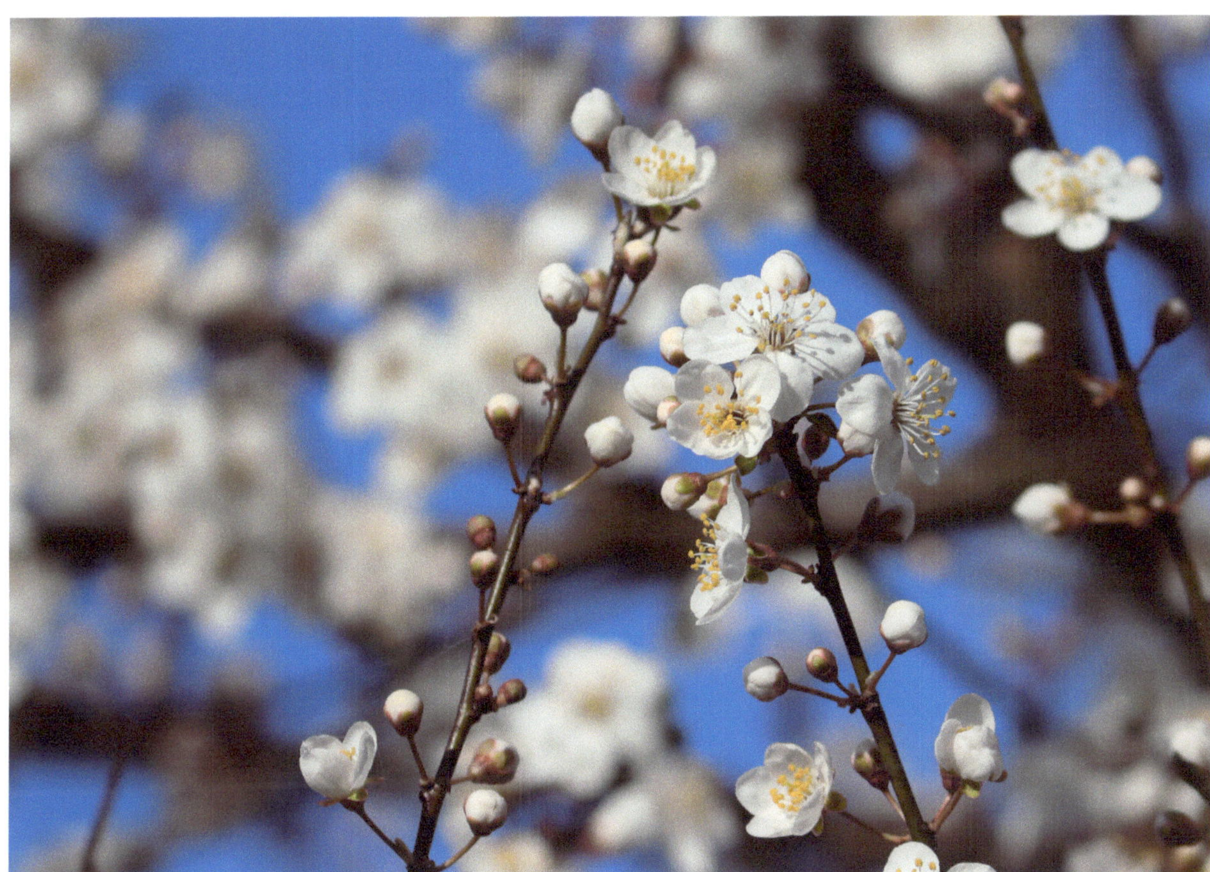

Among these three flower species, the most beloved in Chinese culture are apricot blossoms, because they look particularly dreamy during misty and rainy days in the canal-woven Yangtze River delta region, where spring is often summarized as "apricot blossoms in the misty rain," and a light spring shower is therefore called "an apricot blossom drizzle."

在雨水三候之花之中，最受中國文人偏愛的是杏花，因為杏花在小橋流水的長江三角洲區域每逢煙雨，必然看來格外夢幻。於是，杏花煙雨常常成為概括江南春天的名詞。輕柔的春雨也往往讓人喚作杏花雨。

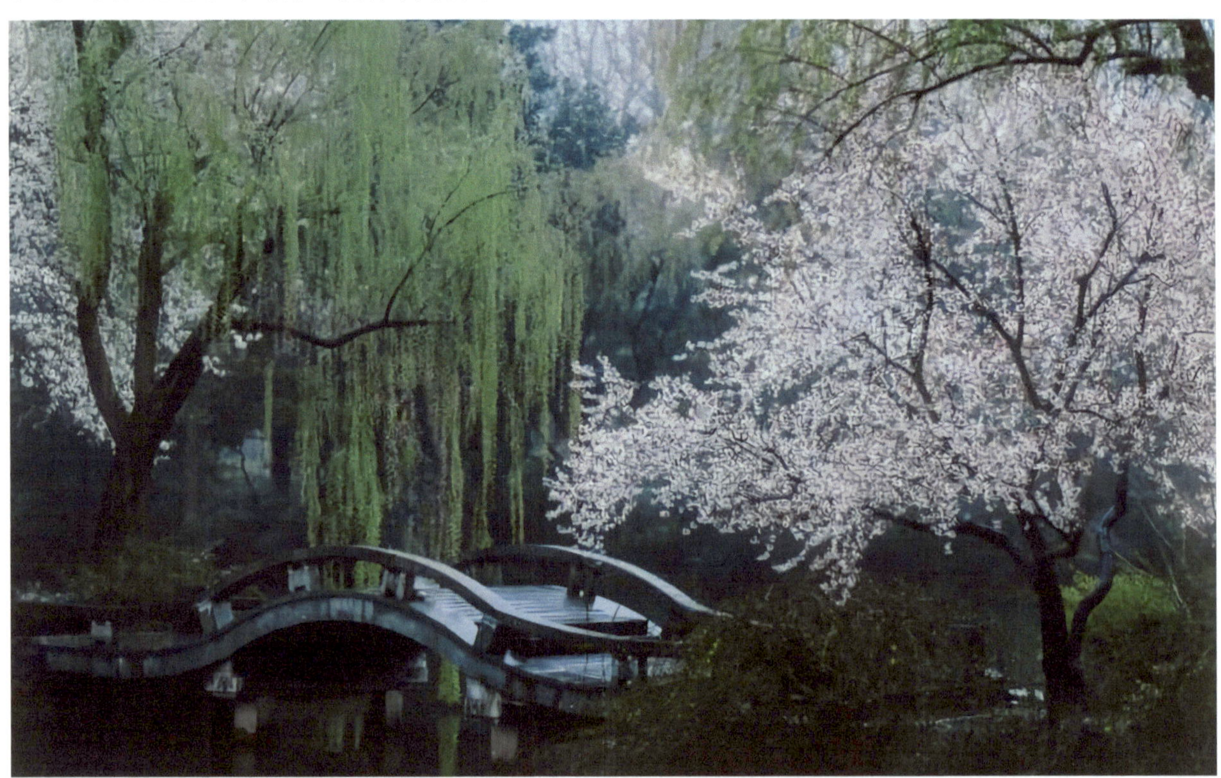

At the end of this chapter is a classical Chinese poem, from which the term "apricot blossom drizzle" originated.

杏花雨的出處是一首恰好題名為《絕句》的絕句，作為終結本章的詩篇。

絕句 A Four-Line Poem

Author：Zhi Nan 志南 (birth and death years unknown)
Translator：Crystal Tai

古木陰中繫短篷 I tied my small boat under an ancient tree in a quiet place.
杖藜扶我過橋東 A cane helped crossing the bridge to the east at a steady pace.
沾衣欲溼杏花雨 A drizzle with apricot blossoms barely dampens my shirt;
吹面不寒楊柳風 A breeze through willow trees never chills my face.

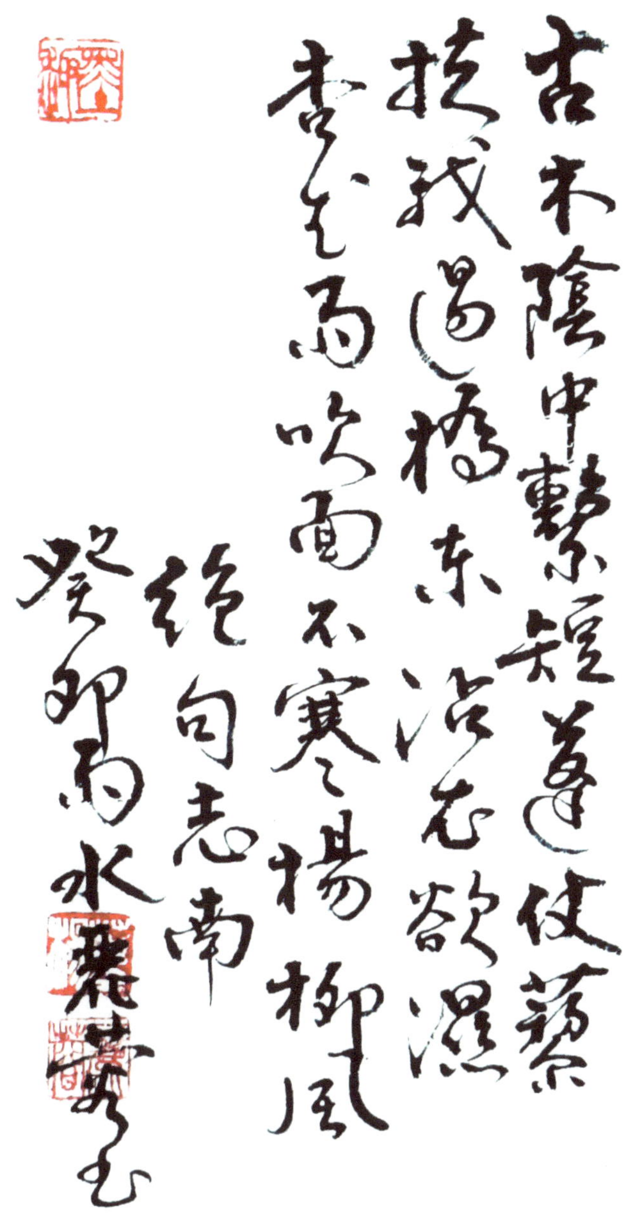

詩意節氣

Chapter 3
Awakening of Hibernating Creatures

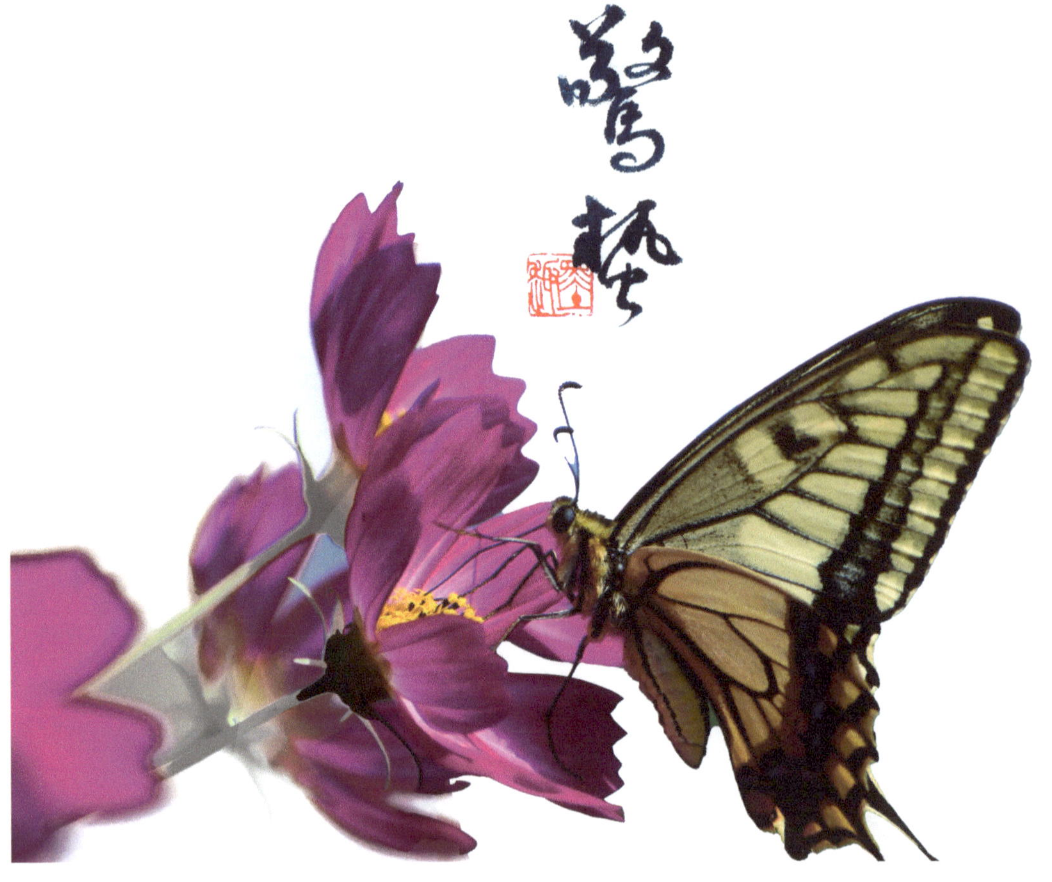

驚蟄

Gardening is a popular hobby, but how many people notice when hibernating insects wake up in their gardens every year? Hibernating creatures are all supposed to wake up in early to mid March, according to a traditional Chinese almanac, which can be applied to other places in the temperate zone of the Northern Hemisphere.

蒔花種樹是很普遍的嗜好，但有多少人注意花園中冬眠的昆蟲每年何時醒來呢？依據黃曆上的節氣，冬眠的動物應當都在陽曆三月上旬到中旬之間甦醒，而這也是能適用於別國北半球溫帶地區的現象。

The solar term that marks the awakening of insects and snakes from hibernation is called Jingzhe in Chinese. It starts on March 4, March 5, or March 6, depending on when the sun reaches 345 degrees of the ecliptic drawn by ancient Chinese astronomers, or when the Earth arrives at 345 degrees of the celestial orbit redrawn by modern Chinese scientists to present the 24 solar terms.

每年此時的節氣稱為驚蟄，始於陽曆三月四日、三月五日，或三月六日，取決於古人所謂太陽到達黃經三百四十五度的日子，亦即現代科學家按照地球繞太陽軌道所重畫的橢圓形二十四節氣圖表上，地球運轉到三百四十五度之時。

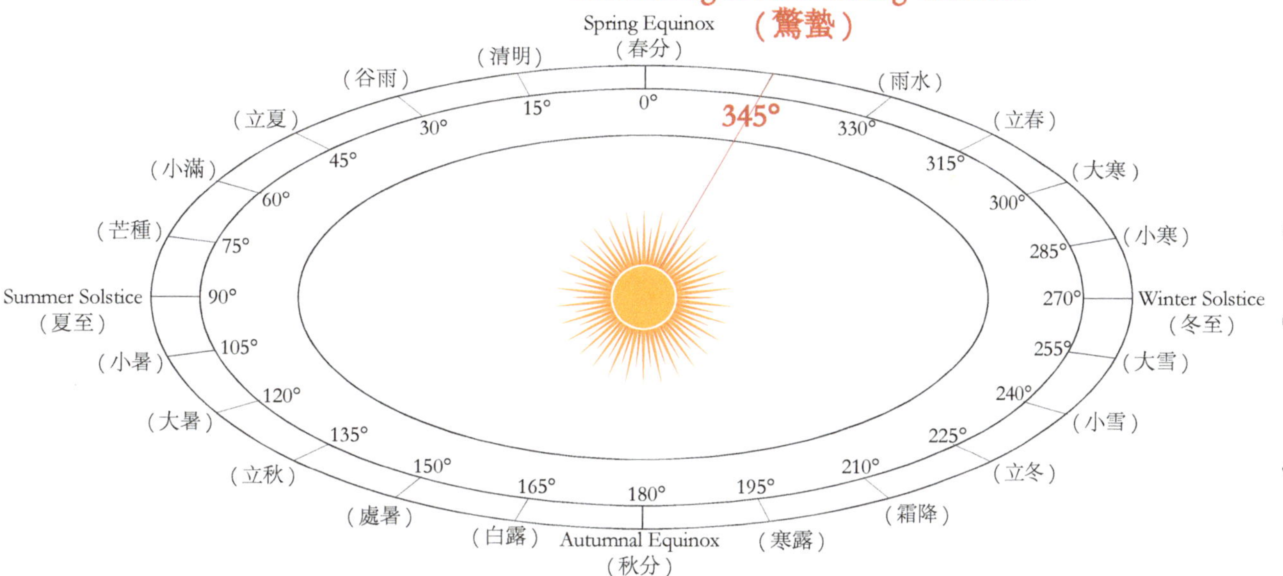

Ancient Chinese meteorologists divided this solar term into three parts. Each part is five or six days long. The first part of the solar term is when peach blossoms come into bloom. The second part is when golden orioles start singing. The third part is when eagles are molting, so they look like turtledoves.

中國古代氣象學家劃分驚蟄為三候。每一候五或六天。驚蟄一候桃始華，二候倉庚鳴，三候鷹化為鳩。

During this time of year, thunder often appears in central and southern China. No wonder residents in central and southern China used to believe it was thunder that woke up hibernating creatures. Some of them even built a shrine for the god of thunder and prayed to him during the solar term from early to mid March. However, those in northern China don't hear thunder during the same solar term. It is still too cold in northern China in early to mid March for thunder.

每年此時，華中和華南時常出現雷聲。難怪華中和華南人民過去相信雷聲驚醒了冬眠的生物。有些民眾甚至建造了雷公廟，並且在驚蟄時節祭拜雷公。然而，華北到了驚蟄時節並無雷響。在陽曆三月上旬到中旬時期，華北天氣還太冷，而打不成雷。

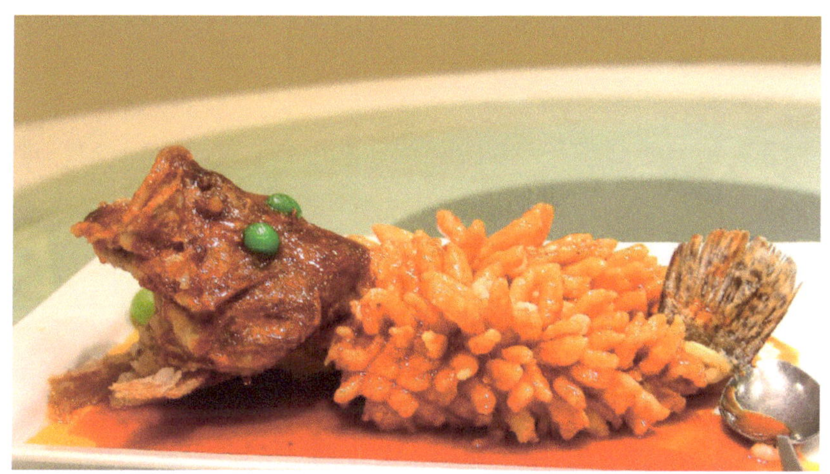

Despite regional differences, many Chinese eat freshwater mandarin fish during the solar term from early to mid March, because they have all heard that freshwater mandarin fish plump up during the peach blossom season.

儘管物候有地域區別，許多華人都在驚蟄時節多吃鱖魚，因為這是桃花流水鱖魚肥的時節。

Peach blossoms are the first of the three flower species that begin blooming during the solar term from early to mid March in China.
桃花是驚蟄第一候之花。

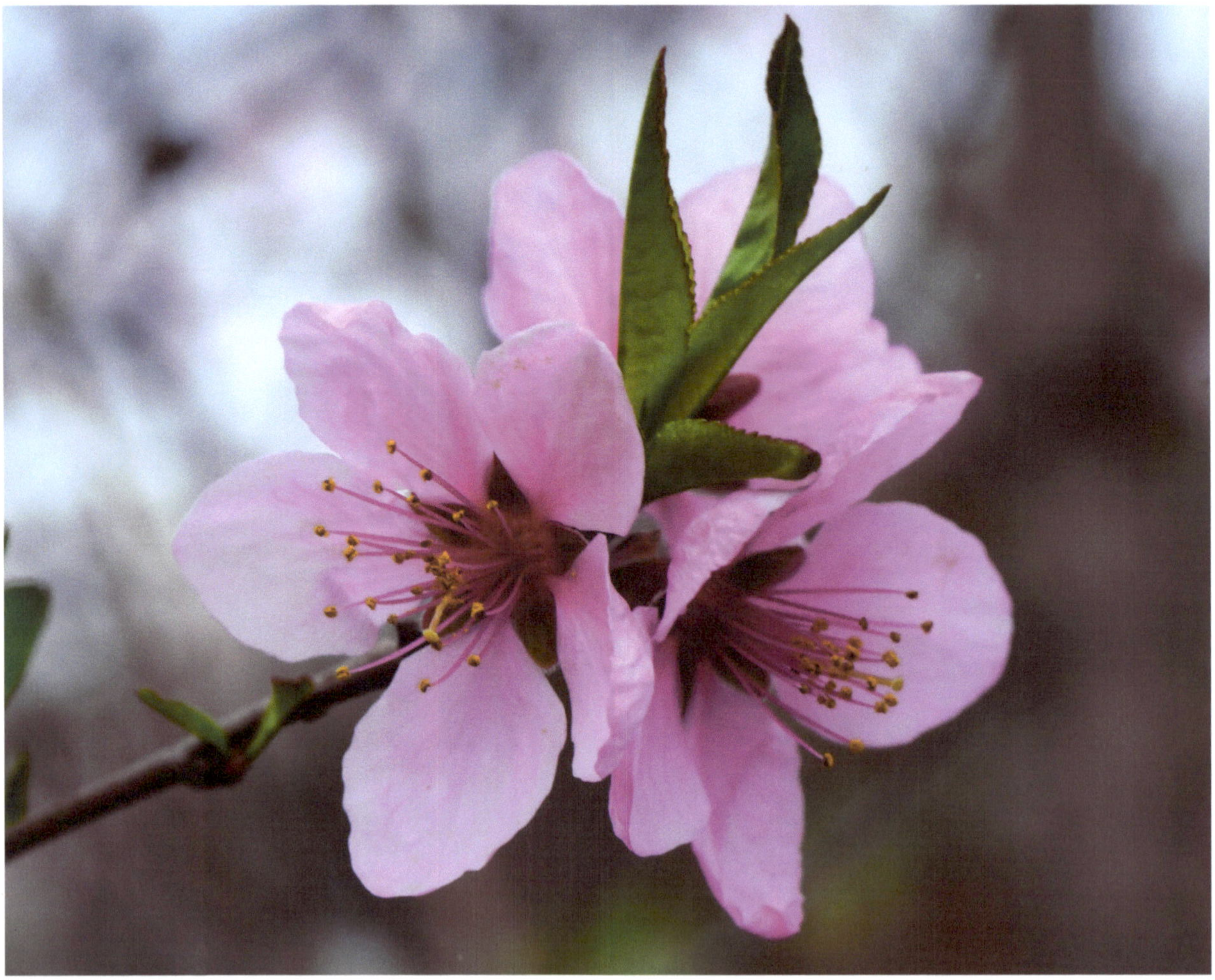

The second flower species blooming during this solar term is kerria japonica.
驚蟄第二候之花是棠棣。

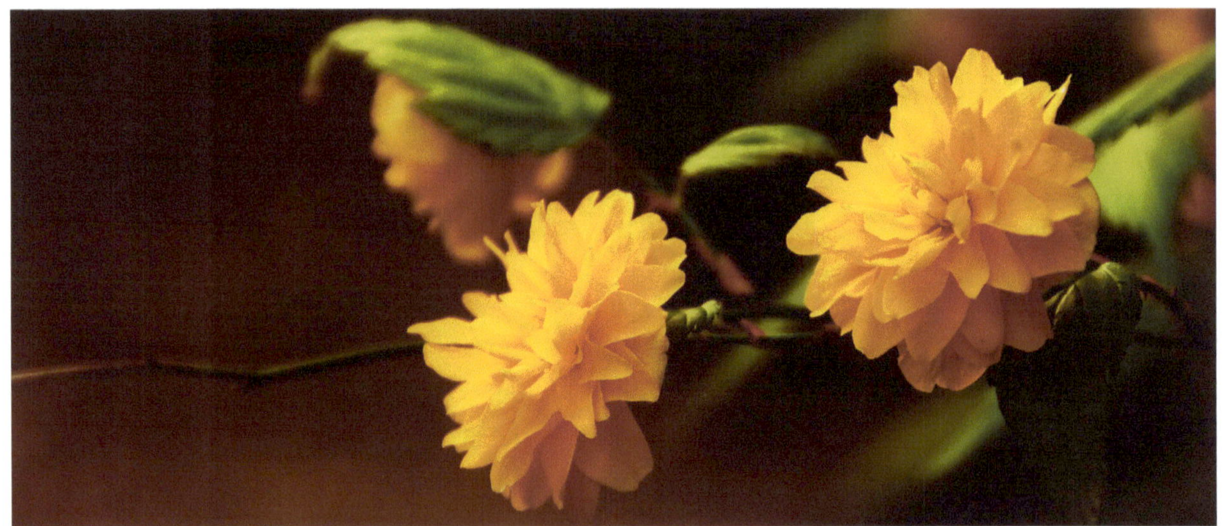

The third is climbing roses.
驚蟄第三候之花是薔薇。

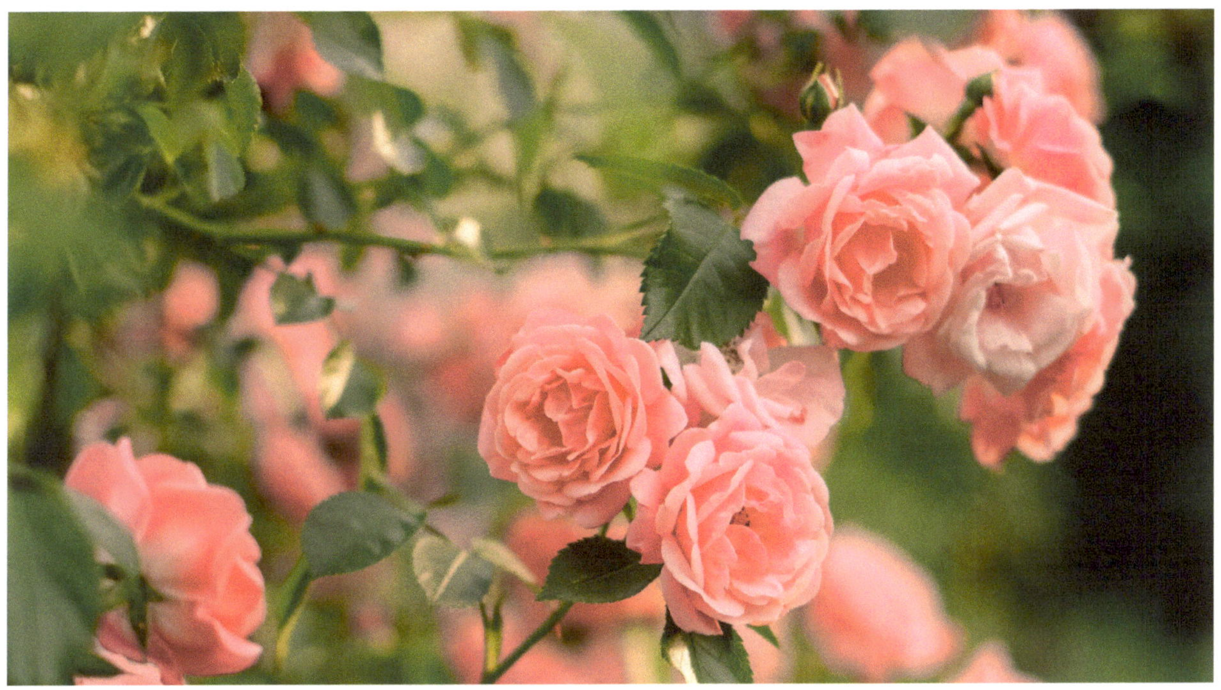

In the meantime, apricot blossoms, which began blooming during the previous solar term, are still in full bloom.
同時，在上個節氣初開的杏花也依然開滿枝椏。

While apricot and peach trees have overlapping bloom periods, it is actually quite easy to tell them apart. Each apricot blossom showcases five broad and curved petals, whereas peach blossom petals have pointy tips, with slender green leaves around them.
儘管杏花和桃花的花期重疊，要分辨兩者其實很容易。杏花五瓣寬圓而微捲，桃花瓣則末梢較尖，還有細長綠葉相襯。

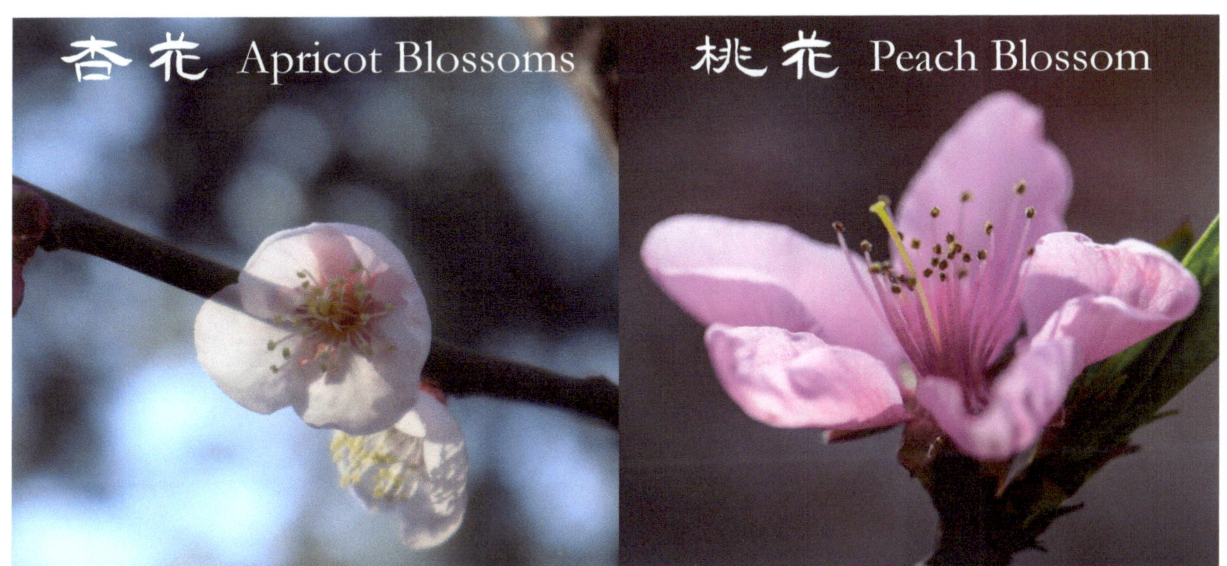

In Chinese culture, peach blossoms are less associated with misty rain or subtle emotions than apricot blossoms but more connected with romance and even marriage. Allegedly, the peak of peach blossom season used to be the most popular time of year for weddings in ancient China.
在中國文化之中，桃花不像杏花那樣帶有煙雨氣息或輕愁遐思，卻有另一種浪漫，總會引起關於愛情與婚姻的聯想。據說桃花巔峰期曾是古中國最經常舉行婚禮的時節。

Nothing summarizes peach blossom season and other natural phenomena during the solar term from early to mid March better than the following poem.
關於桃花，以及驚蟄節氣的其餘自然現象，下一頁的詩篇都以絕佳筆法概括了。

詩意節氣

驚蟄

驚蟄二月節
Awakening of Hibernating Creatures in the Second Lunar Month (Which Overlaps with March)

Author： Yuan, Zhen 元稹 (779-831)
Translator： Crystal Tai

陽氣初驚蟄　The energy of *yang* wakes hibernating creatures up.
韶光大地周　Spring splendor radiates everywhere as a nice setup.
桃花開蜀錦　Peach blossoms come out like silk flowers to show off.
鷹老化春鳩　Old hawks move away for young turtledoves to fly up.
時候爭催迫　Time urges every plant to grow up;
萌芽互矩修　Sprouts encourage each other to keep up.
人間務生事　Farmers must work for a living;
耕種滿田疇　They start plowing the rice field right after getting up.

Note: In the first line of the poem, the word *yang* refers to an invisible natural force that propels everything warm, bright, dry, active, penetrating, and male. The power of *yang* is obviously rising during the solar term that starts in early March.

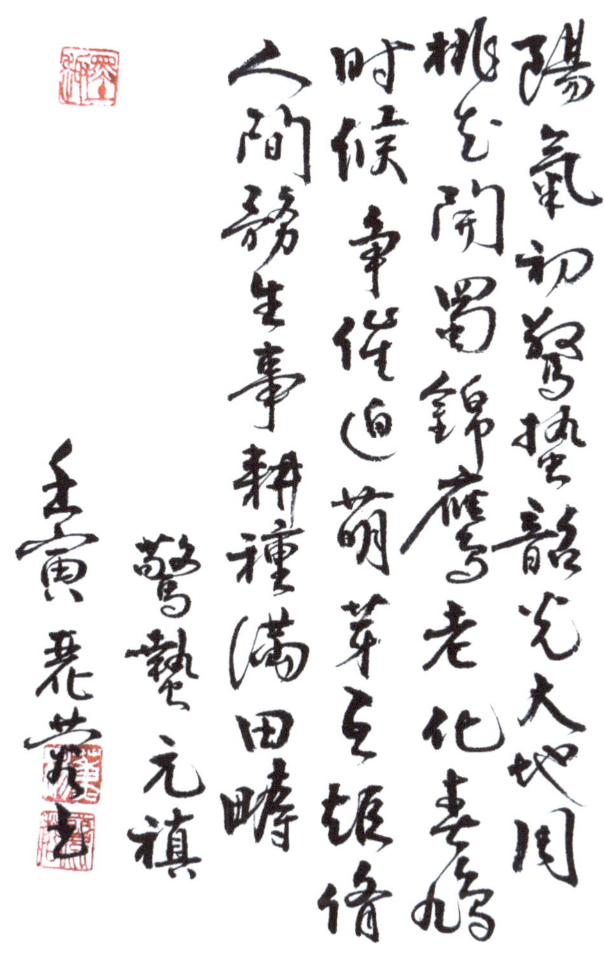

Chapter 4
Spring Equinox

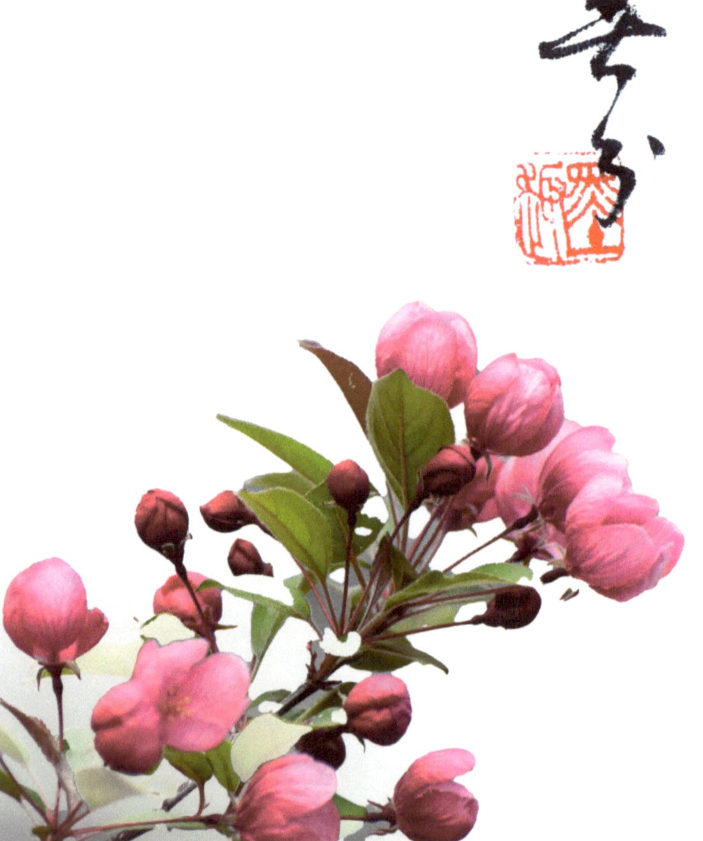

詩 意 節 氣

Who doesn't like flying a kite? It was customary to fly kites during the spring equinox in ancient China. It was also a Chinese tradition that the emperor prayed to the sun on this particular day.

誰不喜歡放風箏呢？古中國曾有春分放風箏的習俗。此外，皇帝總在春分日祭日。

The Temple of the Sun in Beijing is now a historic site open to the public. While monarchy no longer exists in China, Beijing residents still eat the same sweet rice cakes that used to be offered at the sun-worshiping ritual. They are called sun cakes or *taiyang gao* in Chinese, available at some bakeries in Beijing. There is another Beijing dessert for the spring equinox, interestingly called rolling donkey, or *ludaguen* in Chinese, because the vegan cake rolls are covered with soy powder, like playful donkeys with yellow dust all over them.

北京的日壇如今是對大眾開放的古蹟。儘管中國已不復帝制，仍有北京居民在春分食用曾經作為祭日供品的太陽糕。北京有些糕餅店還在做太陽糕，也做另一種名叫驢打滾的春分點心。驢打滾上面沾滿了黃豆粉，就像打過滾的驢子滿身黃沙一樣，故而得名。

春 分

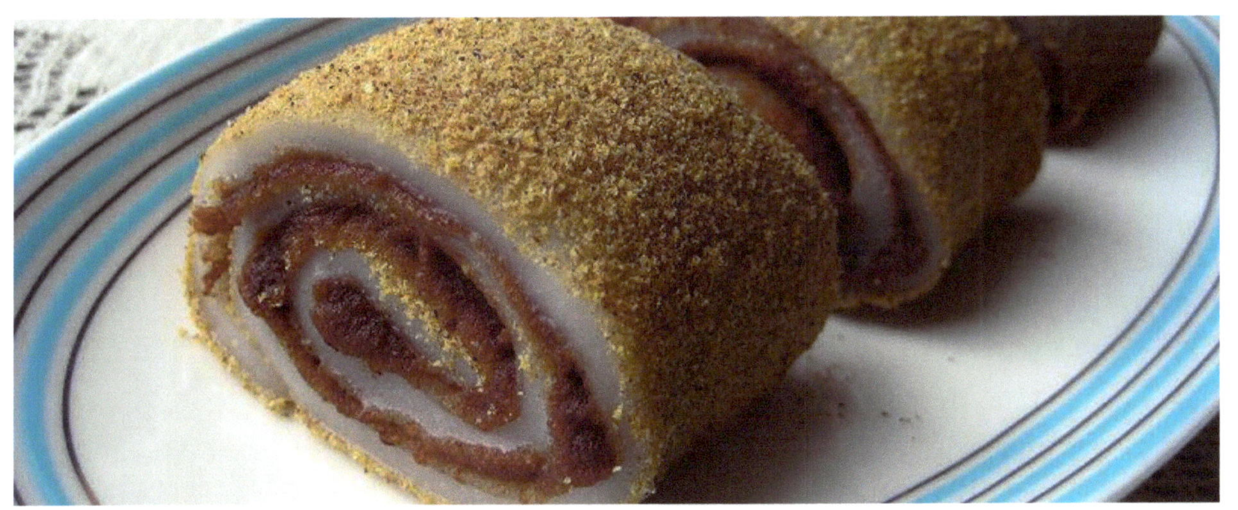

Speaking of food, many Chinese people used to believe that an egg would stand on end during the spring equinox thanks to the Earth's position relative to the sun. However, modern scientists have discovered that there are no changes in gravity alignment between the sun and the Earth on the spring equinox. Even so, balancing an egg is still a fun thing to do.

談到食物，過去曾有很多中國人相信，春分日地面和太陽的相關位置能讓雞蛋站立不倒。然而，現代科學家發現，春分日並不會改變太陽和地球之間的重力關聯。儘管如此，豎立雞蛋仍然有趣。

Many children in China still play the egg balancing game on the spring equinox, which occurs on March 19, March 20, or March 21, depending on when the sun returns to zero degree of the ecliptic drawn by ancient Chinese astronomers, or when the Earth comes back to zero degree of the celestial orbit redrawn by modern Chinese scientists to present the 24 solar terms.

眾多中國兒童仍在春分日玩着豎立雞蛋的遊戲。春分日是陽曆三月十九日、二十日，或二十一日，取決於古人所謂太陽返回黃經零度的日子，亦即現代科學家按照地球繞太陽軌道所重畫的橢圓形二十四節氣圖表上，地球轉回零度之時。

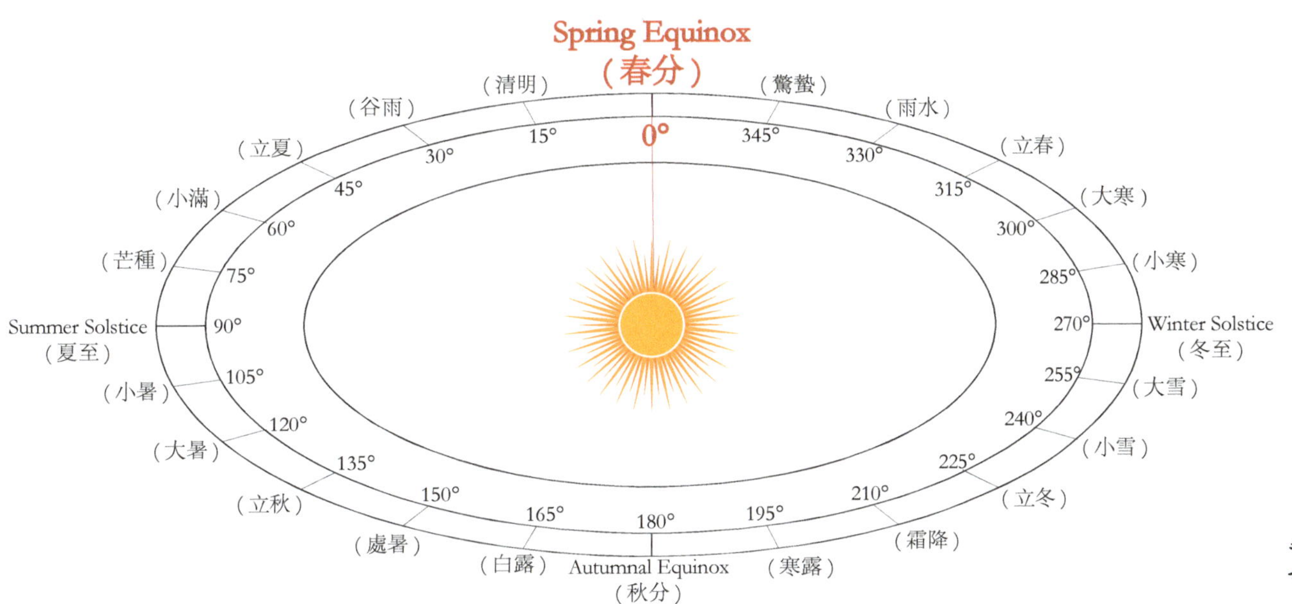

The spring equinox is called *chunfen* in Chinese. The *chun* of *chunfen* refers to spring and *fen* means "divided in half" to show the equal length of day and night.

春分的分字意指分成兩半，顯示白日與黑夜長度相等。

The spring equinox is when *yin* and *yang* are perfectly balanced, according to a traditional Chinese concept, which indicates that night belongs to *yin* and daylight pertains to *yang*. As explained in Chapter 3, *yang* propels everything warm, bright, dry, active, and male. On the other hand, *yin* generates everything cold, dark, wet, passive, receptive, and female. Most notably, a widely accepted Chinese hypothesis stipulates that *yin* and *yang* are the driving forces of the universe.[1]

春分是陰陽平衡之時。依照中國傳統觀念，黑夜屬陰，白日屬陽。如同本書第三章所述，陽推動世間所有溫暖、明亮、乾燥、主動、衝刺、雄性的一切。陰則衍生世間所有寒冷、黑暗、潮溼、被動、容納、雌性的一切。最值得注意的是，一種廣受採納的學說假設陰陽是宇宙運行的動力。

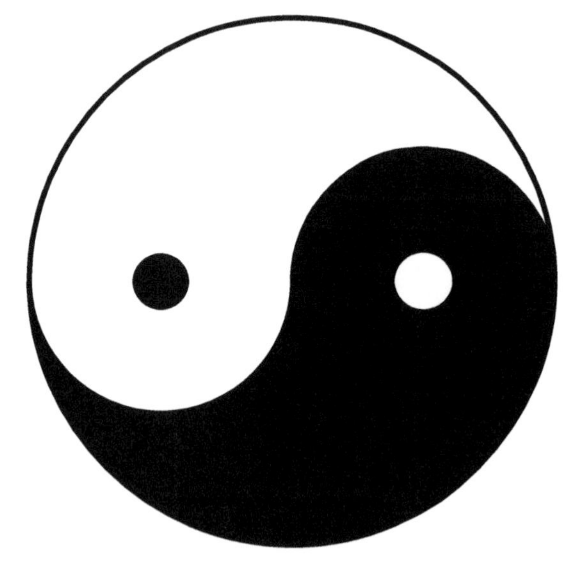

Based on the *yin-yang* theory, *yang* will get stronger in spring and keep rising until reaching its apex on the summer solstice, which was defined as the peak of summer in ancient China. Likewise, the spring equinox has been regarded as the midpoint of the season as well.

根據陰陽理論，陽在春天漸強，不斷上升，直到抵達夏至為止。中國古人定義夏至為夏天過半的頂峰點，也同樣認為春分是春天的中間點。

The spring equinox is not the first day of spring in traditional Chinese culture, but the beginning of the Chinese solar term named after it. This solar term is divided into three parts just like the other 23. Each part is five or six days long. The first part of the solar term following the spring equinox is when migrating swallows arrive in northern China. The second part is when thunder starts to appear in northern China. The third part is when rain comes with lightning in northern China.

春分日雖不是中國傳統文化定義的春季第一天，卻是春分節氣的開端。春分節氣也像其餘二十三個節氣一樣分為三候。每一候五或六天。春分一候玄鳥（燕子）至，二候雷乃發聲，三候始電。

1　Term Bases. "Yin-Yang" (Chinese edition). Key Concepts in Chinese Thought and Culture. https://www.chinesethought.cn/shuyu_show.aspx?shuyu_id=2172

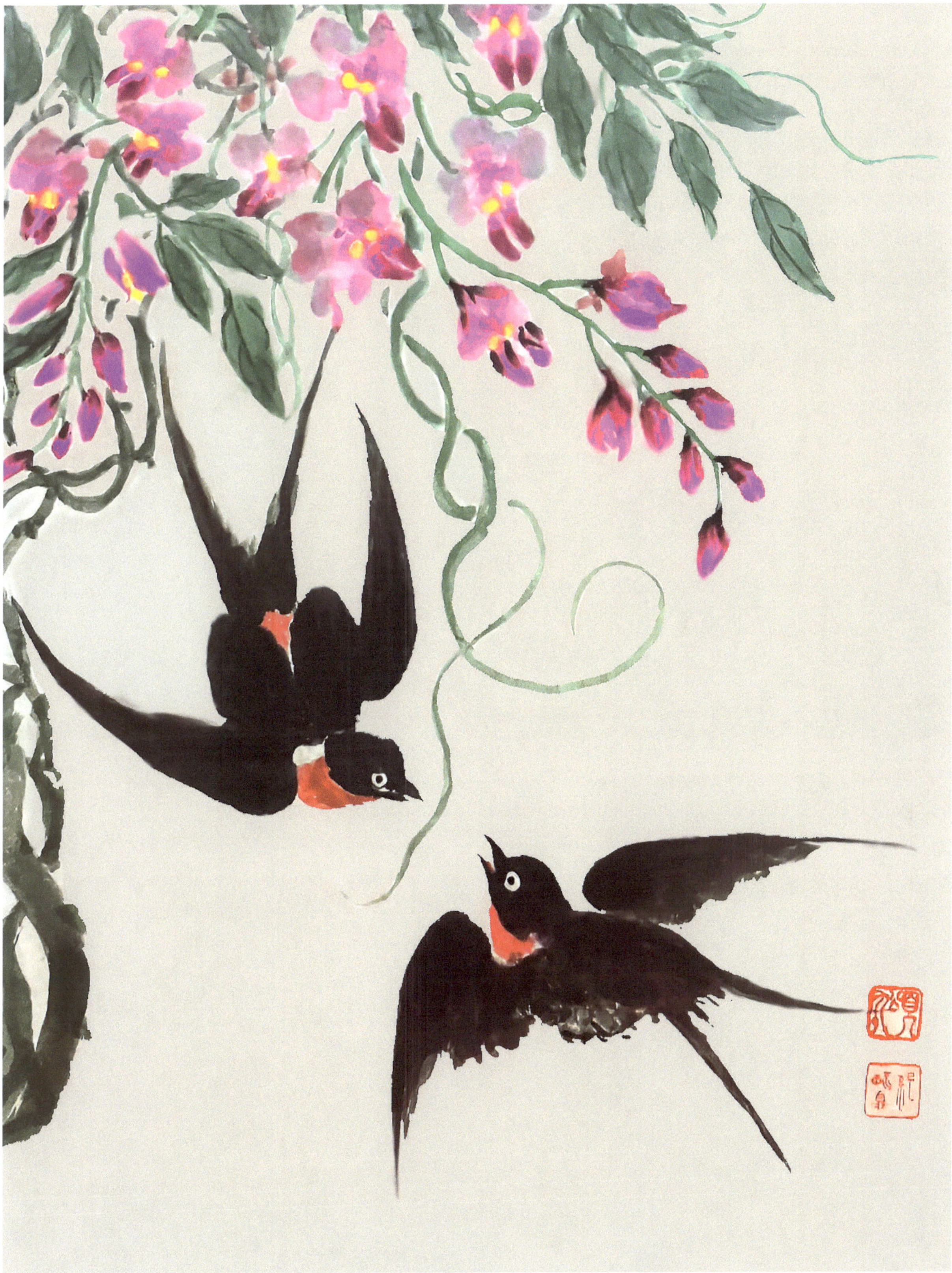

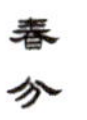

詩意節氣

春分

A painting of swallows and wisteria by Mr. Yu-Ting Chi, the author's maternal grandfather
作者的外公紀毓鼎先生的紫藤雙燕圖

During the solar term following the spring equinox, many flower species begin blooming. Ancient Chinese scholars picked three of them to represent this solar term. The first is Kaido crabapple blossoms, which symbolize wealth and status in Chinese culture. That explains why some classical Chinese gardens have flower-shaped gates that are called crabapple blossom gate or *haitangmen* in Chinese.

春分節氣是百花怒放時期。春分第一候之花是海棠，在中國文化之中象徵着富貴。這就是為何有些古典園林院牆開着海棠形狀的門洞，稱為海棠門。

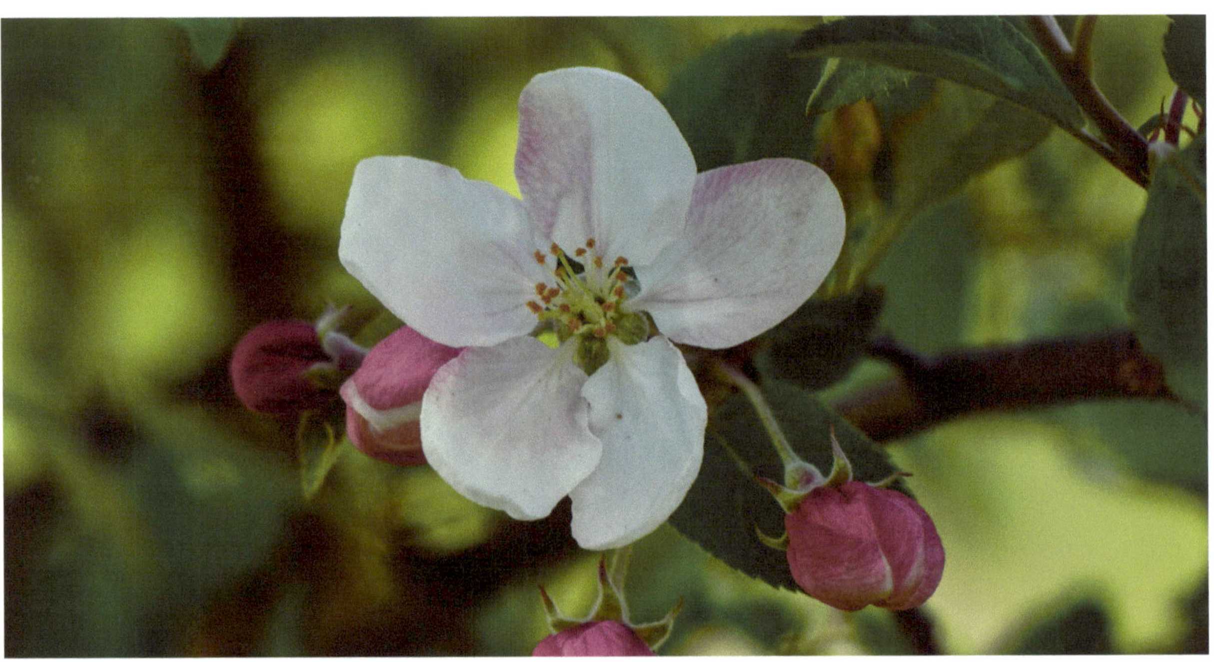

The second flower species that comes into bloom after the spring equinox in China is Asian pear blossoms, which are often metaphorized as snowflakes in spring.

春分第二候之花是梨花，經常被比喻成春雪。

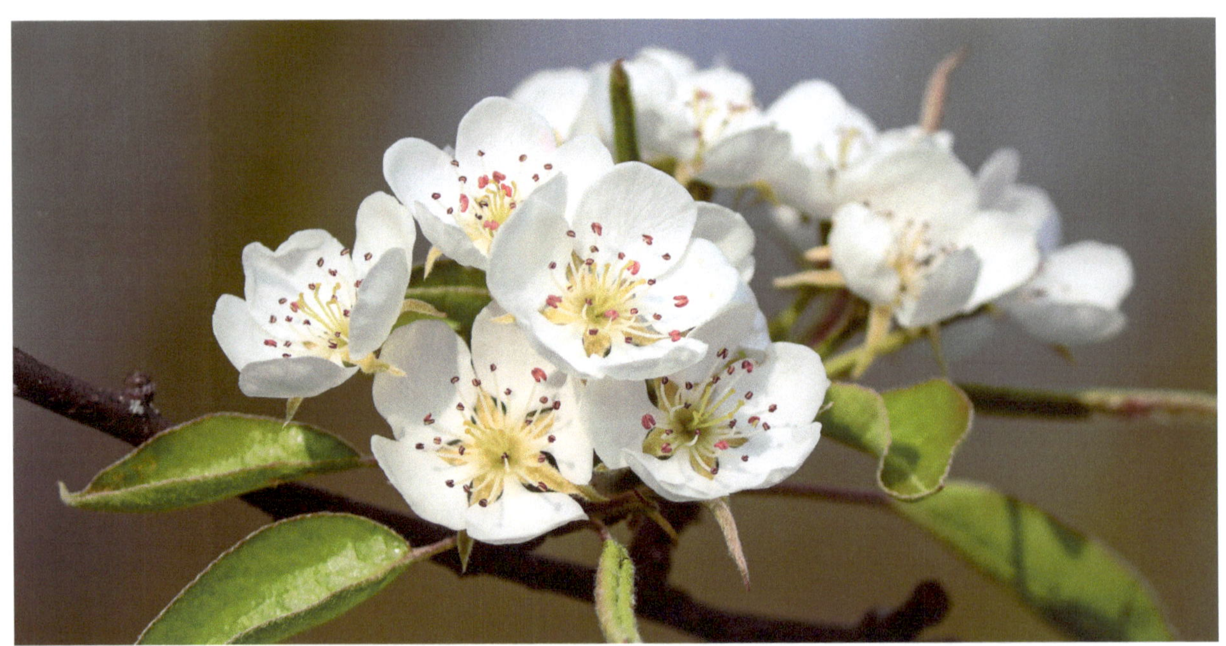

Another flower species that starts blooming during this time of year is lily magnolia, different from Yulan magnolia, which comes into bloom in February. Lily magnolia trees are smaller, so the species can be categorized as a shrub.
春分第三候之花則是木蘭,雖然近似陽曆二月綻放的玉蘭花,但木蘭樹較小,屬於灌木。

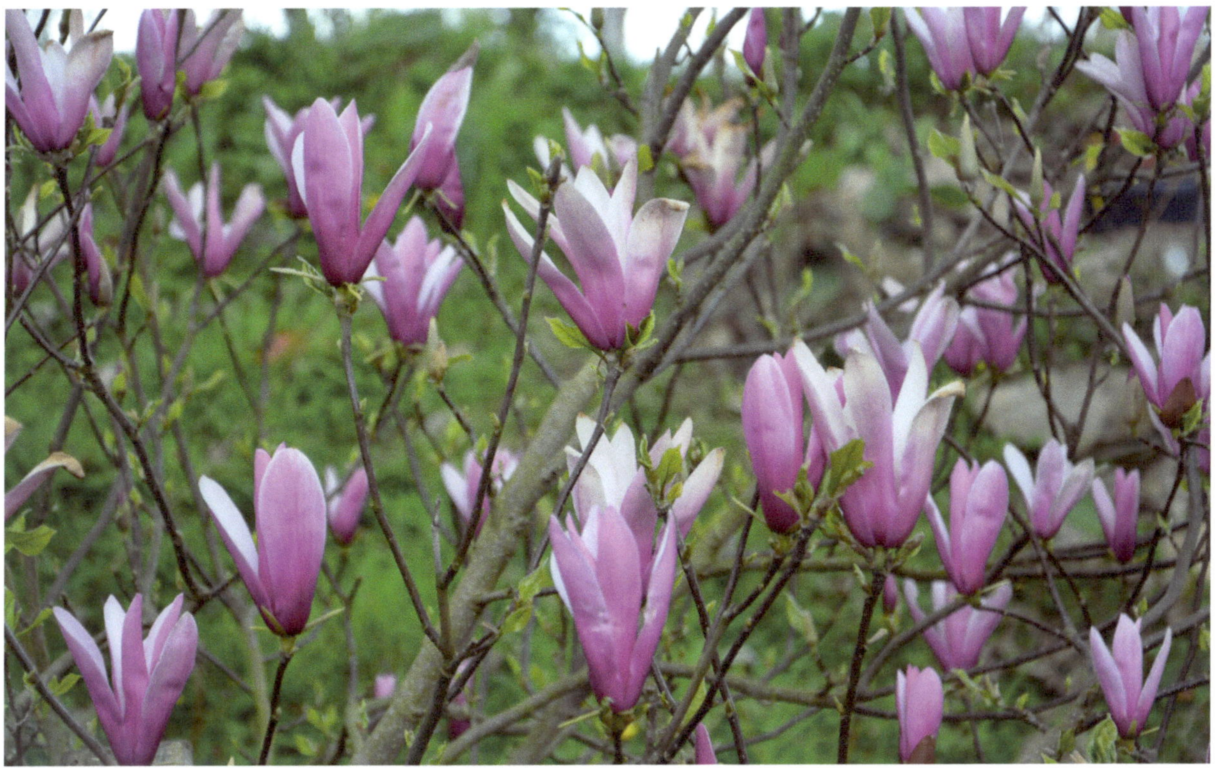

Lily magnolia is called *mulan* in Chinese, just as the heroine of a Chinese folktale that has been adapted into Disney movies. Perhaps Mulan was born during the lily magnolia season?
木蘭花的中文名稱恰巧是花木蘭傳奇女主角的名字。或許花木蘭就是生於木蘭花期?

With various flowers blooming everywhere, the solar term following the spring equinox is a fantastic time of year for outings. On the next page is a classical Chinese poem that pleasantly presents spring equinox activities.
春分時節到處繁花燦開,自然適宜出遊。下一頁就有一首絕句欣然呈現着春分日所有趣味盎然的活動。

春分 Spring Equinox

Author：Liu, Changqing 劉長卿 (709-785)
Translator: Crystal Tai

日月陽陰兩均天 Night and day, *yin* and *yang* look balanced today to every creature;
玄鳥不辭桃花寒 Swallows return north while peach trees bloom in the slightly chilly weather.
從來今日豎雞子 This has always been the day to stand an egg on its end,
川上良人放紙鳶 And the day for good citizens to fly kites along the river.

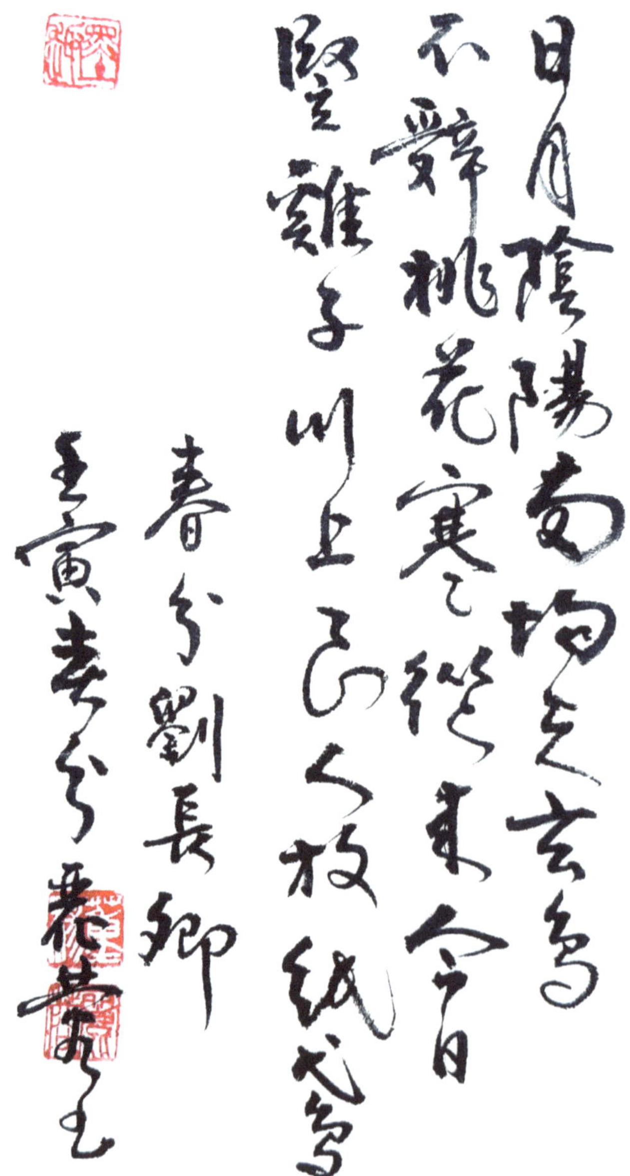

詩意節氣

春分

Chapter 5
Clear & Bright View

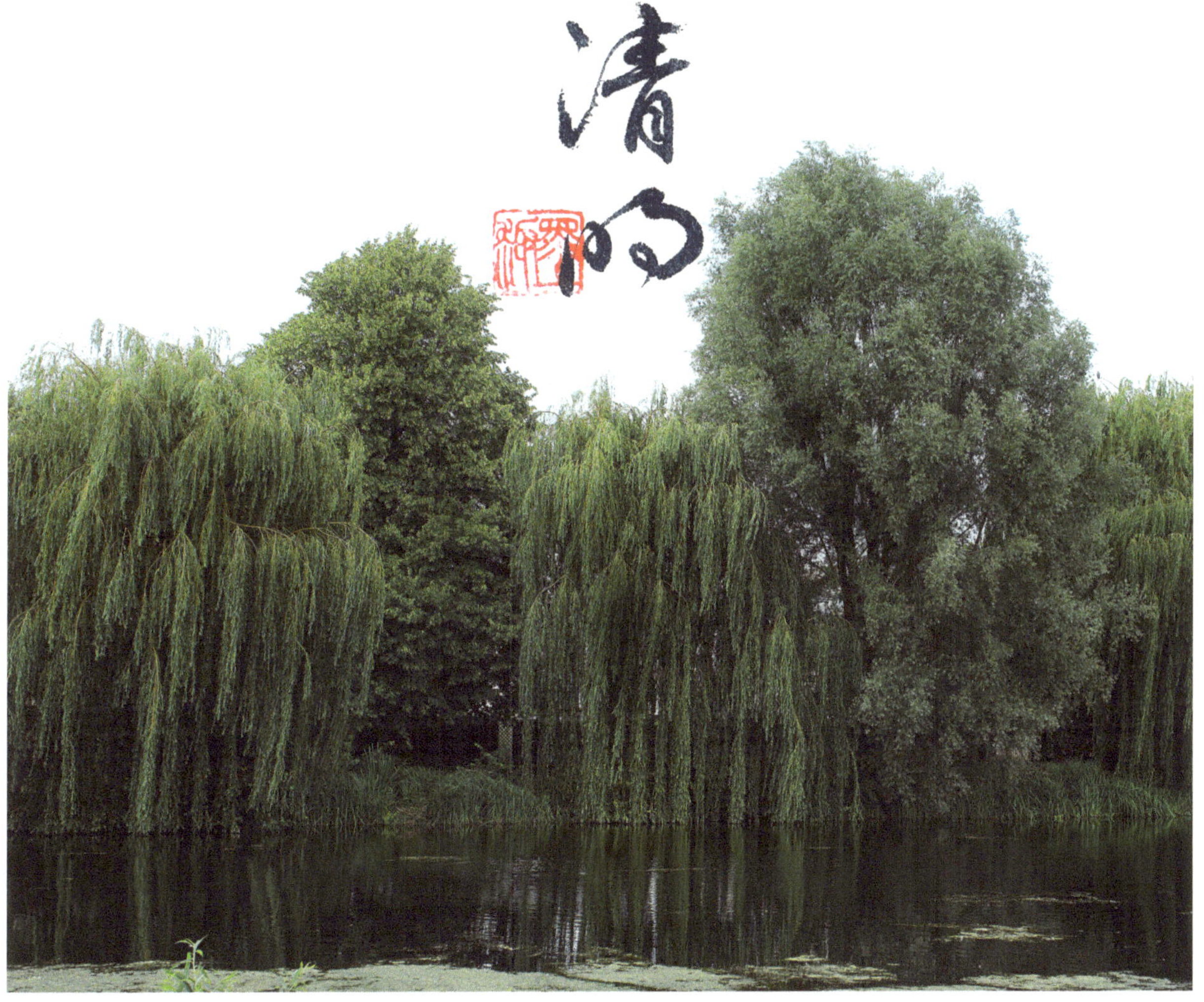

With early April's warmer weather comes a traditional Chinese holiday. Widely known as the Qingming Festival or Tomb Sweeping Day, it is meant for people to pay tribute to their ancestors and deceased family members.

陽曆四月天氣漸暖，一個中國傳統節日隨之來臨。這就是清明節，一個讓人祭拜歷代祖先、緬懷故去親人的節日。

Tomb Sweeping Day may be observed on April 4, April 5, or April 6, depending on when the sun reaches 15 degrees of the ecliptic drawn by ancient Chinese astronomers, or when the Earth arrives at 15 degrees of the celestial orbit redrawn by modern Chinese scientists to present the 24 solar terms.

清明節可能在陽曆四月四日、四月五日，或四月六日，取決於古人所謂太陽到達黃經十五度的日子，亦即現代科學家按照地球繞太陽軌道所重畫的橢圓形二十四節氣圖表上，地球運轉到十五度之時。

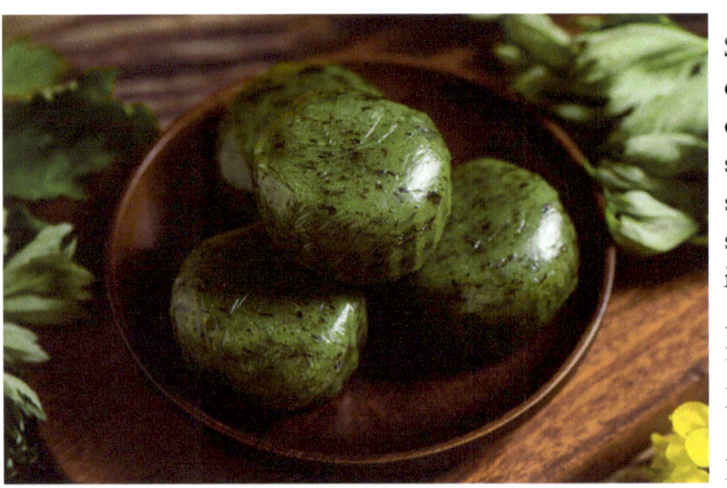

On Tomb Sweeping Day, Chinese cemetery visitors often bring green rice balls as tomb offerings and picnic food. It is mugwort juice or another wild plant juice that gives the rice balls their green color.

清明節掃墓祭品以及野餐食物都經常包括青糰。青糰的綠色是艾草或別的野生植物汁液所染成。

Shanghai-style green rice balls are especially famous. Most of them contain azuki bean paste or another sweet filling, but some of them are savory, with salted duck egg yolk or shredded vegetables and minced meat inside.

上海青糰特別有名，多數包着豆沙餡或別種甜餡，另外也有鹹蛋黃或菜肉之類鹹味餡料。

It is notable that green rice balls are seasonal, only available in spring. Why? As stated in Chapter 2, Chinese medicine practitioners believe that the nutrients of green vegetables will do good to the liver, which works extra hard in spring. That explains why Tomb Sweeping Day's rice balls are all dyed with natural green juice.

值得注意的是，青糰只有在春天才買得到。為什麼呢？如同本書第二章所述，中醫相信綠色蔬菜的養份入肝，而肝臟在春天工作量特大，養肝有額外需要。因此，清明的青糰都用天然綠葉汁液染色。

Following Tomb Sweeping Day is a solar term, also called Qingming in Chinese, which literally means "clear and bright." It definitely indicates a clear and bright view of spring scenery.

緊接在清明節之後的是清明節氣。清明意指春天視野清晰、光線明亮的景色。

During the solar term of Qingming, many different types of flowers are blooming, but ancient Chinese scholars only picked three of them to represent this solar term. The first is tung blossoms.

在清明時節，繁花怒放，但是古中國學者只選出了三種花來代表清明。清明第一候之花是桐花。

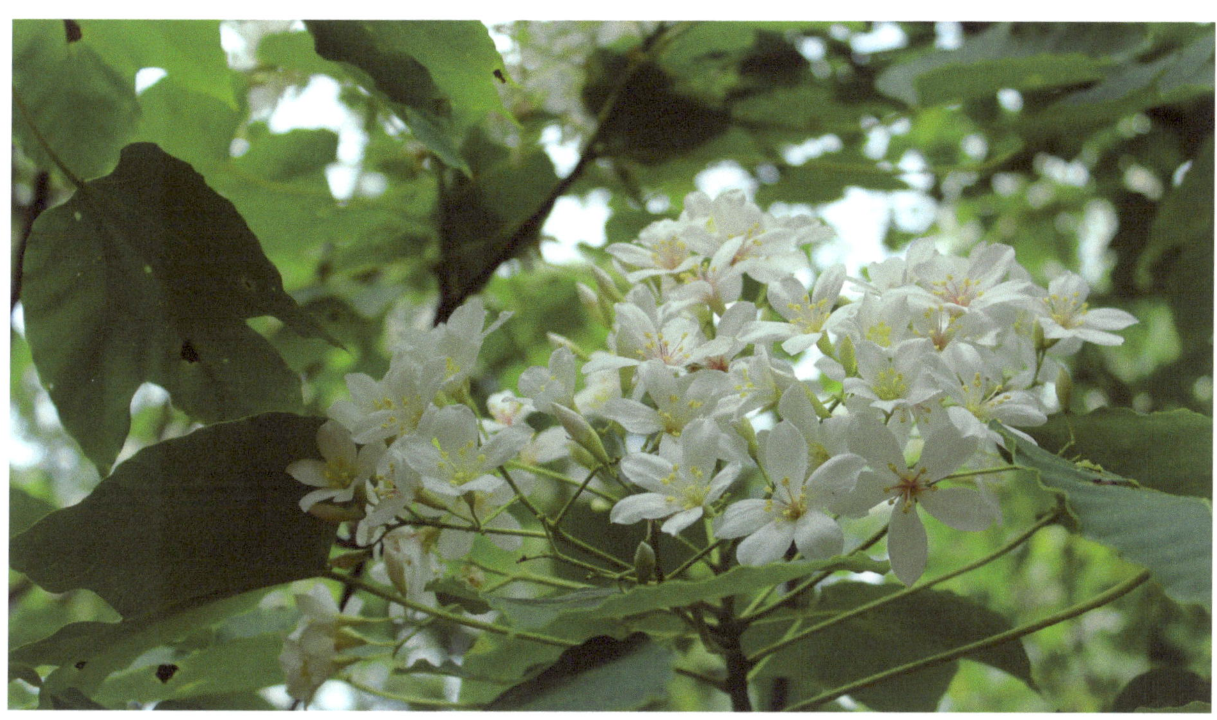

The second flower species blooming during this solar term is wheat flowers.

第二候之花是麥花。

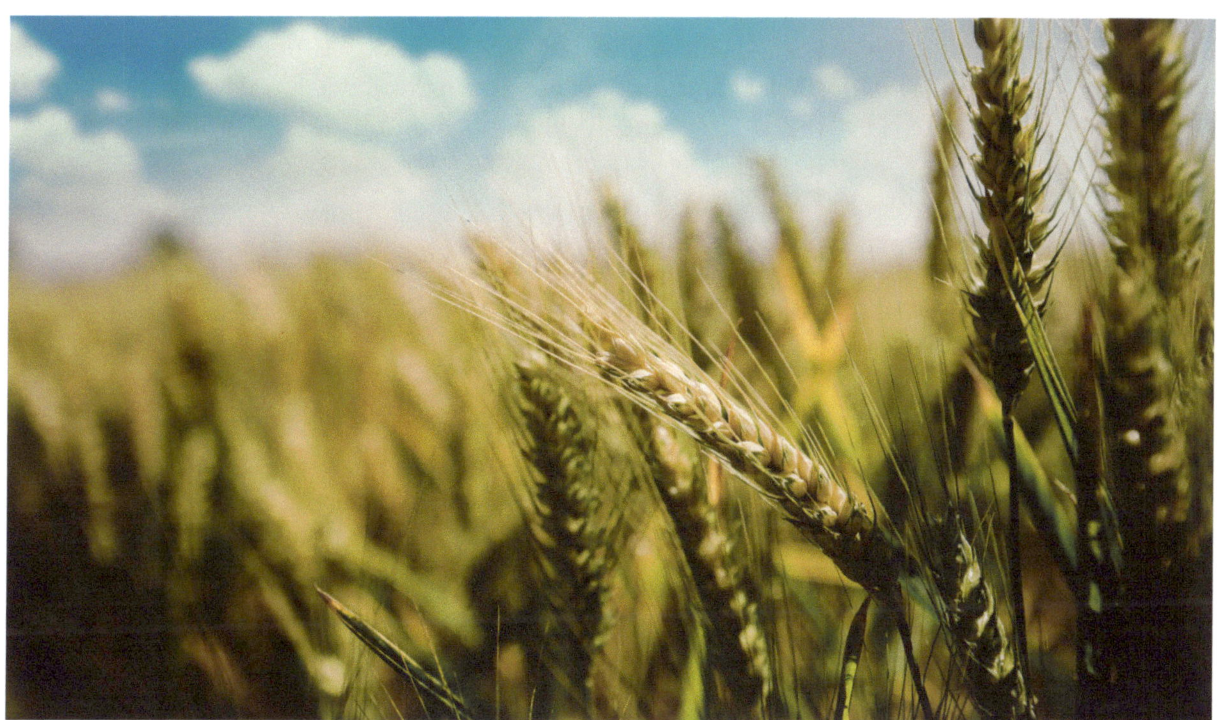

The third is Chinese willow flowers.
第三候之花是柳花。

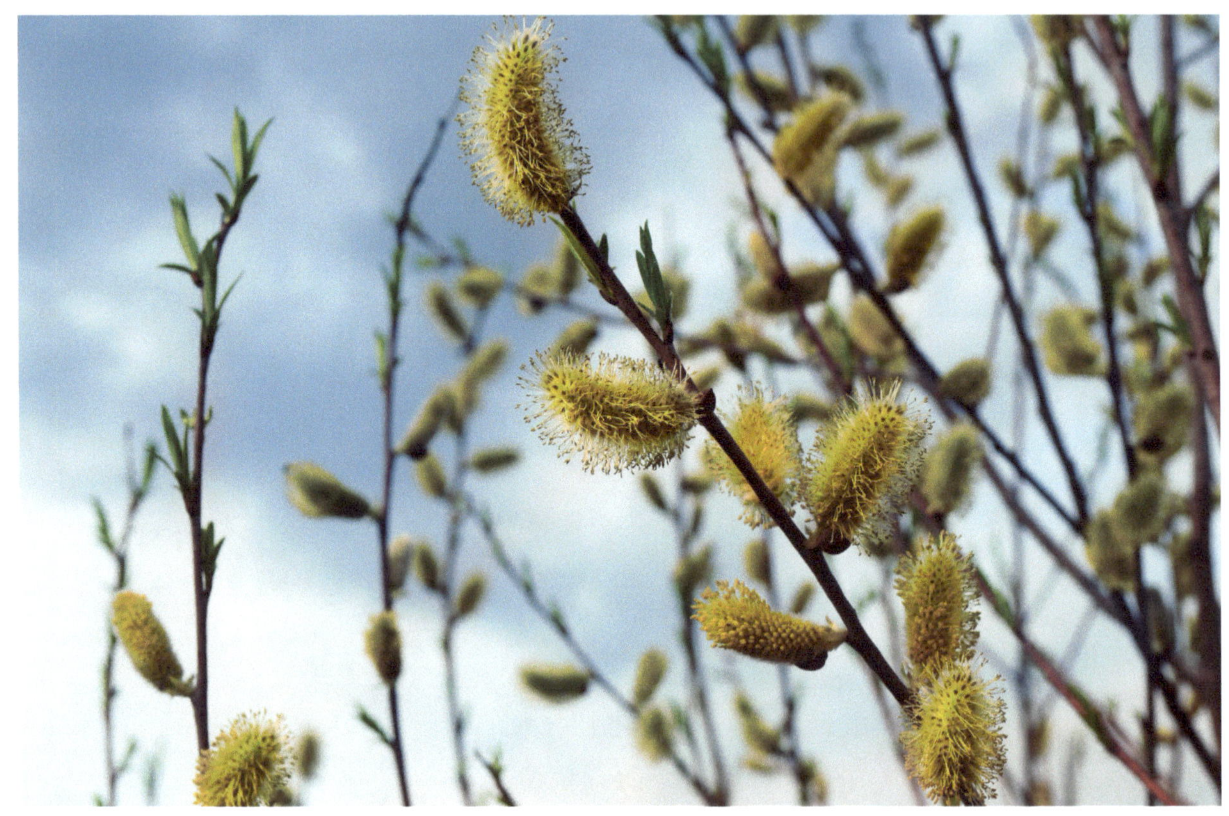

Among the three, wheat flowers only bloom in the countryside. Since most people nowadays live in cities and don't see a wheat field very often, some Chinese bloggers have suggested replacing wheat flowers on the list with a flower species commonly seen at city parks. The alternatives include Chinese wisteria, which has a disturbingly brief bloom period. Although Chinese wisteria may stay in bloom in May in northern China, it only blooms in April in central China.
在這三種花之中，麥花只開在鄉村。因此，有些人建議以城市公園常見的春花來取代麥花，例如換成紫藤。紫藤花期可謂匆促得令人感傷。儘管紫藤在華北到陽曆五月還開花，在華中花期卻只限於陽曆四月。

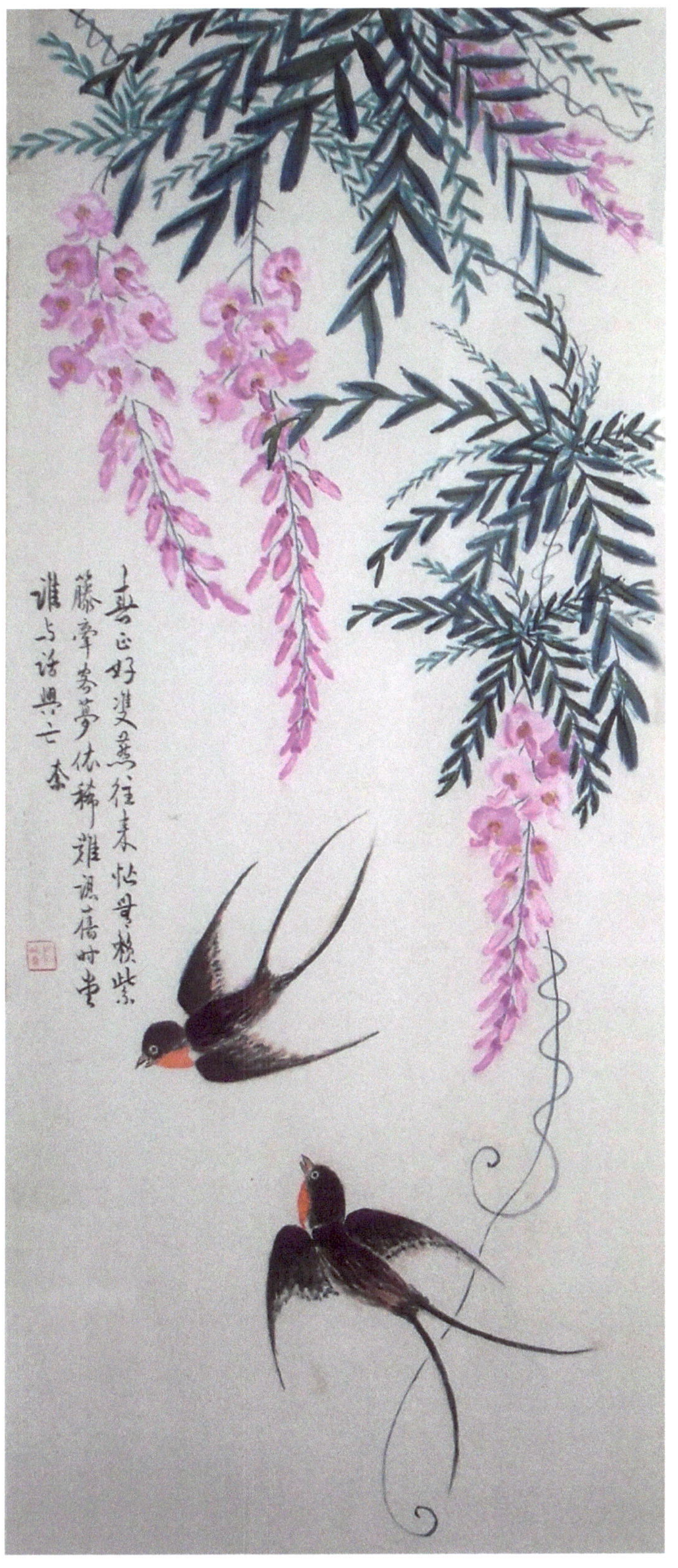

A painting of swallows and wisteria by Mr. Yu-Ting Chi, the author's maternal grandfather
作者的外公紀毓鼎先生的紫藤雙燕圖

The solar term from early to mid April can be divided as three parts, just like the other 23 solar terms. Each part is five or six days long. The first part is when tung trees burst into bloom. The second part is when quails become active and replace voles in the field. The third part is when the rainbow season starts.

清明節氣如同另外二十三個節氣，可分為三候，每一候為時五或六天。清明一候桐始華，二候田鼠化為鴽，三候虹始見。

Ancient Chinese meteorologists observed that the weather would have to be warm enough for rainbows to appear after the rain, but they didn't know why. Modern scientists have found out why. This is because there must be sunshine and raindrops at the same time for a rainbow to show up, but when the weather is cold, water droplets within clouds are often frozen ice particles that are incapable of scattering sunlight.

中國古代氣象學家觀察到了天氣要夠暖才會有雨後彩虹，但只知其然，不知所以然。現代科學家找到了原因。原來，天氣較冷時，雲間水珠往往結冰，而冰珠無法像雨珠一樣發散所反射的陽光，就形成不了彩虹。

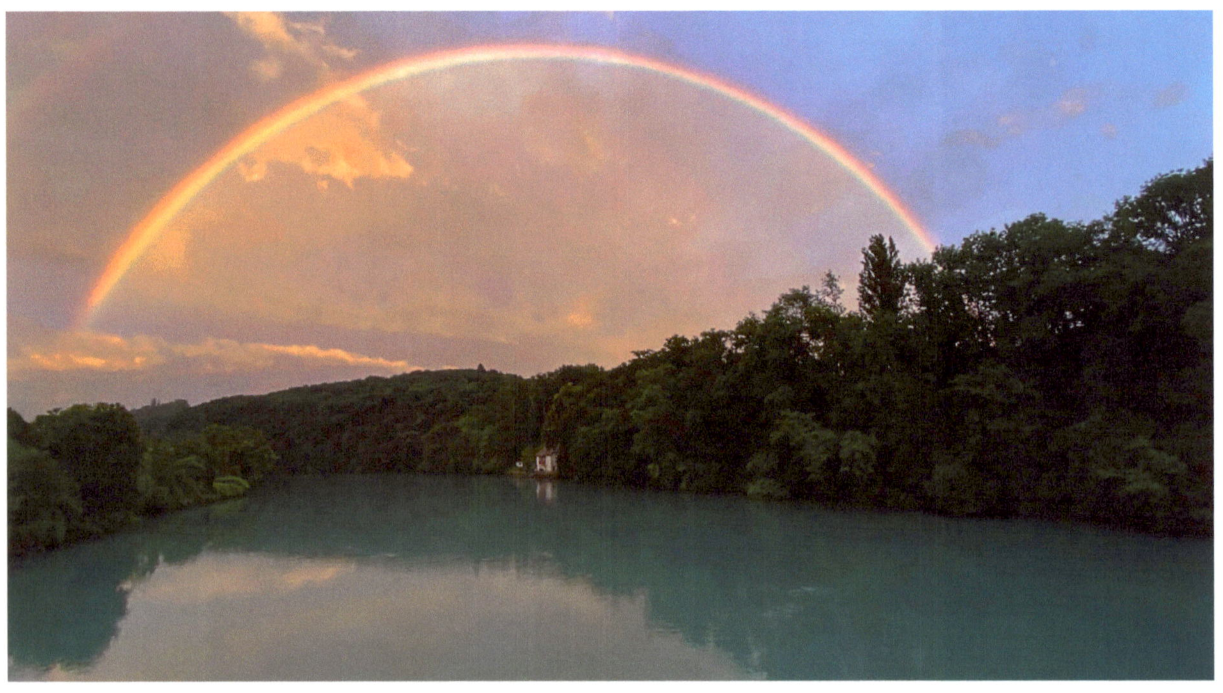

About the rainy weather during the solar term from early to mid April, the following poem poignantly paints a word picture.

談到清明時節多雨的天氣，下一頁的詩篇就在傳神描繪清明雨景：

清明 Tomb Sweeping Day

Author： Du, Mu 杜牧 (803-852)
Translator：Crystal Tai

清明時節雨紛紛 It rains nonstop on Tomb Sweeping Day
路上行人欲斷魂 Much to the pedestrians' dismay.
借問酒家何處是 When they ask where the nearest inn is,
牧童遙指杏花村 A cowboy points to Apricot Blossoms Village far away.

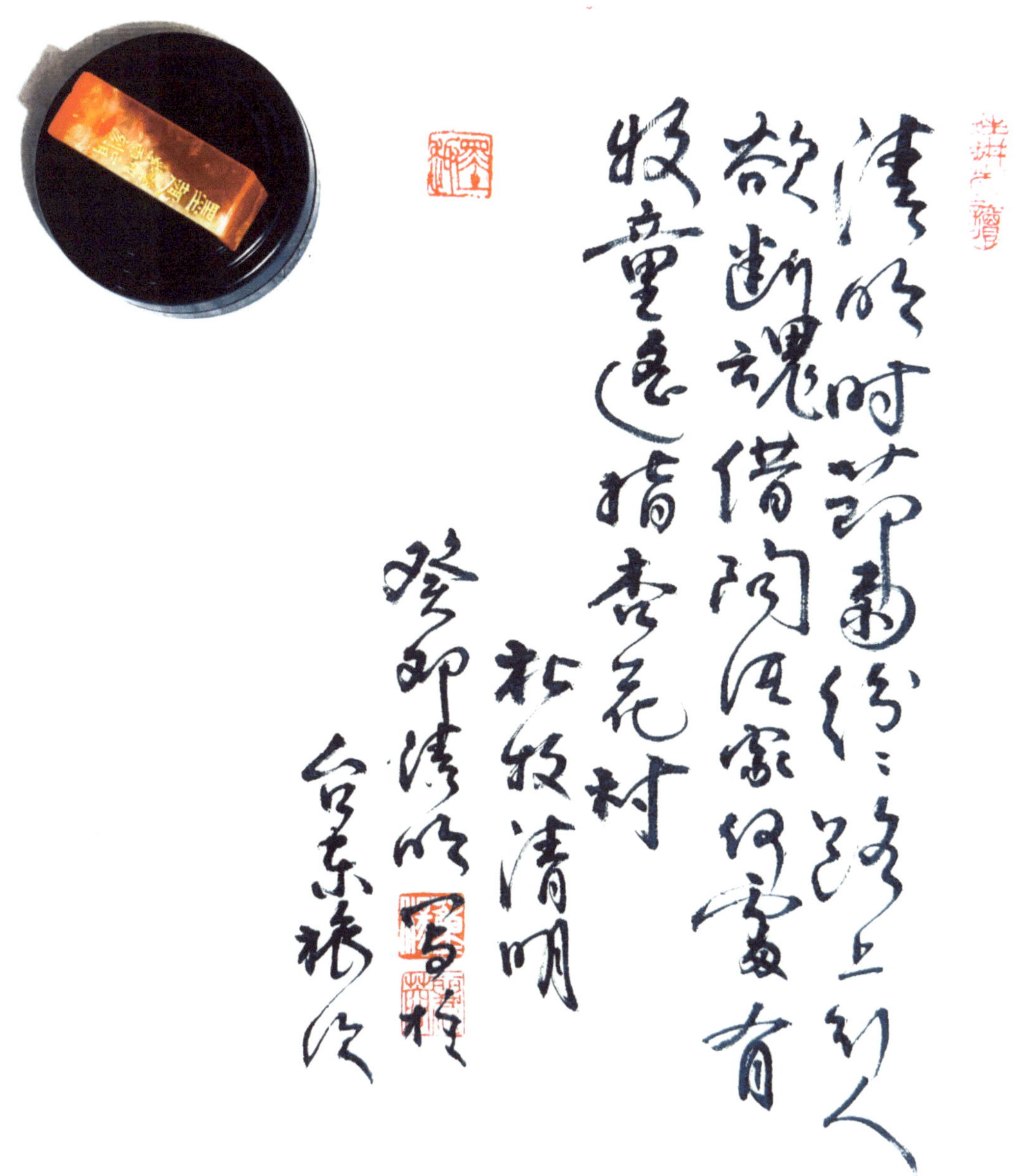

Chapter 6
Rain for Crops

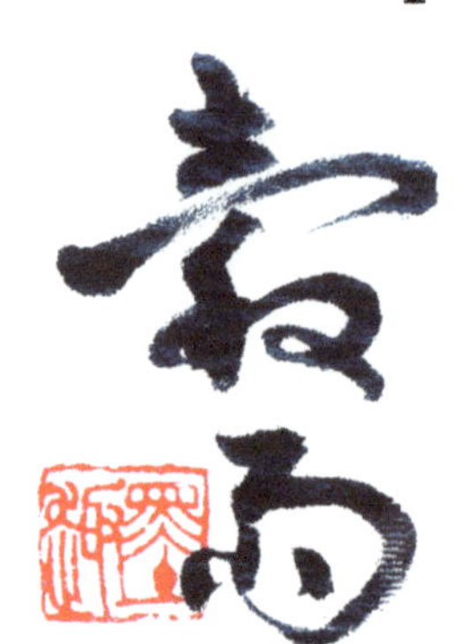

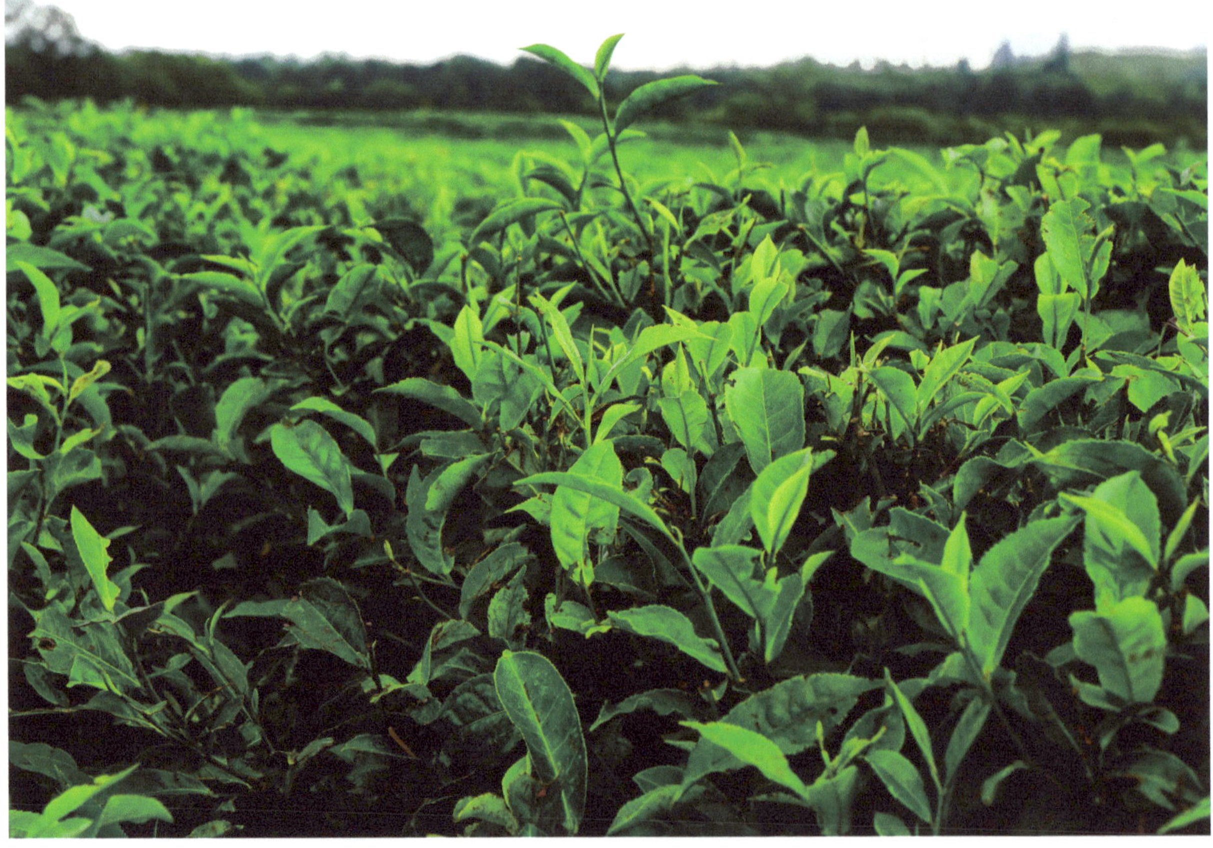

To tea lovers, stir-fried shrimp with tea leaves must look appetizing. This is a famous dish that originated from Hangzhou, China. It incorporates an exquisite type of tea named *longjing*, which means "dragon well" in Chinese. The shrimp dish with dragon well tea leaves tastes the best in late April, because April is the month when spring tea leaves are picked from tea plantations in China. That makes many fresh tea leaves readily available in late April.

穀雨 對於愛茶人士，龍井蝦仁必然是很有吸引力的美食。這是杭州名菜，在陽曆四月下旬特別美味。因為陽曆四月是春茶採收時節，所以陽曆四月下旬有特多新鮮茶葉。

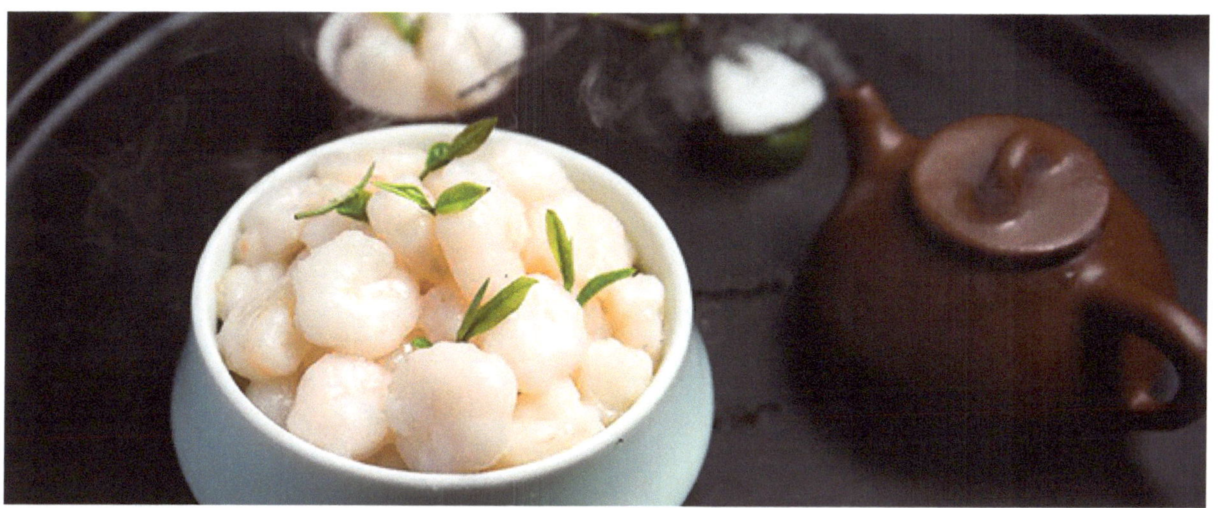

In Chinese tea culture, it is preferable to harvest spring tea either right before or on a special day in April. This day can be April 19, April 20, or April 21, depending on when the sun reaches 30 degrees of the ecliptic drawn by ancient Chinese astronomers, or when the Earth arrives at 30 degrees of the celestial orbit redrawn by modern Chinese scientists to present the 24 solar terms.

在中國的茶文化之中，春茶最好在陽曆四月一個特殊的日子之前或當天採摘。這一天可能是陽曆四月十九、二十，或二十一日，取決於古人所謂太陽到達黃經三十度的日子，亦即現代科學家按照地球繞太陽軌道所重畫的橢圓形二十四節氣圖表上，地球運轉到三十度之時。

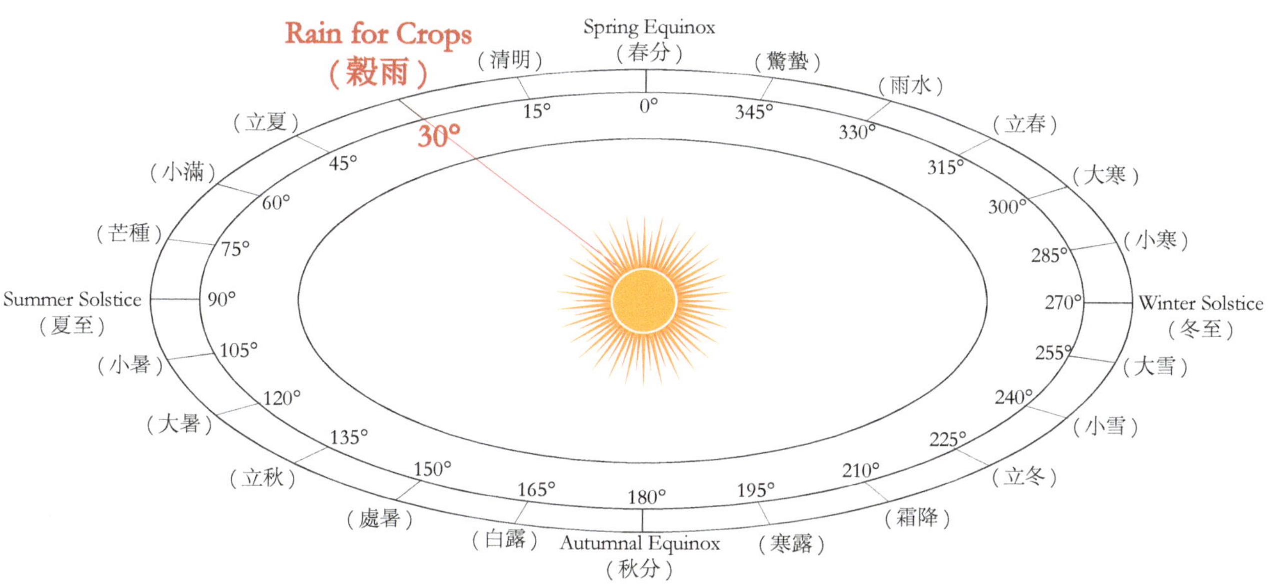

According to folklore, the inventor Cangjie completed his creation of Chinese words on a rainy spring day, which coincided with the sun at the celestial longitude of 30 degrees. From then on, Chinese people paid tribute to Cangjie on this particular day called *guyu* for thousands of years, but the custom has gradually faded away by now.

根據傳說，倉頡造字就是在太陽到達黃經三十度的一個雨中春日完成。從此，中國人民常在這個稱為穀雨的日子祭祀倉頡，但歷經數千年的此一傳統已在現代式微。

Guyu Day is the beginning of a solar term with the same name, in which *gu* refers to grains and *yu* indicates rain. Guyu represents frequent rain showers for growing crops from late April to early May.
穀雨日是同名節氣的第一天。穀雨之名顯示陽曆四月下旬到五月初之間多雨，可以滋養正在成長的農作物。

This solar term can be divided into three parts. Each part is five or six days long. The first part of the solar term from late April to early May is when duckweed begins to cover the water surface. The second part is when cuckoos are singing and fluttering their wings. The third part is when hoopoes perch on mulberry trees.
穀雨節氣可分為三候。每一候五或六天。穀雨第一候萍始生；第二候鳴鳩拂其羽；第三候戴勝降於桑。

Aside from recording these natural phenomena, ancient Chinese meteorologists named three types of flowers that always bloom during the solar term from late April to early May. The first includes all the tree peonies, which symbolize wealth and status in Chinese culture.
中國古代氣象學家除了記下這些自然現象以外，也選出了代表穀雨節氣的花。穀雨一候之花是牡丹，象徵着富貴。

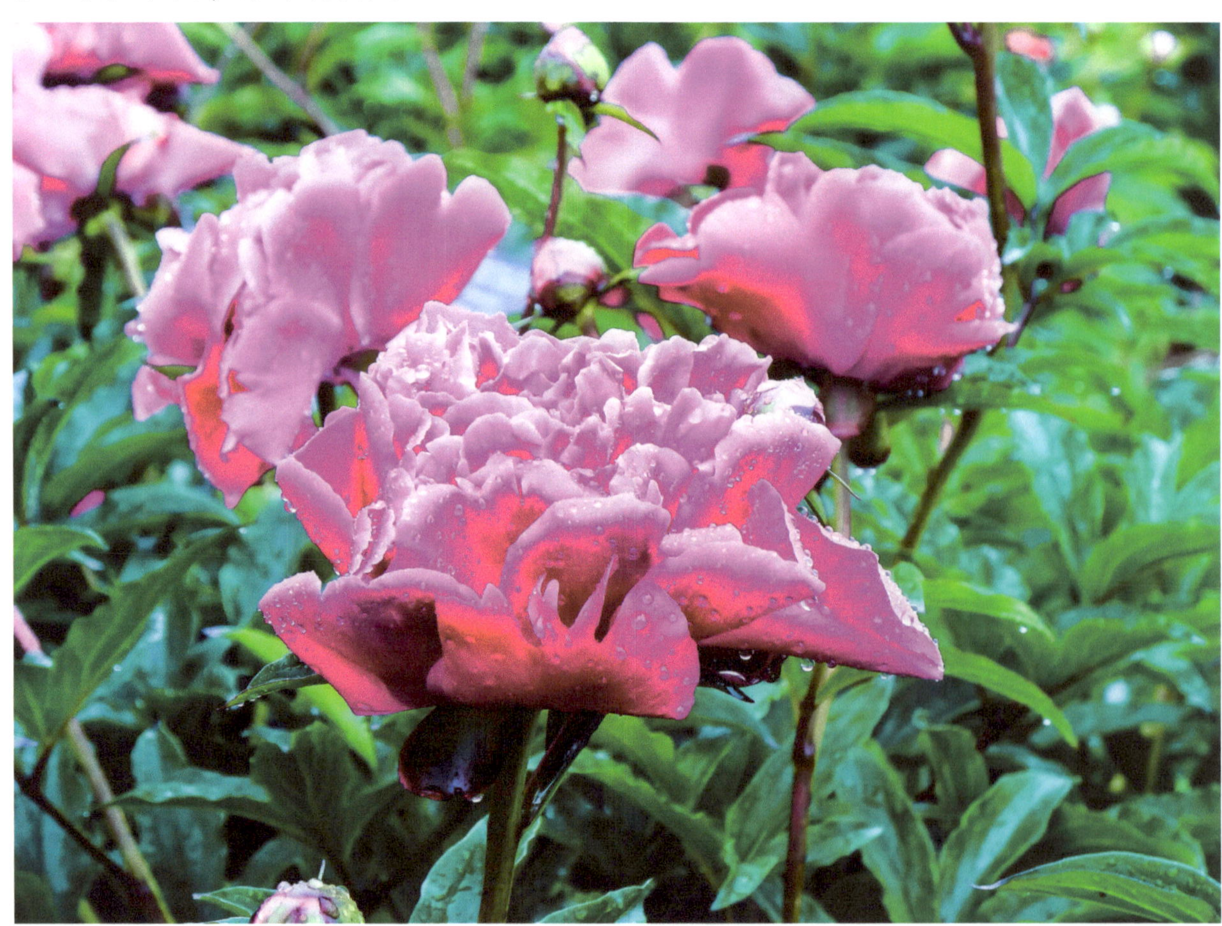

The second is rosa rubus, which belongs to the rose family and can be used for making perfumes.
穀雨二候之花是荼蘼，屬於薔薇科，適合用來製造香水。

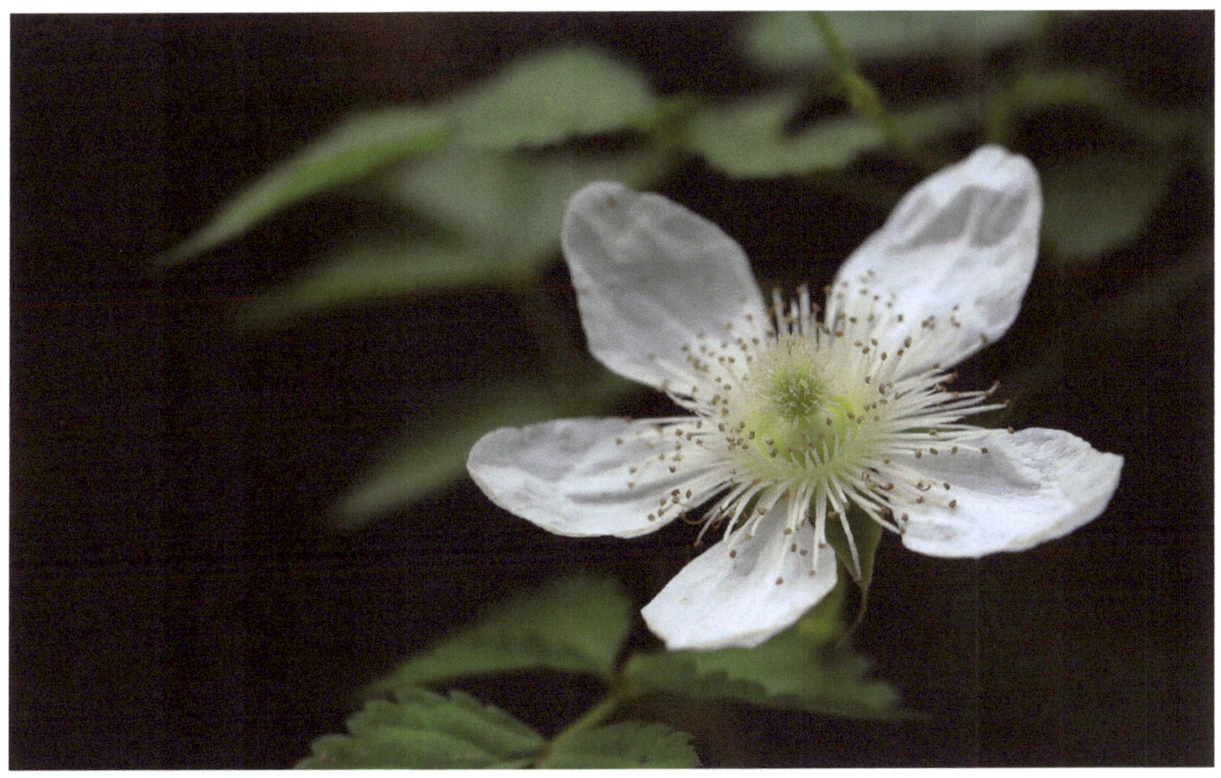

The third is neem flowers, which can work as an insect repellent. 穀雨三候是楝花，有驅蟲的作用。

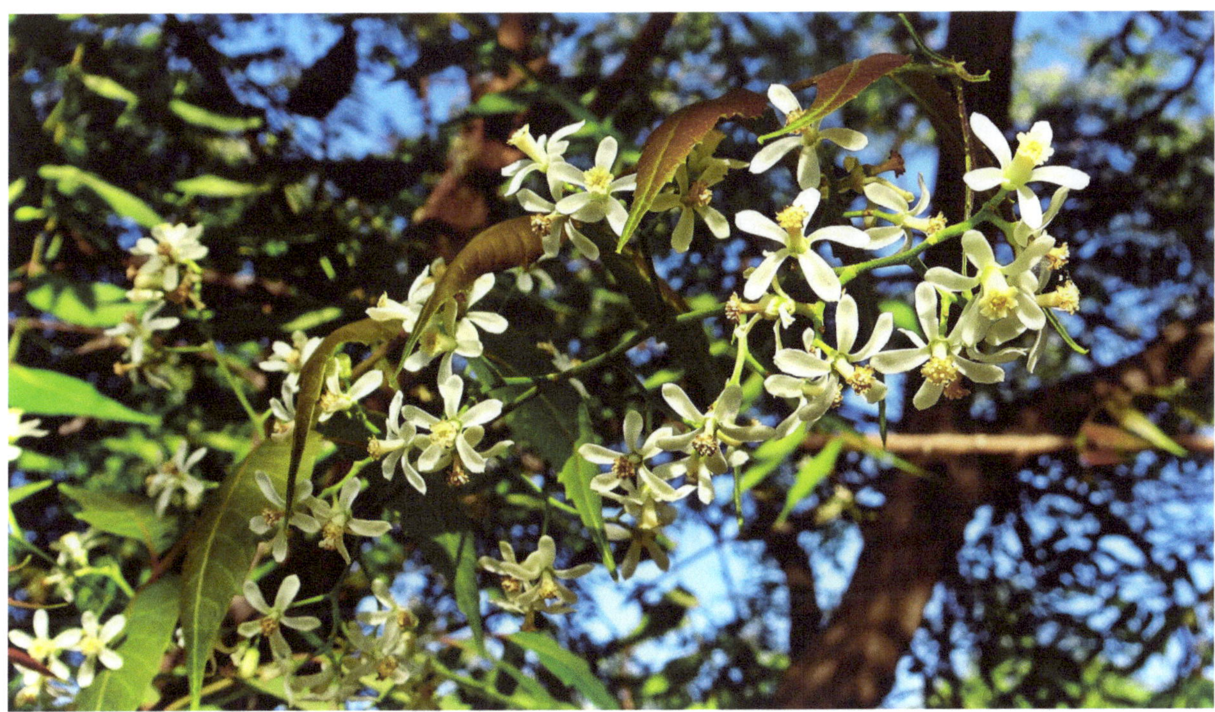

Among these three, please note that a tree peony is different from an herbaceous peony. In China, Luoyang has always been the city of tree peonies, and Yangzhou the city of herbaceous peonies.

在這三種花之中，牡丹是木本，但長得很像草本的芍藥。在中國，洛陽是牡丹之城，揚州則是芍藥之城。

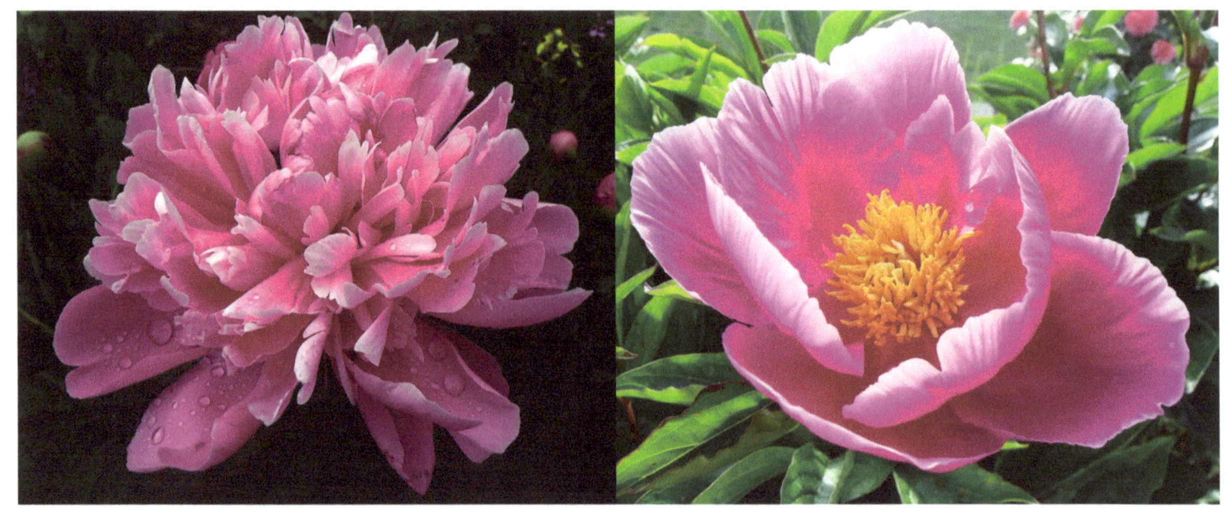

| Tree Peony | Herbaceous Peony |

Compared with herbaceous peonies, tree peonies are of course taller, with bigger flowers, too. Tree peonies usually come into bloom during the first five or six days of the solar term named Rain for Crops. By contrast, herbaceous peonies begin blooming toward the end of this solar term.

牡丹和芍藥長得很像，但木本的牡丹當然較高，花朵也較大。牡丹在穀雨節氣初期綻放，芍藥則在穀雨末期才初開。

Speaking of peony flowers, the following poem mesmerizingly metaphorizes them. Please take some time to savor it before delving into the solar terms of summer...

談到牡丹花，下一頁的詩篇就是以迷人的暗喻手法來予以讚美。敬請在進入夏季節氣之前好好欣賞一番 ...

牡丹 Peony Flowers

Author: Xu, Ning 徐凝 birth and death years unknown but probably in the 9th century
Translator: Crystal Tai

何人不愛牡丹花 Who doesn't love peony flowers?
占斷城中好物華 They outshine all the others among the city's eye-catchers.
疑是洛川神女作 I wonder if the goddess of the Luo River created them,
千嬌萬態破朝霞 Making thousands of them burst like dawn breaking into vibrant colors.

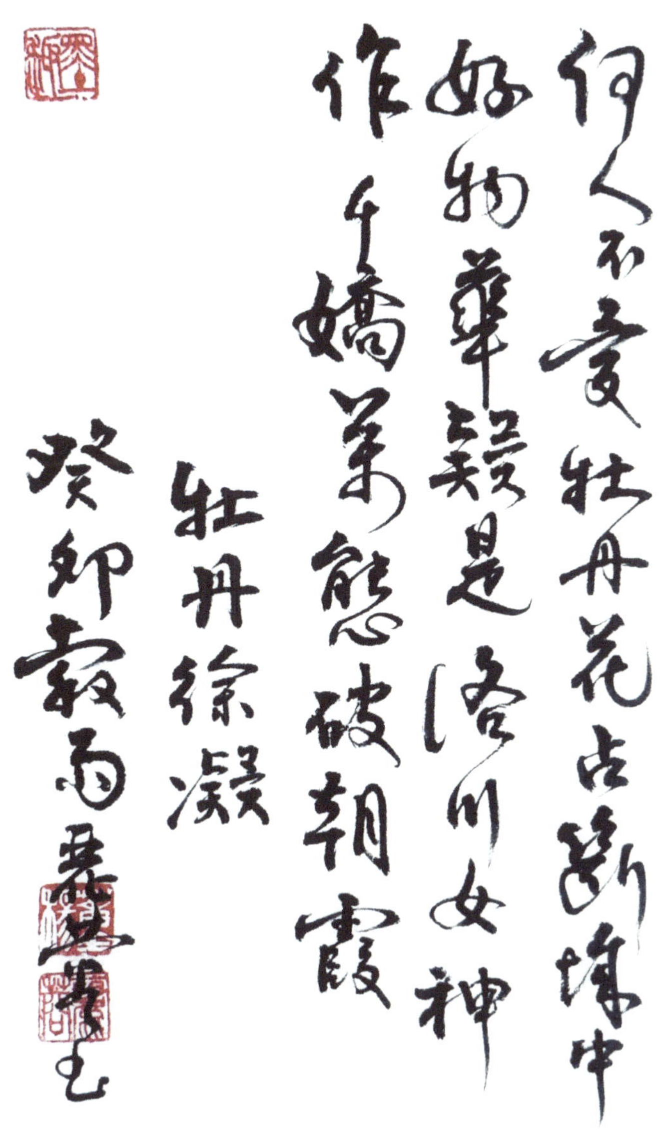

Chapter 7
First Signs of Summer

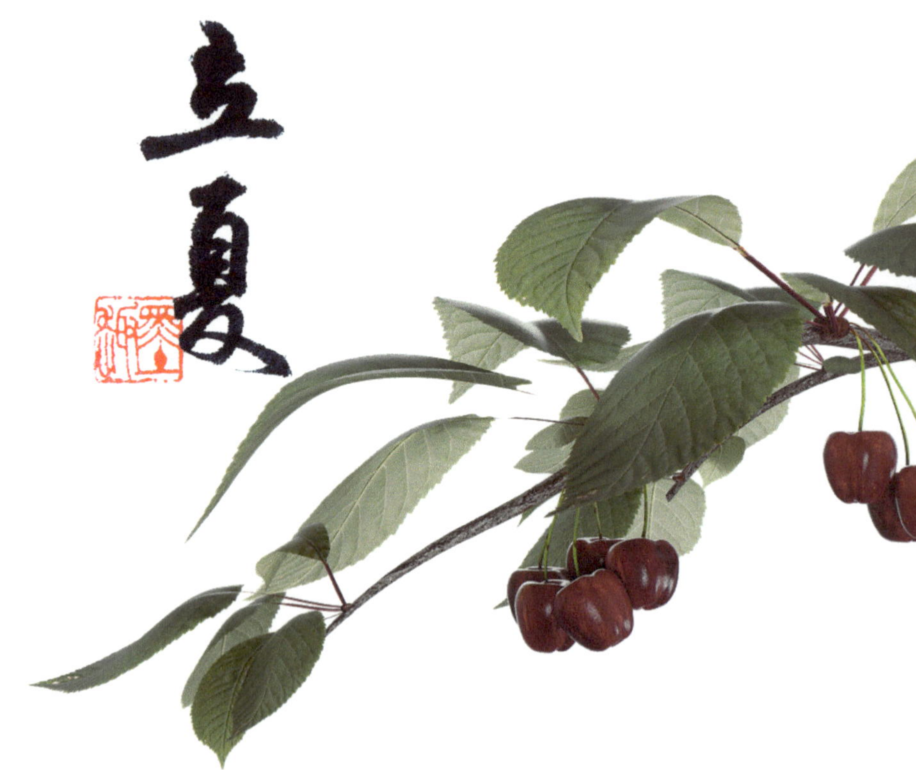

Those who have read William Shakespeare's Sonnet 18 may remember this famous quote:

Shall I compare thee to a summer's day?
Thou art more lovely and more temperate.
Rough winds do shake the darling buds of May,
And summer's lease hath all too short a date.

如果讀過莎士比亞的第十八首十四行詩，大概記得其中前四句名言：「吾可否將汝比擬作夏日？汝較之更為可人而溫柔。狂風必搖撼五月之嫩蕊，夏之短租約匆匆引離愁。」

From this sonnet, everyone can tell that May was a summer month in Shakespeare's time. That was before the Societas Meteorologica Palatina defined summer as the months of June, July, and August based on weather conditions in 1780, as mentioned in Chapter 1. Prior to the meteorological definition of the four seasons, the summer solstice was generally considered the peak of summer in Europe for having the longest daylight of the year.

從這首十四行詩，可以看出陽曆五月在莎士比亞時代是夏天的月份。這是在本書第一章提過的某個國際氣象組織於西元 1780 年定義夏天為陽曆六、七、八月之前。在氣象定義的四季廣受採納之前，夏至在歐洲乃是夏季的中途至高點，因為夏至是一年之中白晝最長的一天。

The ancient Chinese also saw the summer solstice as the midpoint of summer for the same reason, and that made summer start in early May. It comes when the sun reaches 45 degrees of the ecliptic drawn by ancient Chinese astronomers, or when the Earth arrives at 45 degrees of the celestial orbit redrawn by modern Chinese scientists to present the 24 solar terms. It can be any time between May 4 and May 7.

中國古人也認為夏至在夏天的中間點，那麼夏天就從陽曆五月初開始。夏天起於古人所謂太陽到達黃經四十五度的日子，亦即現代科學家按照地球繞太陽軌道所重畫的橢圓形二十四節氣圖表上，地球運轉到四十五度之時，這在陽曆五月四日到五月七日之間都有可能。

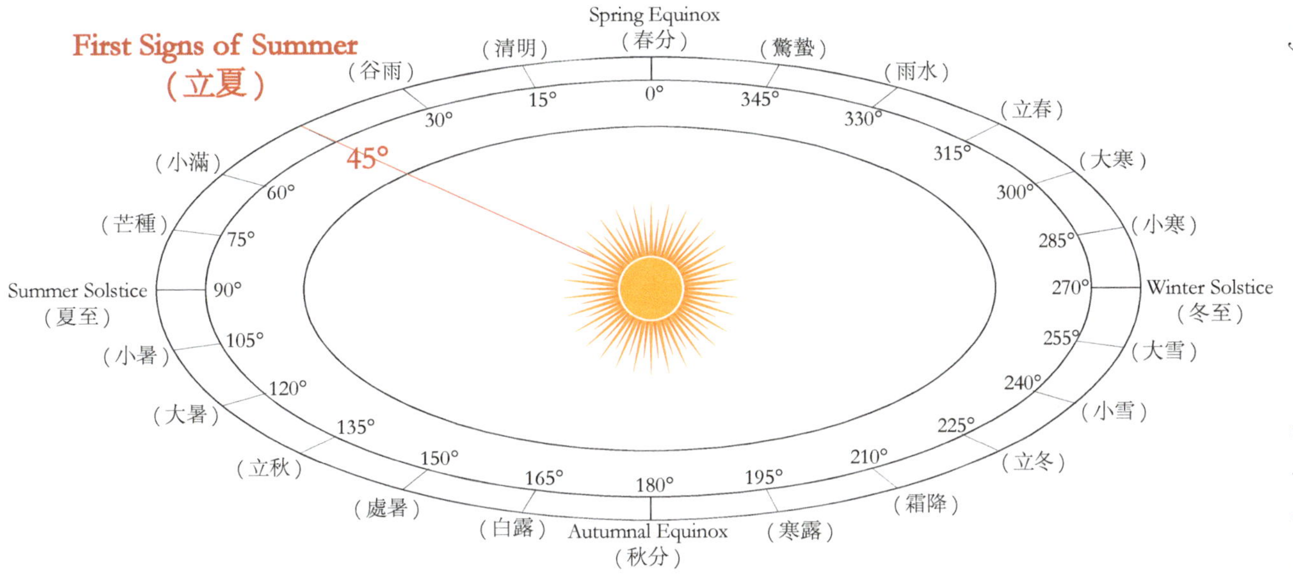

On the ancient-Chinese-defined first day of summer, namely Lixia in Chinese, many people in China eat boiled eggs. This is because a tradition has taught them that eating eggs can increase their intake of nutrients right before the weather gets hot and causes a loss of appetite. With this concept in mind, Chinese people used to weigh themselves on this day, hoping to prevent themselves from losing weight over the summer, but this custom has become outdated. Nowadays, most Chinese people would rather lose weight. Even so, they still indulge in traditional treats on the ancient-Chinese-defined first day of summer.

很多華人在立夏這一天吃雞蛋，為的是在天氣漸熱、胃口降低之前補一補。舊時習俗要在這一天量體重，希望夏天不會瘦，但那已過時。現代大多數華人寧願減肥。儘管如此，立夏日的傳統食物依然風行。

In addition to eggs, early summer must-haves include three varieties of freshwater fish or shellfish, depending what's locally available. There are also amaranth leaves, broad beans, and garlic sprouts as three seasonal vegetables. As for fresh fruit, apricots, cherries, and loquats are three new arrivals.

除了雞蛋以外，立夏食物還有稱為水三鮮的三種水產，也有當令的蔬菜，包括莧菜、蠶豆、蒜苗。剛上市的水果則有杏子、櫻桃、枇杷。

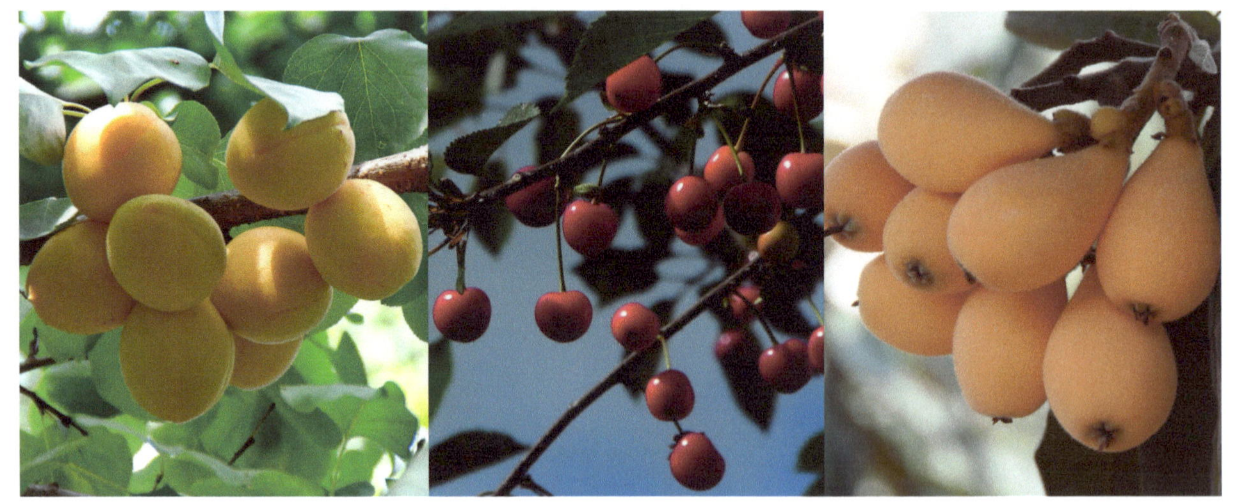

杏子 Apricots　櫻桃 Cherries　枇杷 Loquats

It is notable that amaranth leaves have red spots. Cherries are even all red. Chinese medicine practitioners encourage the consumption of red foods during the three months from around May 4 to around Aug. 5. These three months are traditionally defined as summer, the season during which the heart works extra hard and needs more care, based on Chinese medicinal classics. Chinese medicine practitioners believe that the nutrients of red foods will enter the heart meridian and improve heart function.[1]

值得注意的是，莧菜綠葉上有紅色部份，櫻桃更是整顆紅色。中醫提倡在陽曆五月初到八月初這三個月多吃紅色食物，因為這三個月是傳統定義的夏天，而根據中醫典籍記載，夏天心臟特別辛苦，需要養心。中醫相信，紅色食物的養份能入心經，改善心臟功能。

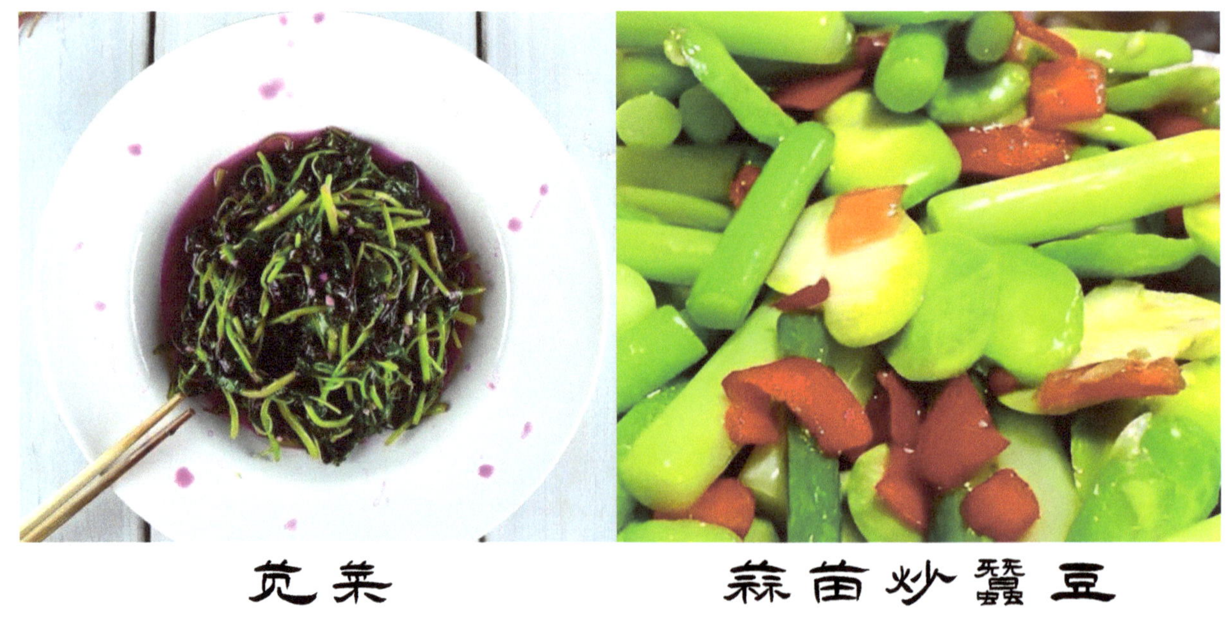

莧菜

蒜苗炒蠶豆

Amaranth Leaves　　Broad Beans & Garlic Sprouts

1　Chinese Medical Culture. "The Heart is Connected with the Air of Summer." （Chinese edition）. Nanjing Hospital of Traditional Chinese Medicine. https://www.njszyy.cn/djwh/detail.aspx?id=4075&mtt=MKBZ5770

This Chinese medical theory has been proven true. Modern science has found lycopene, a natural red pigment in foods, to support cardiovascular health.[1] That means red foods indeed do good to the heart. Why not buy more in-season cherries in May?
這項中醫理論已獲證實。現代科學已發現紅色食物中的茄紅素能維持心血管健康。紅色食物確實有益於心臟。何不在陽曆五月份多買一些當令的櫻桃？

In May, the first solar term of summer starts with the ancient-Chinese-defined first day of summer. Like the other 23 solar terms, this one can be divided into three parts. Each part is five or six days long. The first part of the solar term from early to mid May is when frogs begin to croak. The second part is when earthworms come out. The third part is when cucumbers produce fruit. Please note that cucumbers have the highest water content of any solid food.[2] It will be wonderfully hydrating to incorporate cucumbers into summer meals.
在陽曆五月，立夏節氣隨着立夏日展開。如同另外二十三個節氣，立夏節氣可分為三候。每一候五或六天。立夏一候螻蟈鳴，二候蚯蚓出，三候王瓜（黃瓜）生。請注意黃瓜在固體食物之中含水量排名第一，可在夏天多多食用來好好補充水份。

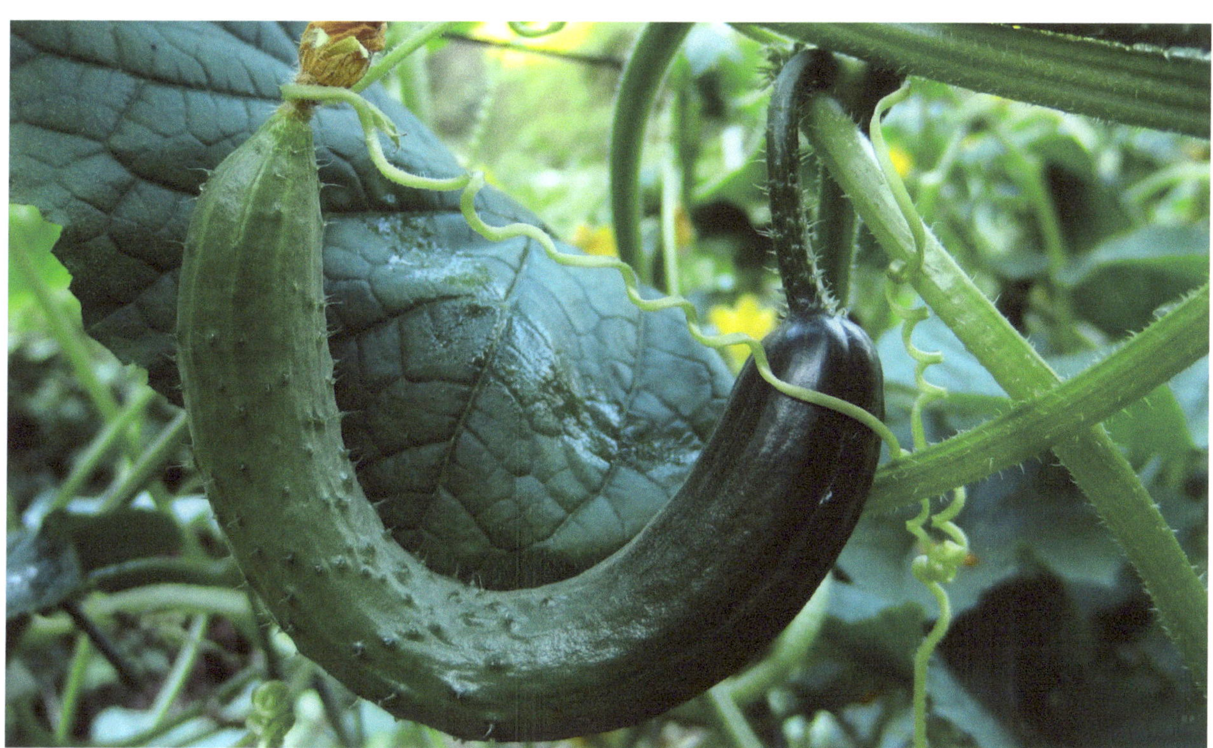

While the springlike weather doesn't feel like summer in May, one of the summer's initial signs, according to a Song-Dynasty poet named Yang Wanli (1127-1206), is the beginning of pomegranate flower season.
儘管陽曆五月份天氣還像春天，但夏天初始的跡象已顯現。 如同南宋詩人楊萬里所指出，石榴花初開是立夏的徵兆。

1　Przybylska, Sylwia and Grzegorz Tokarczyk. "Lycopene in the Prevention of Cardiovascular Diseases." National Library of Medicine, Feb 10, 2022. https://www.ncbi.nlm.nih.gov/pmc/articles/PMC8880080/

2　UCLA Health. "15 Foods That Help You Stay Hydrated." University of California, Los Angeles, June 17, 2022. https://www.uclahealth.org/news/15-food-that-help-you-stay-hydrated

Unlike roses and herbaceous peonies, which have already been beautifully in bloom for weeks, pomegranate flowers are newcomers among May flowers. Pomegranate flower season generally spans from May to August, roughly coinciding with the six solar terms of summer.
石榴花不像五月的玫瑰或芍藥已經絢麗開放了好幾週。石榴花在五月花之中是新來者。
石榴花季通常是從陽曆五月到八月，大致吻合夏天的六個節氣。

On the next page is the previously mentioned poet's poem about how the first pomegranate flower of the year embodies the earliest sign of summer.
下一頁就展示着楊萬里的絕句，其中點出了一年中第一朵石榴花代表初夏。

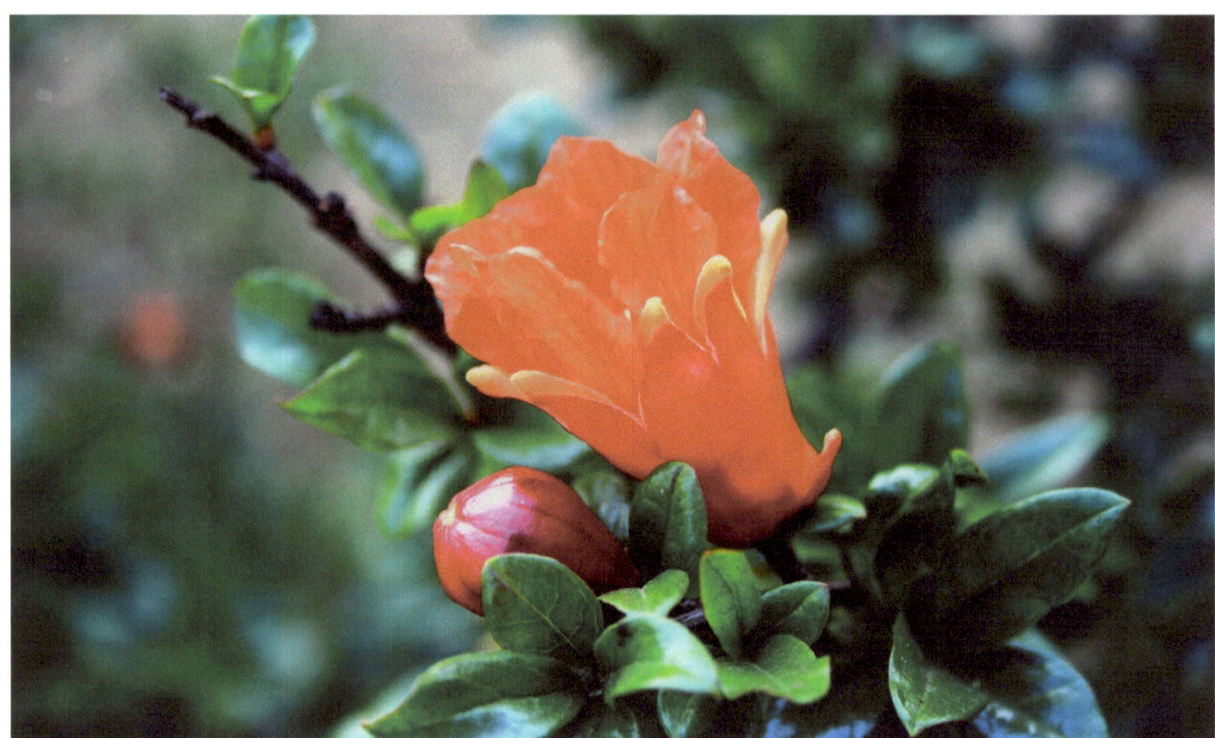

初夏即事 Phenomena of Early Summer

Author：Yang, Wanli 楊萬里 (1127-1206)
Translator：Crystal Tai

從教節序暗相催 Time pushes seasonal changes quietly;
曆日塵生懶看來 I let my calendar collect dust, unaware of time's velocity.
卻是石榴知立夏 But the pomegranate knows when to call it the first day of summer,
年年此日一花開 With a flower bursting into bloom on the same day annually.

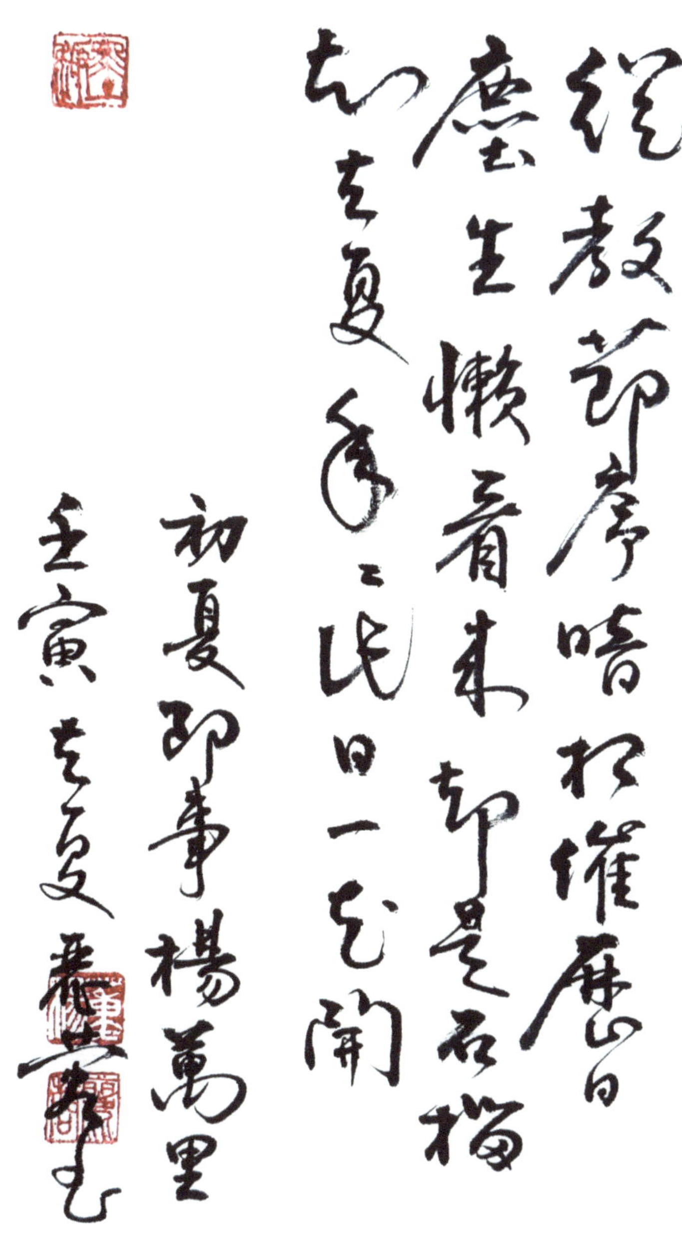

Chapter 8
Maturing Crops

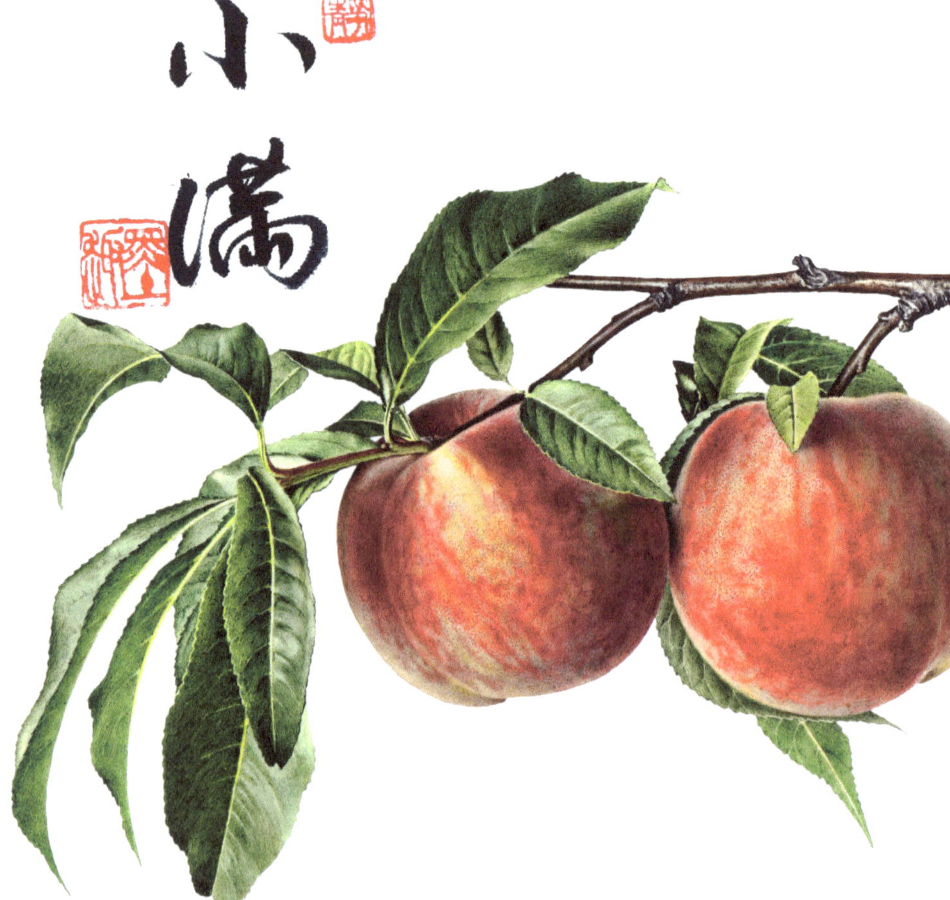

In the Northern Hemisphere, peach season may run from May through September, depending on regional climate. In China, where the peach originated, the peach season generally begins in late May. Starting from late May, there is a 15-or-16-day period called Xiaoman in Chinese, which literally means "a little full" and descriptively refers to maturing crops.

在北半球，桃子產季可從五月到九月，因各地氣候相異而有所不同。不過，在桃子原產地，亦即中國，桃子產季一般都始於五月下旬。從五月下旬起始的節氣稱為小滿，字面意義是有一點滿，引申意義則是農作物接近成熟。

The solar term that comes with maturing crops may begin on May 20, May 21, or May 22, depending on when the sun reaches 60 degrees of the ecliptic drawn by ancient Chinese astronomers, or when the Earth arrives at 60 degrees of the celestial orbit redrawn by modern Chinese scientists to present the 24 solar terms.

小滿節氣開端可能在陽曆五月二十日、二十一日，或二十二日，取決於古人所謂太陽到達黃經六十度的日子，亦即現代科學家按照地球繞太陽軌道所重畫的橢圓形二十四節氣圖表上，地球運轉到六十度之時。

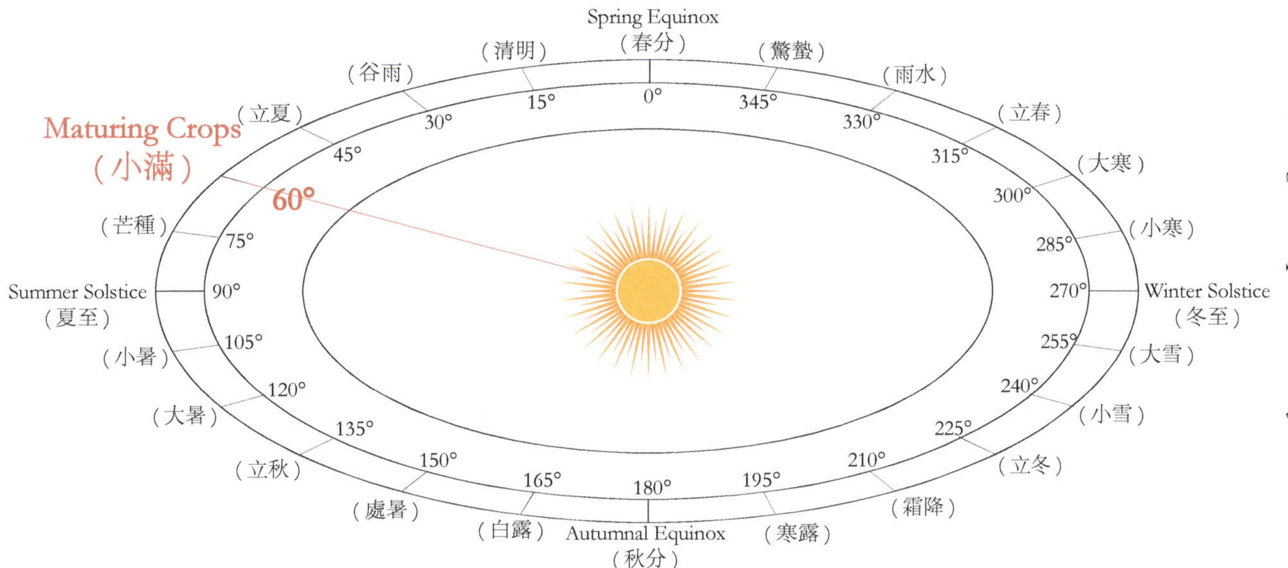

During the solar term from late May to early June, temperatures are generally rising in the Northern Hemisphere, making aquatic plants flourish. This is when water lilies dreamily come into bloom. Before the weather gets too hot, why not take a walk around a picturesque pond of water lilies?

在小滿時節，氣溫上升，水生植物欣欣向榮。睡蓮就在此時如夢如幻綻開了。在天氣變得太熱之前，何不到景色如畫的睡蓮池畔散散步？

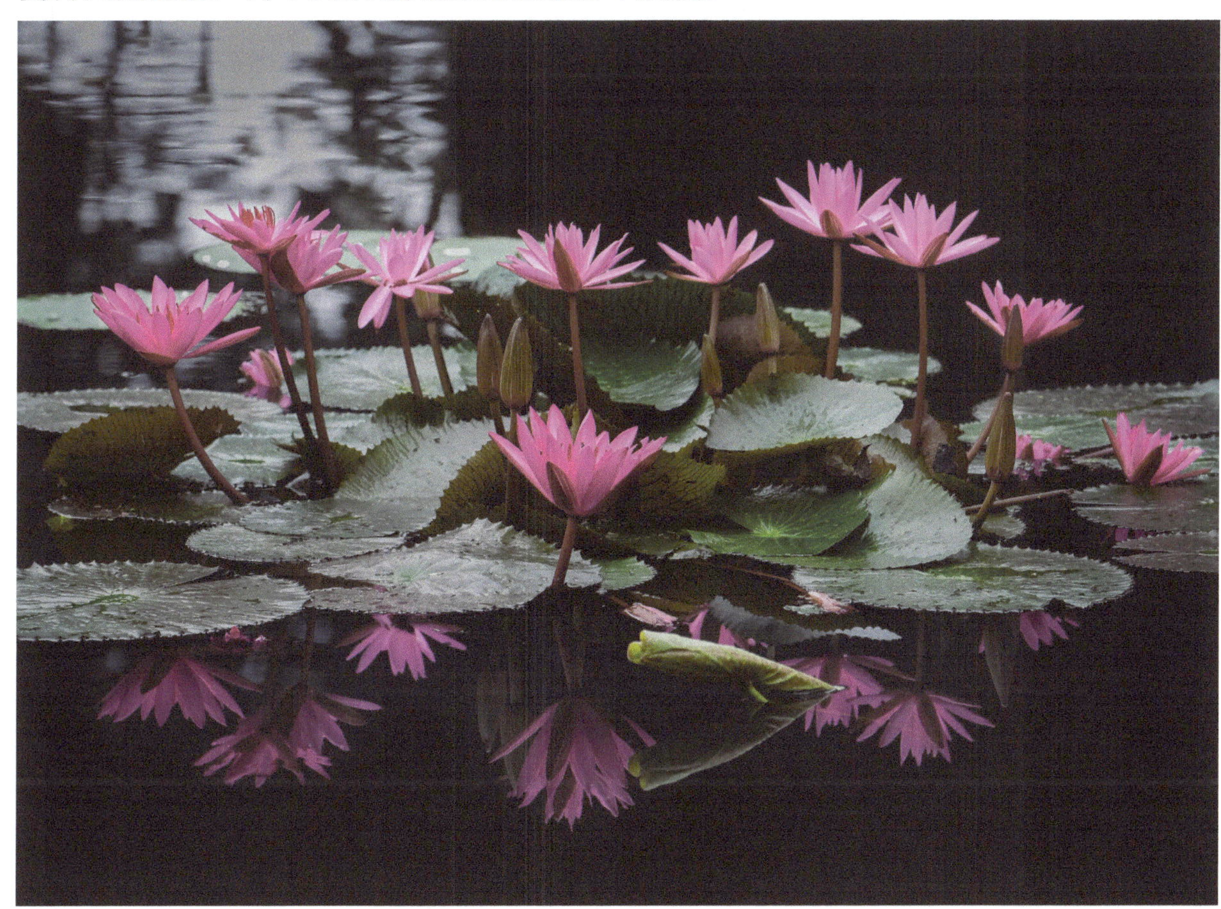

This solar term, just like the other 23, can be divided into three parts. Each part is five or six days long. The first part of the solar term with maturing crops is when bitter lettuce thrives. The second part is when some tender grasses wither under the hot sun. The third part is the beginning of wheat harvest.

小滿節氣恰如另外二十三個節氣，可分為三候。每一候五或六天。小滿一候苦菜秀，二候靡草死，三候麥秋至。

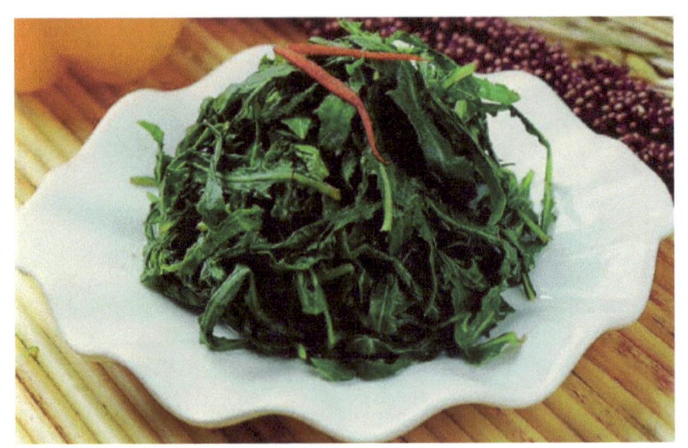

In celebration of wheat harvest, Chinese farmers used to go on a picnic with wheat buns, pancakes, and bitter lettuce salad. However, this tradition has faded away. Nowadays, the solar term from late May to early June is time to enjoy seasonal fruit, which of course includes peaches, plus those from the previous solar term, such as apricots, cherries, and loquats. As for new arrivals at the fruit market, watermelons are definitely popular. It's worth noting that there are yellow-fleshed watermelons in Asia.

為了慶祝麥子收成，舊時中國農民會帶着麥包、麥餅，以及涼拌苦菜去野餐。如今此一傳統已式微。現代小滿節氣是享用水果之時。當令水果當然有桃子，也有上個節氣就有的杏子、櫻桃、枇杷，還有剛上市的西瓜。值得一提的是，西瓜不都是紅瓤，亞洲西瓜也有些是黃瓤的小玉西瓜。

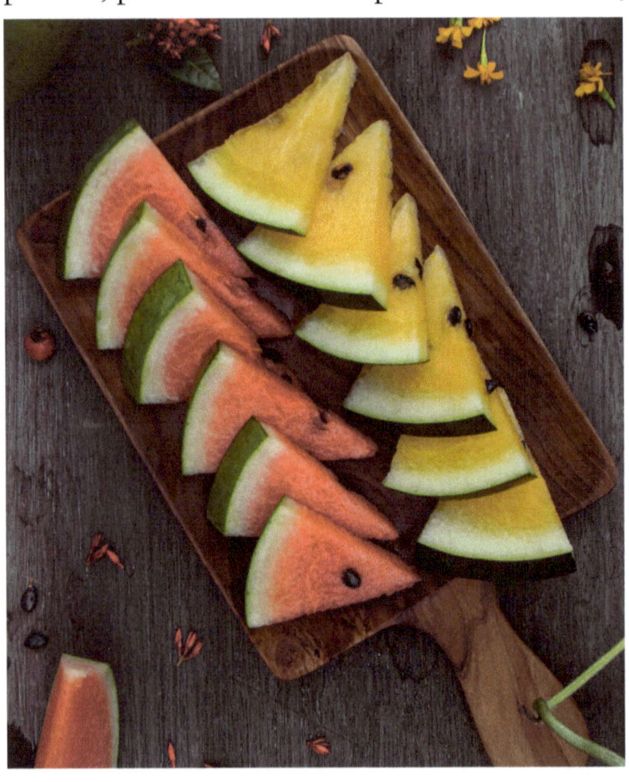

More exotic than yellow-fleshed watermelons are lychees and red bayberries. Red bayberries in particular are hard to find in the West, whereas lychees may be available at some Asian markets in America.

在西方，比黃瓤西瓜更具異國風味的水果是荔枝和楊梅。其中楊梅在西方很難找，荔枝則在美國的某些亞洲超市有售。

There is an interesting Chinese folktale about lychees. Allegedly, a Tang-Dynasty emperor had fresh lychees shipped from southern China to the capital in the North every day during the lychee season, and he demanded super speedy deliveries of lychees, because they were his beloved concubine's favorite fruit. This charming concubine was widely known as Consort Yang. As shown in her portraits, she was a curvy lady. In her time, being a little plump was considered attractive, so she never had to lose weight. Doesn't that sound enviable?

荔枝有個傳說是關於唐朝的楊貴妃。唐明皇為了她愛吃荔枝，命令屬下在荔枝產季天天從嶺南送荔枝進京。從楊貴妃的畫像可以看出她身材豐滿。在她的時代，審美標準崇尚微胖。難怪她無須減肥。那是否很令人羨慕呢？

Another notable fact about lychees is, Chinese medicine practitioners believe they will generate heat in the body, so it is better not to overeat them, especially when the weather is warm.
不過，荔枝不能多吃。中醫認為荔枝上火。尤其在天氣暖和時，不宜吃太多荔枝。

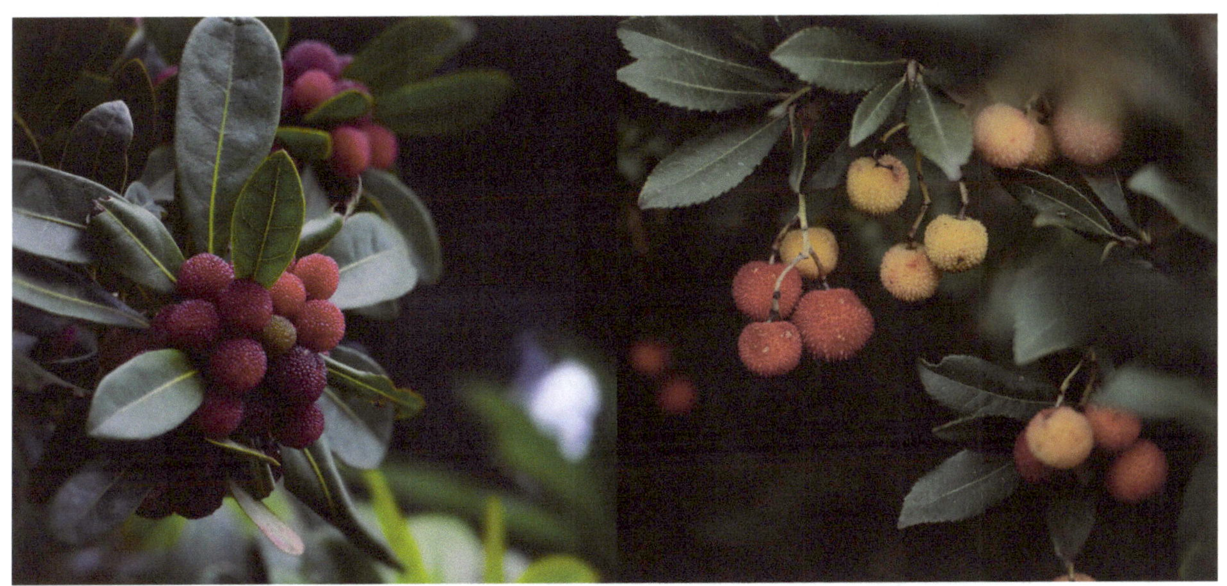

杨梅

Chinese Bayberries

荔枝

Lychees

About abundant fruits and grains at this time of year, on the next page is a classical Chinese poem that delicately describes an idyllic farm during this solar term.
關於每年此時豐盛的水果和穀物，下一頁就有一首細膩描述小滿節氣田園風光的絕句。

小滿 Maturing Crops

Author：Wang, Taixie 王泰偕 (1832-1896)
Translator：Crystal Tai

調劑陰晴作好年 Cloudy times and sunny days take turns to make a good year;
麥寒豆暖兩周旋 Cold wheat and warm beans grow together here.
枇杷黃後楊梅紫 Bayberries turn purple after the harvest of yellow loquats;
正是農家小滿天 It is the time of maturing crops farmers hold dear.

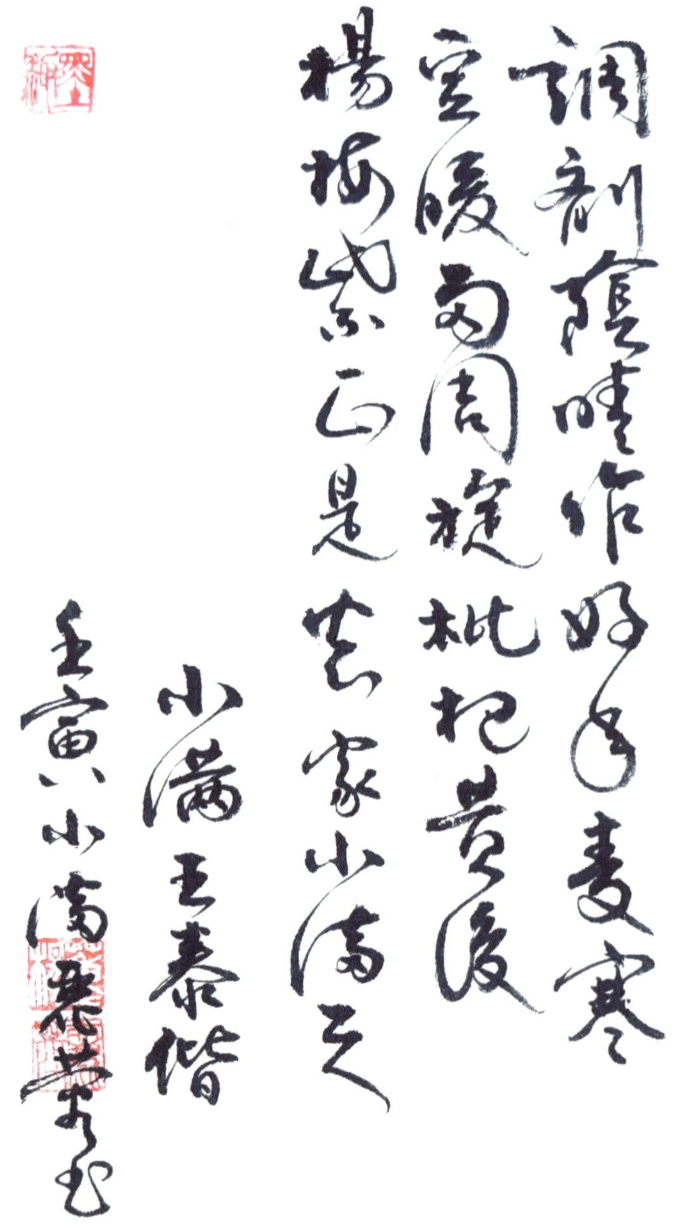

Chapter 9
Awned Ears of Grain

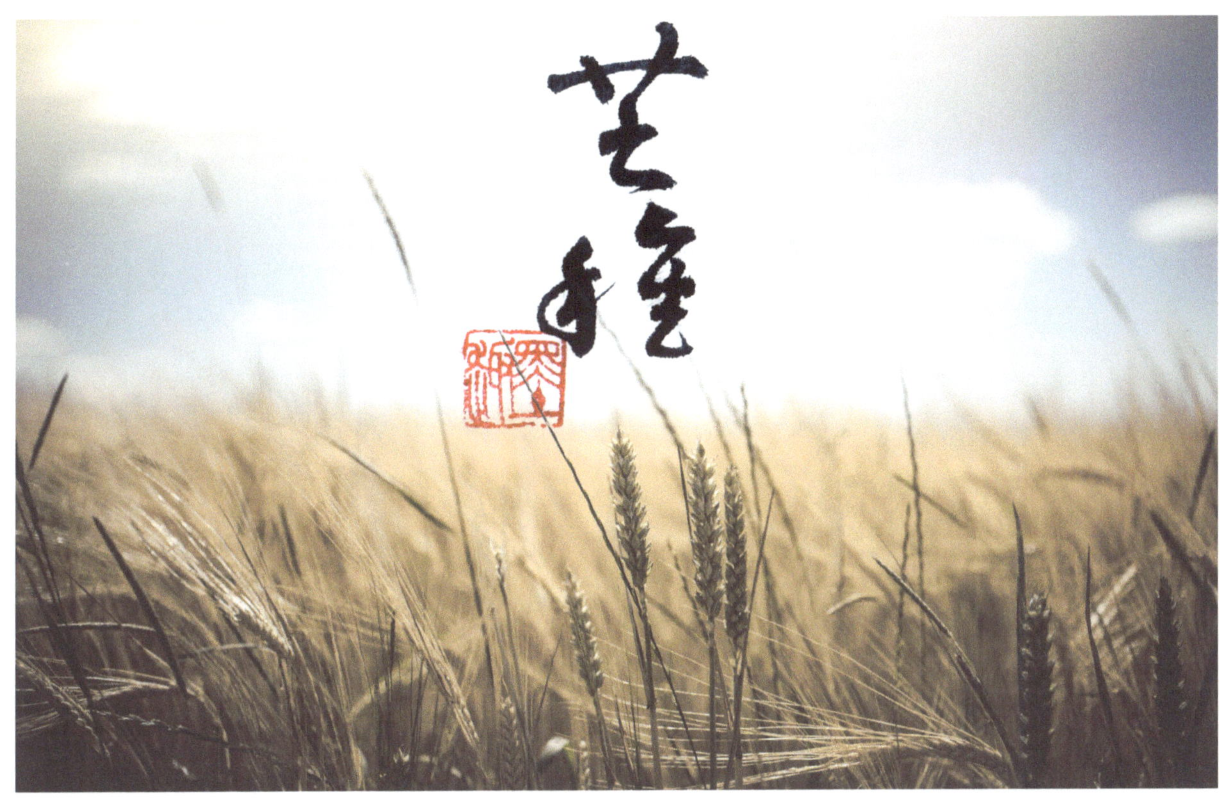

From breakfast toast to pasta dinner, wheat products are essential to everyone not allergic to gluten. However, how many people pay attention to when wheat is harvested every year?
從早餐的吐司麵包，到晚餐的意大利麵，小麥產品之於不對麥蛋白過敏的人士都是不可或缺。然而，有多少人會注意小麥何時收成？

In many places of the Northern Hemisphere, the peak of wheat harvest occurs in June. No wonder a 15-or-16-day period in June is called Mangzhong in Chinese, which means "awned ears of grain."
在北半球許多地區，小麥收成的巔峰期都在陽曆六月份。難怪陽曆六月有個節氣稱為芒種，意指有芒的穀物。

The solar term that features awned ears of grain may start on June 5, June 6, or June 7, depending when the sun reaches 75 degrees of the ecliptic drawn by ancient Chinese astronomers, or when the Earth arrives at 75 degrees of the celestial orbit redrawn by modern Chinese scientists to present the 24 solar terms.
芒種節氣可能始於陽曆六月五日、六月六日，或六月七日，取決於古人所謂太陽到達黃經七十五度的日子，亦即現代科學家按照地球繞太陽軌道所重畫的橢圓形二十四節氣圖表上，地球運轉到七十五度之時。

詩
意
節
氣

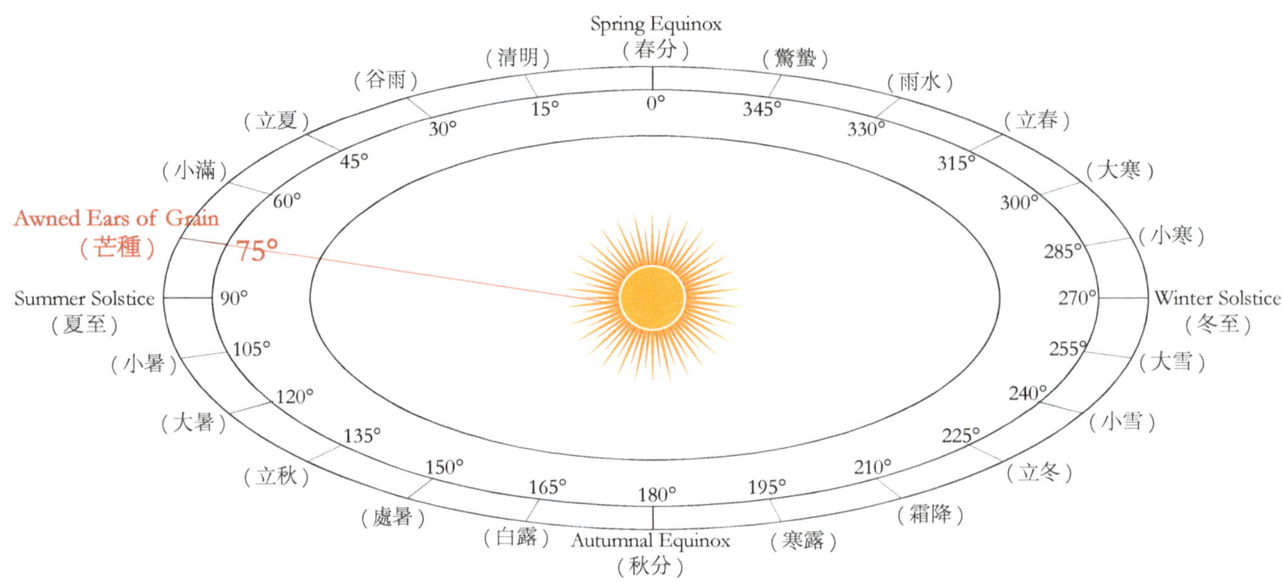

Like the other 23 solar terms, this one can also be divided into three parts. Each part is five or six days long. The first part is when praying mantises come out. The second part is when butcher birds start singing. The third part is when mockingbirds become silent.
如同另外二十三個節氣，芒種節氣亦可分為三候。每一候五或六天。芒種一候螳螂生，二候鵙始鳴，三候反舌無聲。

During the solar term named Mangzhong, many seasonal fruits are available. Aside from those from the previous two solar terms, new arrivals include mangoes and mulberries.
芒種時節還有很多當令水果。除了上兩個節氣已有的水果以外，也有新上市的芒果和桑葚。

Please note that mulberries look very similar to blackberries but have a longer shape. Both blackberries and mulberries are rich in anthocyanins, which can lower blood pressure, prevent diabetes, improve vision, reduce cancer cell proliferation, and inhibit tumor formation.[1] Those who cannot find mulberries in the West can go for blackberries, which are also in season in June in the Northern Hemisphere.
請注意桑葚很像黑莓，但桑葚較長。兩者皆富含花青素，能夠降血壓、預防糖尿病、改善視力，減少癌細胞擴散機率，以及抑制腫瘤。在西方買不到桑葚的人士可以買黑莓。北半球的黑莓產季也在陽曆六月份。

芒
種

---

1   Martins, Mariana et al. "Blackberries and Mulberries: Berries with Significant Health-Promoting Properties."
National Library of Medicine, July 27, 2023. https://pubmed.ncbi.nlm.nih.gov/37569399/

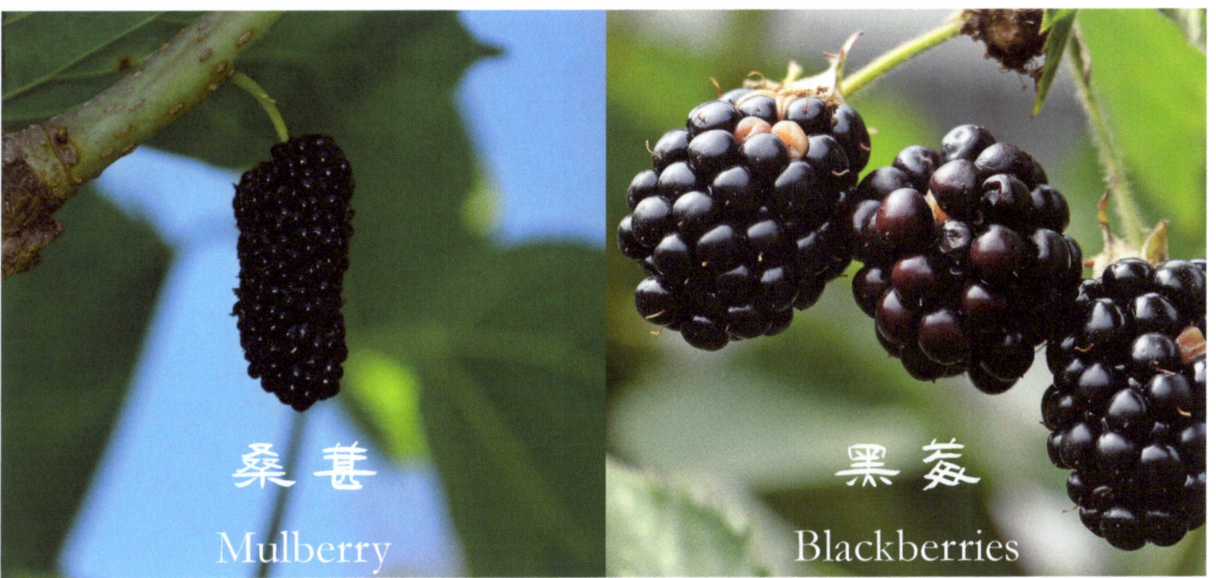

The solar term from early to mid June normally overlaps with the fifth month of the East Asian Lunar Calendar, so the Dragon Boat Festival on the fifth of the fifth lunar month usually falls in this particular solar term. The Dragon Boat Festival is of course celebrated with dragon boat racing. In addition, Chinese people eat a special rice dish named *zongzi* for the traditional holiday. The rice dish may be savory or sweet. The savory ingredients may go with or without pork, but they usually include black mushrooms, duck egg yolk, and peanuts. The sweet option is usually vegan, with azuki bean paste or pieces of jujube fruit inside. The rice dish is generally wrapped in bamboo leaves.

陽曆六月的芒種時節通常和陰曆五月有交集，因此，陰曆五月初五端午節經常處於芒種時節。端午節又名龍舟節，當然有龍舟比賽。此外，華人也在端午節吃粽子。粽子有鹹也有甜。鹹粽或許包豬肉，或許不放肉類，但通常都有香菇、鴨蛋黃，以及花生米。甜粽子則必定是素的，常包豆沙或紅棗。粽子一般都裹在竹葉之中。

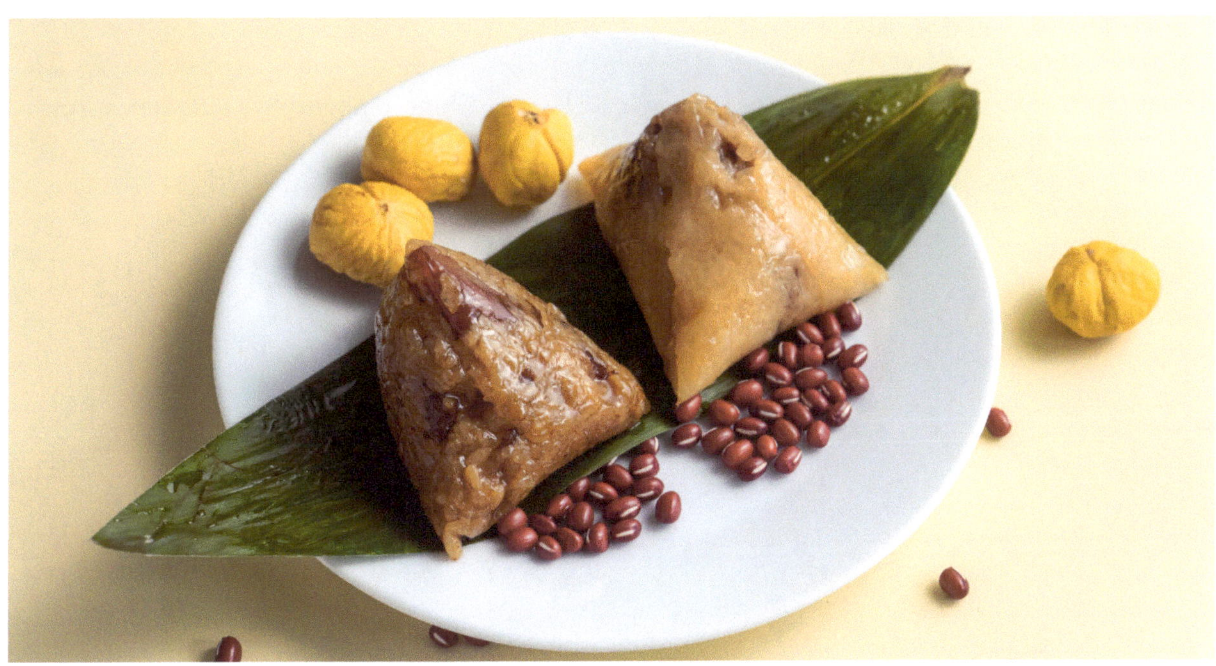

Bamboo groves thrive during this time of year in the Northern Hemisphere. So do many other plants, including pomegranate trees, which first came into bloom in early May in China as well as many other places. Pomegranate flowers reach peak bloom in June. Less vibrant but more fragrant are certain types of white flowers, such as gardenia, champaca, and jasmine.

每年此時，竹林在北半球都長得很茂密。別的植物亦然。其中石榴樹在陽曆五月初已開始開花，但石榴花期巔峰在陽曆六月。此外，不如石榴花鮮艷卻較香的一些白花也在陽曆六月盛開，例如梔子、白蘭、茉莉。

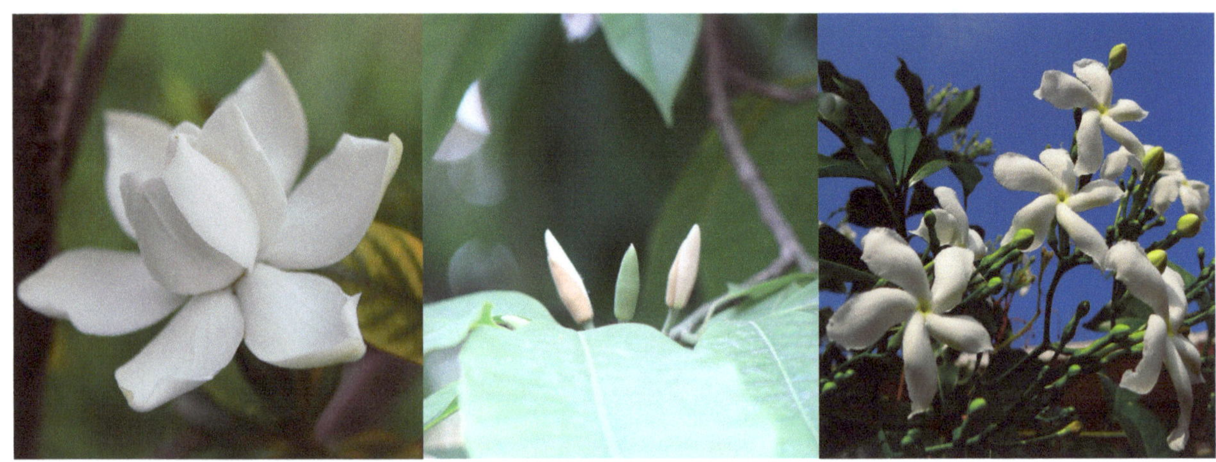

Gardenia   Champaca   Jasmine

These fragrant flowers can be used for making essential oils and perfumes, which are in high demand during this time of year, because it is when people sweat a lot. Farmers definitely perspire more during this busy time on the farm.

這些香花可以用來製成精油和香水，正好每年此時需求量很高，因為這是眾人容易大量出汗的時候。農夫在農忙時節尤其會流更多汗。

About farmers' perspiration, on the next page is a classical Chinese poem that directly expresses deep compassion for hardworking farmers.

關於農夫的汗水，下一頁有一首絕句就直白表達了對辛勤農民的深刻同情：

憫農 Compassion for Farmers

Author: Li, Shen 李紳 (772—846)
Translator：Crystal Tai

鋤禾日當午 Farmers plow the land when the noon sun starts to boil.
汗滴禾下土 Their sweat drips down the rice stalks into the soil.
誰知盤中飧 Who can see in a plate of rice,
粒粒皆辛苦 Every grain comes from their toil?

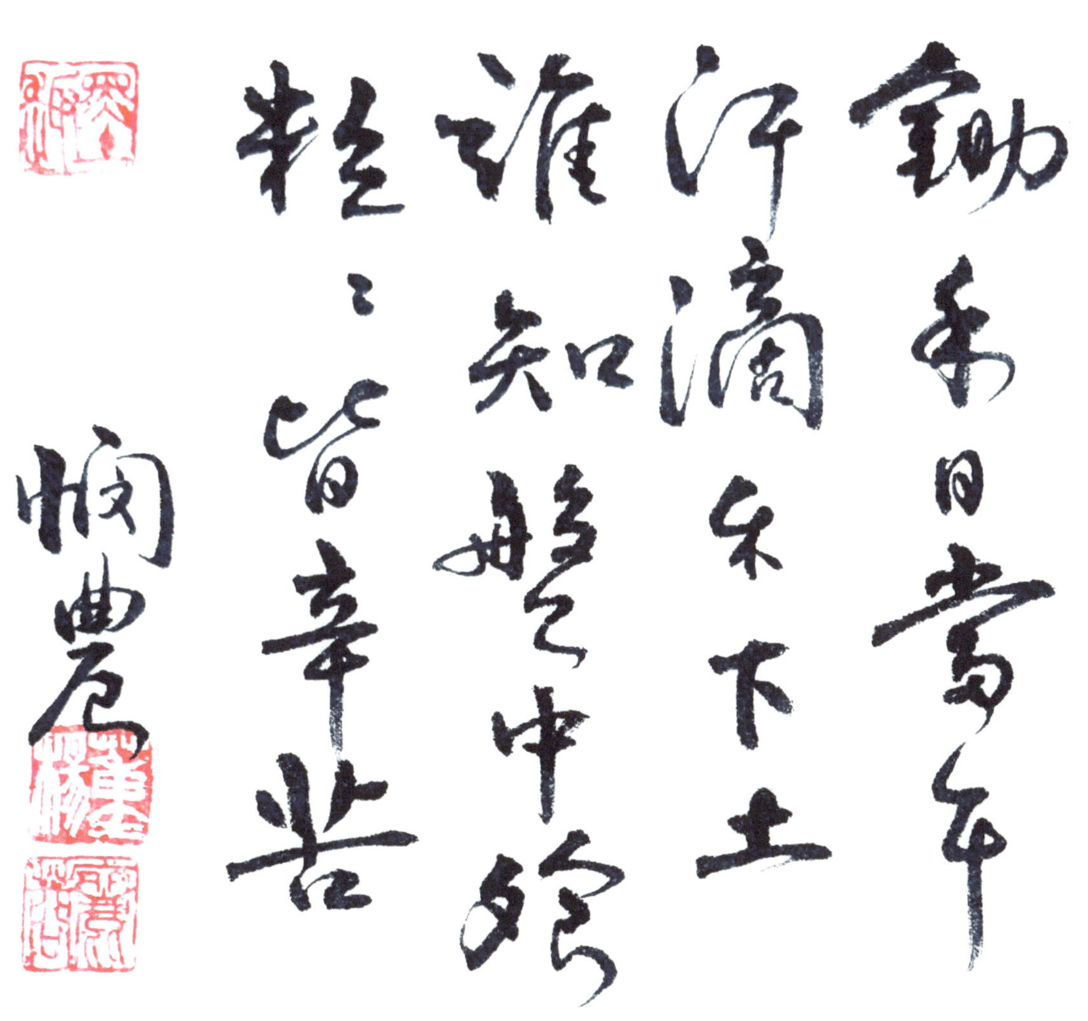

Chapter 10
Summer Solstice

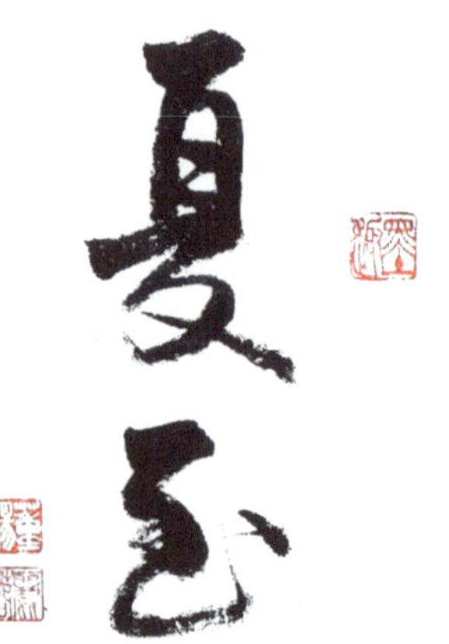

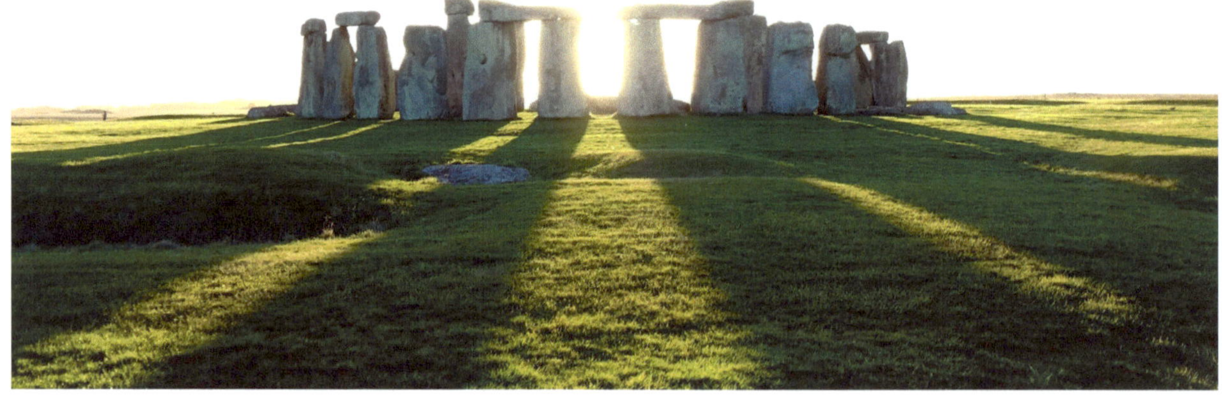

Stonehenge is a prehistoric monument in England. Thousands of visitors from around the world gather here right before the summer solstice every year to cheer sunrise. Stonehenge was apparently designed to let the rays of the rising sun exactly strike the altar stone in the center at dawn on the longest day of the year. That means human beings in prehistoric times were already aware of the summer solstice.

英國有一座巨石陣，乃是史前遺跡。每年夏至都有成千上萬旅客到此處來歡迎日出。巨石陣的設計能讓夏至朝陽的光芒準確射到祭壇中央的石柱。那表示人類在史前時代就曉得夏至。

In the East, the ancient Chinese also discovered the summer solstice, which is called Xiazhi in Chinese. It arrives when the sun reaches 90 degrees of the ecliptic drawn by ancient Chinese astronomers, or when the Earth arrives at 90 degrees of the celestial orbit redrawn by modern Chinese scientists to present the 24 solar terms. This day may be June 20, June 21, or June 22.

在東方，中國古人也發現了夏至。夏至何時來臨取決於古人所謂太陽到達黃經九十度的日子，亦即現代科學家按照地球繞太陽軌道所重畫的橢圓形二十四節氣圖表上，地球運轉到九十度之時。這一天可能是陽曆六月二十日、二十一日，或二十二日。

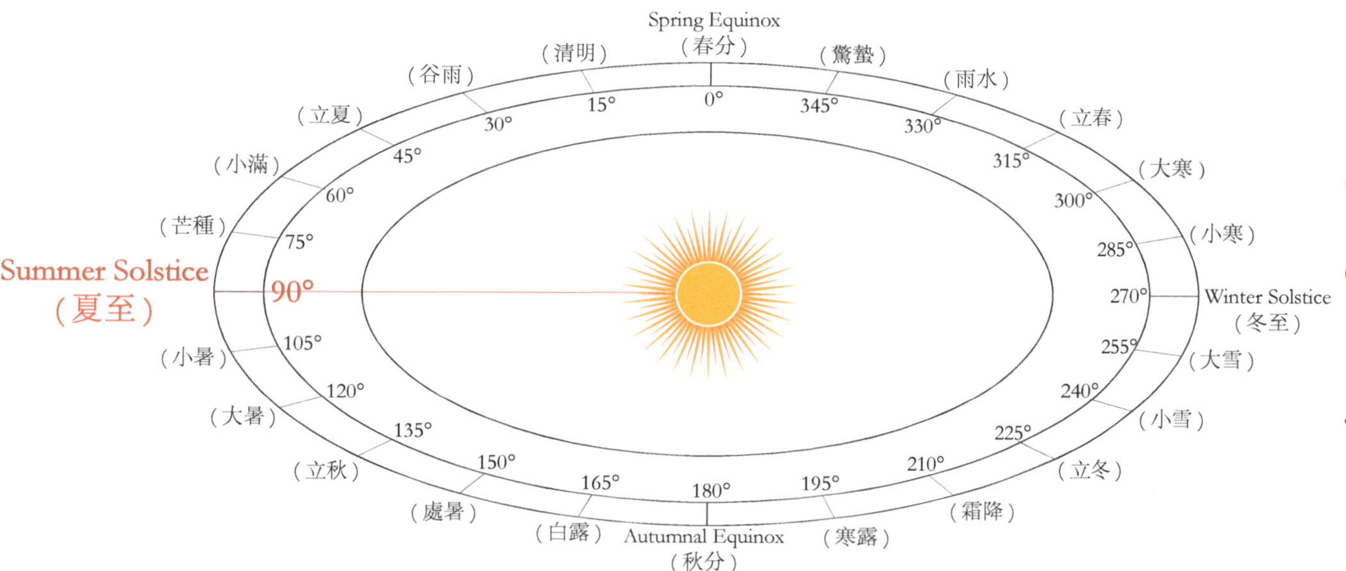

The summer solstice is the first day of a 15-or-16-day solar term named Xiazhi in Chinese, which means "the peak of summer." Like the other 23 solar terms, this one can be divided into three parts. Each part is five or six days long. The first part is when deer shed their antlers. The second part is when cicadas start singing. The third part is when an herb called pinellia ternata grows. Interestingly, the Chinese name of the herb, *bianxia*, means "midsummer."

從夏至日起始的夏至節氣有十五或十六天，就像另外二十三個節氣一樣可分為三候。每一候五或六天。夏至一候鹿角解，二候蟬始鳴，三候半夏生。有趣的是，半夏草的名字顯示夏天已過半。

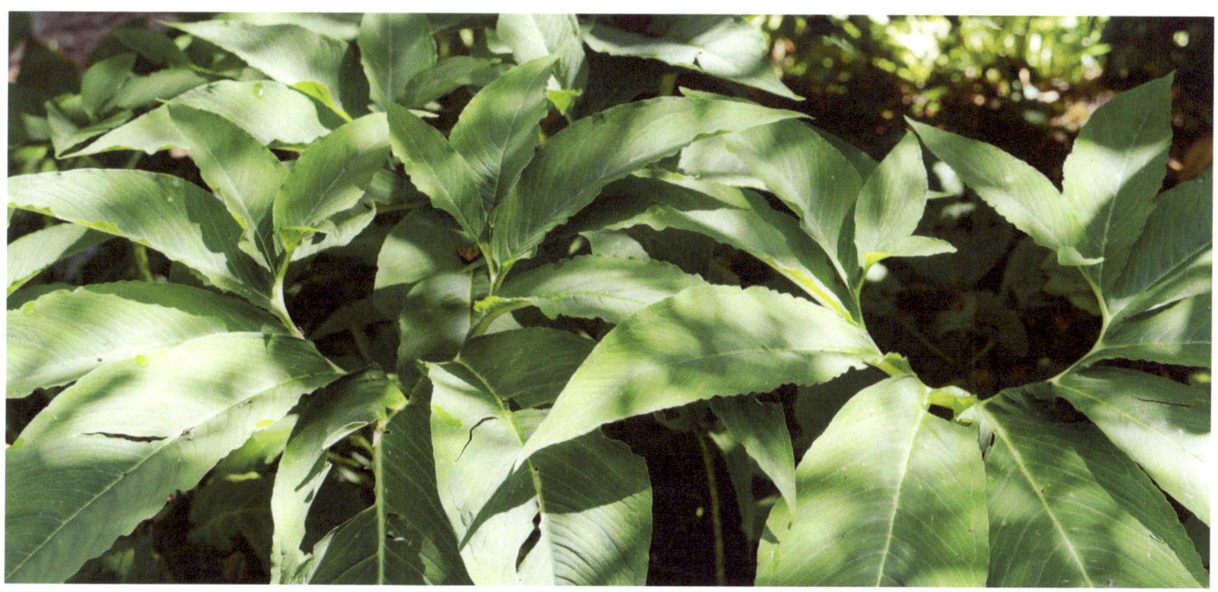

While it is already midsummer by ancient definition, this is not the hottest time of year yet. The weather will get even hotter later because of thermal lag, the delay for heat to be conducted, like the time it takes to boil a pot of water.

古代定義的夏至雖在夏天的中間點，夏至節氣卻並非一年最熱的時候。天氣在夏至之後還會更熱，因為有個物理現象叫做加熱延遲，好比燒開水需要時間來燒熱。

During the solar term starting with the summer solstice, Chinese people often make cold noodles, which will be appetizing in the increasingly hot weather.
夏至節氣常常有人做涼麵，才好在越來越熱的時候提起胃口。

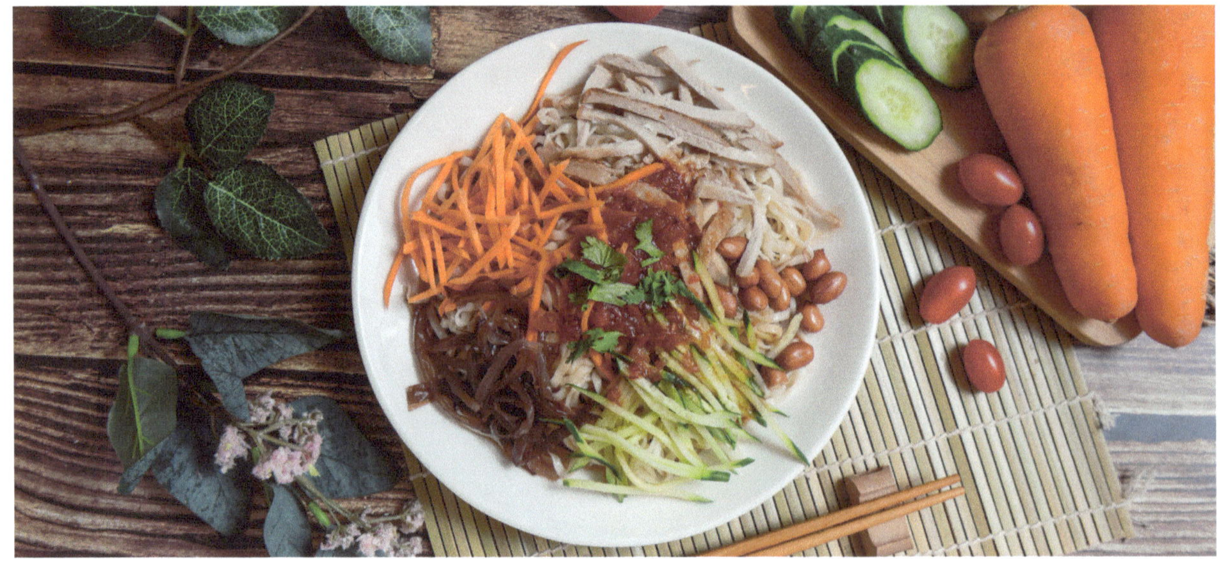

In addition, there are lots of seasonal fruits. Aside from those already available during the previous three solar terms, new arrivals include cantaloupe, honeydew, and papaya.
此外，還有很多當令水果。除了上三個節氣上市的水果以外，亦有新來的哈密瓜、香瓜、木瓜。

In the meantime, lavender fields are in full bloom. This is a great time of year for road trips, thanks to long daylight hours.
同時，薰衣草開滿了原野。這是開車旅行的好時節，因為這段時期白晝較長。

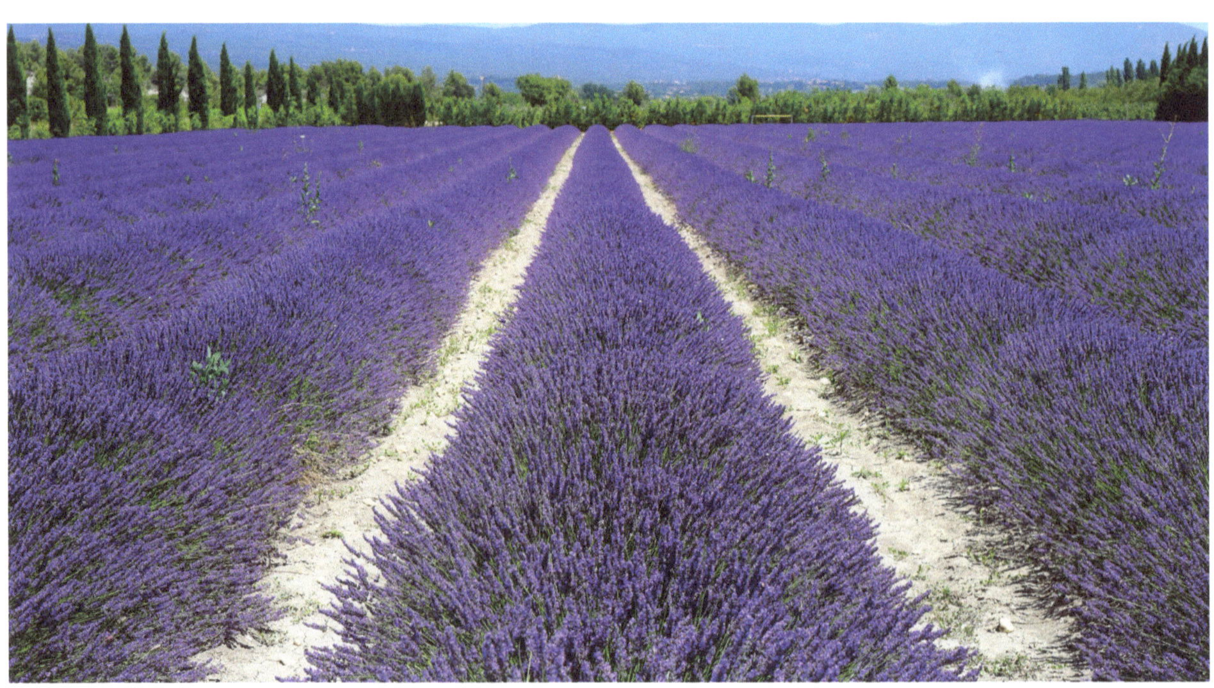

Surprisingly, ancient Chinese saw the day with the longest daylight of the year as the starting point of the so-called *yin*, which can be roughly defined as the passive energy of the universe and is associated with darkness, as stated in Chapter 4. However, it is conceivable that the nights will get longer and longer right after the summer solstice. That explains why ancient Chinese philosophers thought of darkness on the longest day of the year. Those intelligent philosophers wisely saw what was coming next.

令人驚訝的是，中國古人認為一年之內白晝最長的一天是陰的起始點！所謂陰，如同本書第四章所言，可以大致定義為宇宙間被動的力量，與黑暗相關。不過，夏至過後黑夜就會越來越長。那就是為何中國古代哲學家在一年中最長的白晝想到了黑暗。他們很有智慧，預見了接踵而至的現象。

On the next page is a classical Chinese poem that clearly conveys such wisdom.

下一頁的一首絕句就清晰呈現了這種智慧。

夏至日作 A Poem about the Summer Solstice

Author: Quan, Deyu 權德輿（759 ～ 818）
Translator: Crystal Tai

璿樞無停運 The Big Dipper never stops rotating;
四序相錯行 The four seasons always keep alternating.
寄言赫曦景 While we talk about bright scenery on the longest day of the year,
今日一陰生 Today is when *yin* begins burgeoning.

詩意節氣

夏至

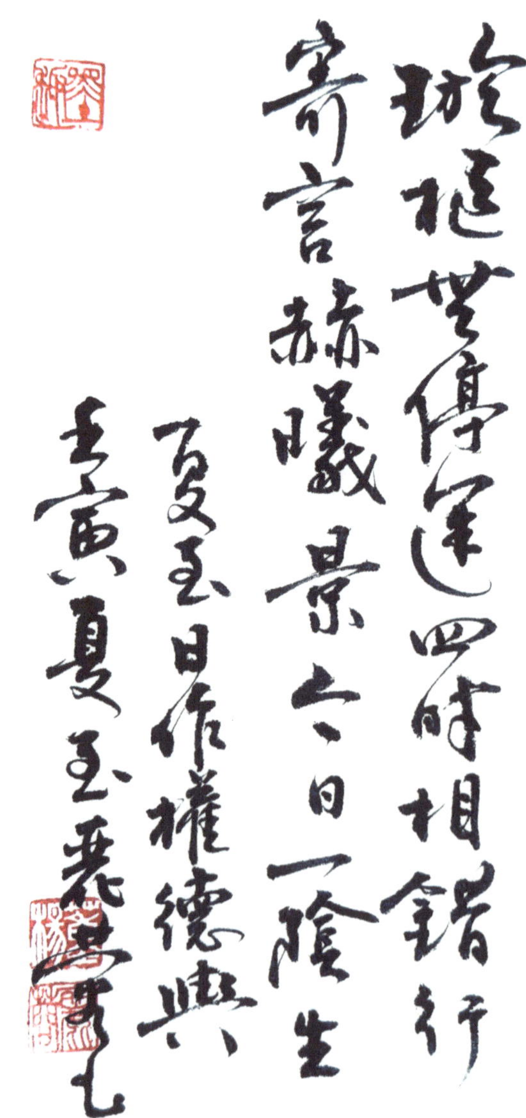

Chapter 11
Mild Summer Heat

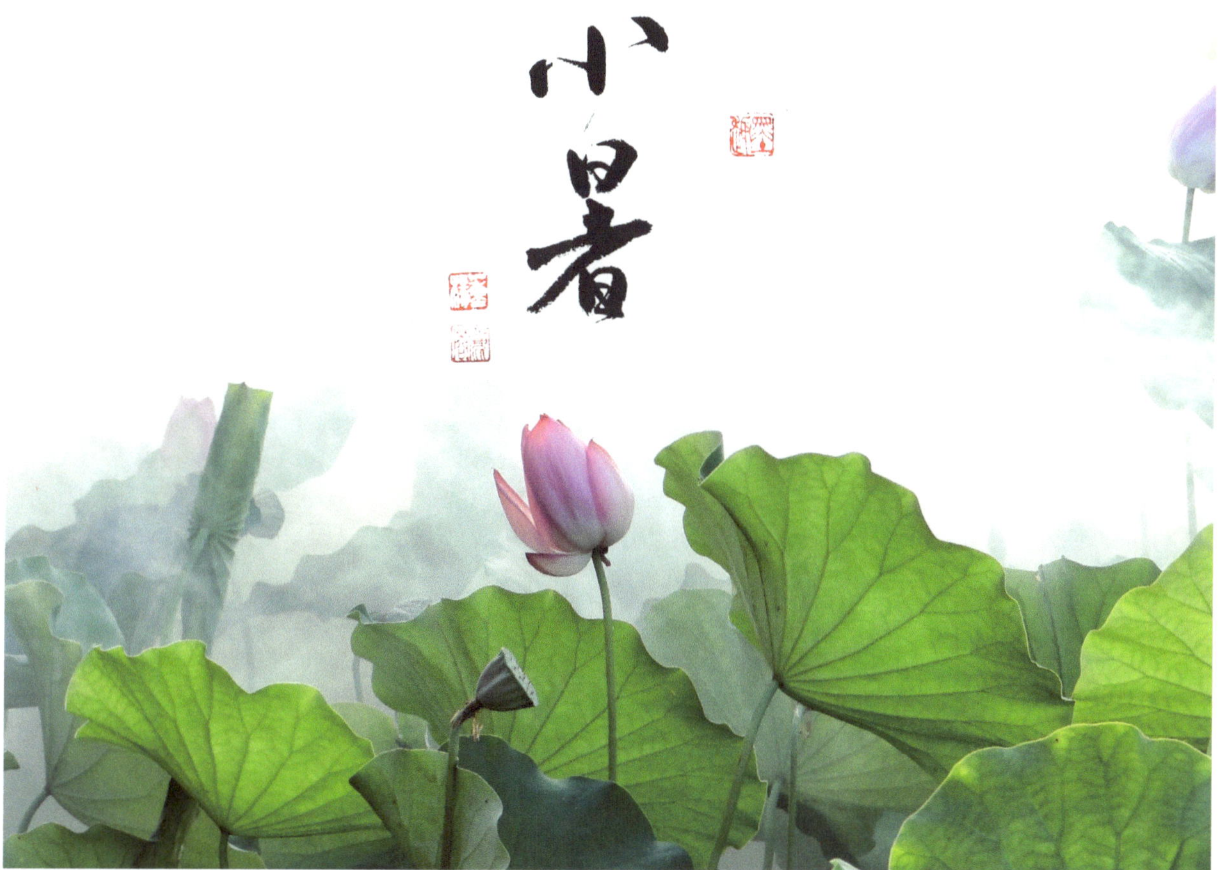

Breezes usually bring coolness, but breezes in early to mid July may start to feel warm in the temperate zone of the Northern Hemisphere. Ancient Chinese meteorologists were also aware of this phenomenon, so they called the 15-or-16-day solar term from early to mid July "Xiaoshu" in Chinese, which means "mild summer heat."

微風通常帶來涼意，但在北半球溫帶，陽曆七月上旬到中旬的微風開始含有暖意。中國古代氣象學家注意到了此一現象，而為這段時期的節氣取名為小暑。

This solar term begins when the sun reaches 105 degrees of the ecliptic drawn by ancient Chinese astronomers, or when the Earth arrives at 105 degrees of the celestial orbit redrawn by modern Chinese scientists to present the 24 solar terms. This day may be July 6, July 7, or July 8.

小暑節氣始於古人所謂太陽到達黃經一百零五度的日子，亦即現代科學家按照地球繞太陽軌道所重畫的橢圓形二十四節氣圖表上，地球運轉到一百零五度之時。這一天可能是陽曆七月六日、七月七日，或七月八日。

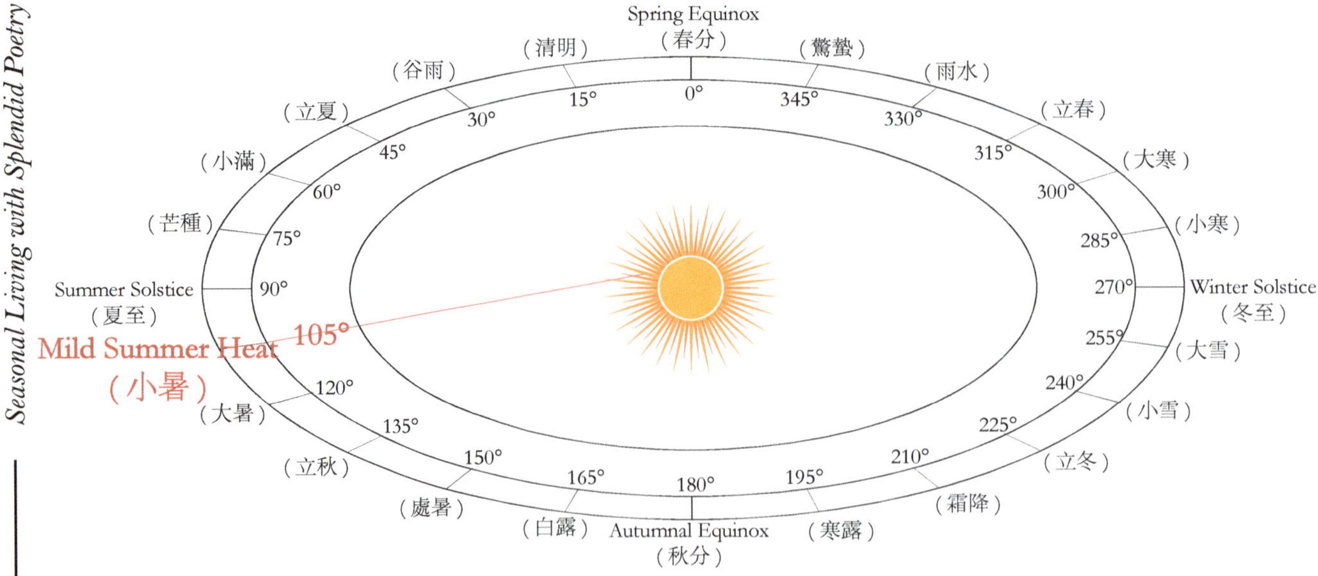

Like the other 23 solar terms, this one can be divided into three parts. Each part is five or six days long. The first part of the solar term from early to mid July is when warm winds arrive, as stated earlier. The second part is when crickets seek shade. The third part is when eagles fly high.
如同另外二十三個節氣，小暑節氣可分為三候。每一候五或六天。小暑一候溫風至，二候蟋蟀居宇，三候鷹始鷙。

During the solar term with mild summer heat, many Chinese customarily eat freshwater eels. They believe eating freshwater eels during this time of year will bring energy, just like the way ginseng soup would work in winter. Since summer is too hot for the consumption of ginseng soup, freshwater eels should be consumed instead. Freshwater eels are just as delicious as saltwater eels. Freshwater eels are available at many Shanghai-style restaurants in America.
在小暑時節，華人有個習俗是多吃鱔魚，相信小暑黃鱔賽人參。鱔魚就像海鰻一樣美味。炒鱔糊在美國很多上海餐館亦可吃到。

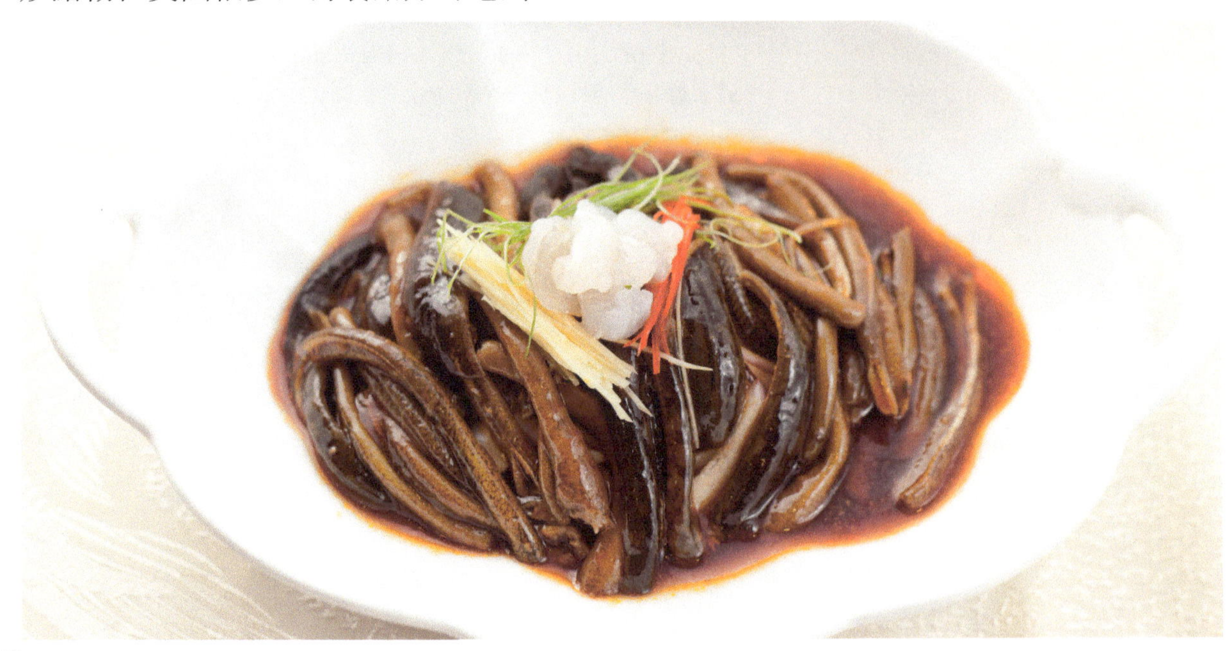

After a summer meal, many Chinese people like to have shaved ice for dessert. There are various toppings for shaved ice.
夏日飯後，華人喜歡吃刨冰作為甜點。刨冰上面可變很多花樣。

Among the toppings, Aiyu jelly is made from the seeds of a plant in the fig family. The businessman who first discovered the fig in the 19th century named it after his daughter, Aiyu, which means "beloved jade."[1] Aiyu juice will naturally congeal into jelly, which is not very sweet but really refreshing. Rich in pectin, vitamins, and dietary fiber, it is often available at Asian bubble tea cafes in America.
刨冰常用的愛玉是用一種無花果的種子所製成的果凍。首先發現愛玉果的商人以自己女兒的名字為之命名。愛玉子汁液所凝成的果凍並不太甜，而很清爽可口。愛玉凍富含果膠、維生素，以及纖維，經常在美國的亞洲式泡沫茶坊有售。

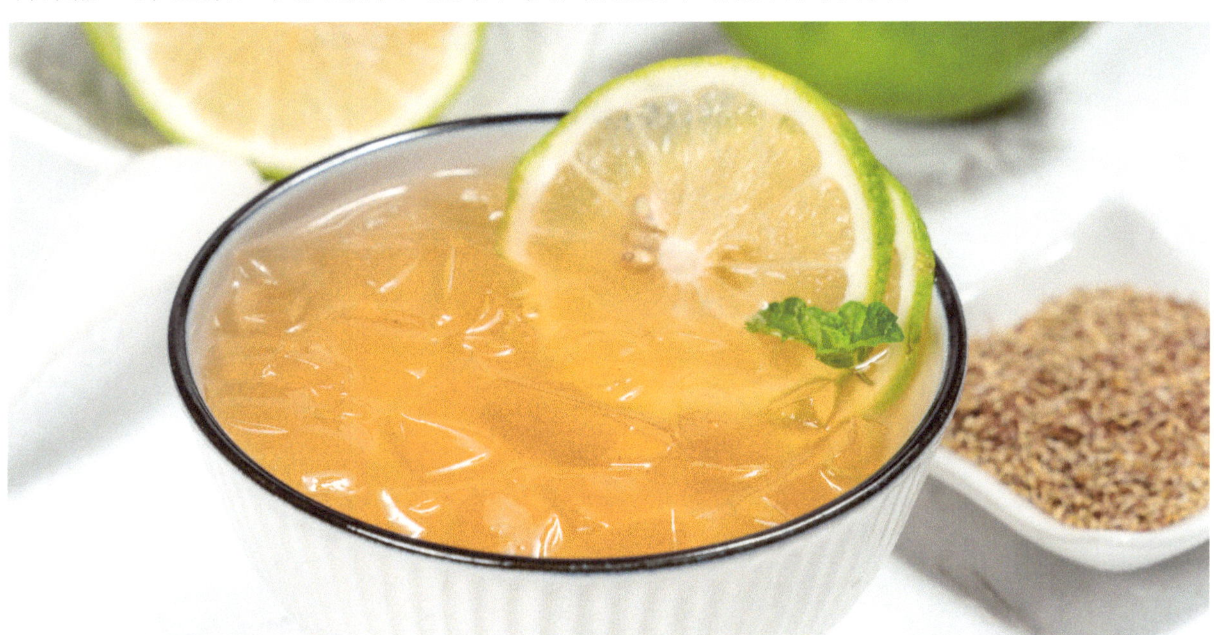

In East Asia, the solar term from early to mid July is a great time of year to go to a park where there is a lotus pond. This is when lovely lotus flowers generally reach their peak bloom.
在東亞，小暑時節很適合到有荷花池的公園去散步。這正是可人的荷花巔峰期。

On the next page is a classical Chinese poem that lyrically describes a large lotus pond during this time of year.
下一頁就有一首深具韻律美的小暑荷花絕句。

1　Wikipedia. "Aiyu Seeds" (Chinese edition). Wikipedia Foundation. https://zh.wikipedia.org/zh-hant/%E6%84%9B%E7%8E%89%E5%AD%90

曉出淨慈寺送林子方
Seeing My Friend Lin Zifang Off near Jingci Temple on a Summer Morning

Author: Yang, Wanli 楊萬里 (1127-1206)
Translator: Crystal Tai

畢竟西湖六月中 It's the sixth lunar month (overlapping with July) by West Lake;
風光不與四時同 No other seasons can compare with this time of year at dawn's break.
接天蓮葉無窮碧 Green lotus leaves luxuriantly reach the horizon, never limited;
映日荷花別樣紅 Pink lotus flowers distinctively reflect the sun, just awake.

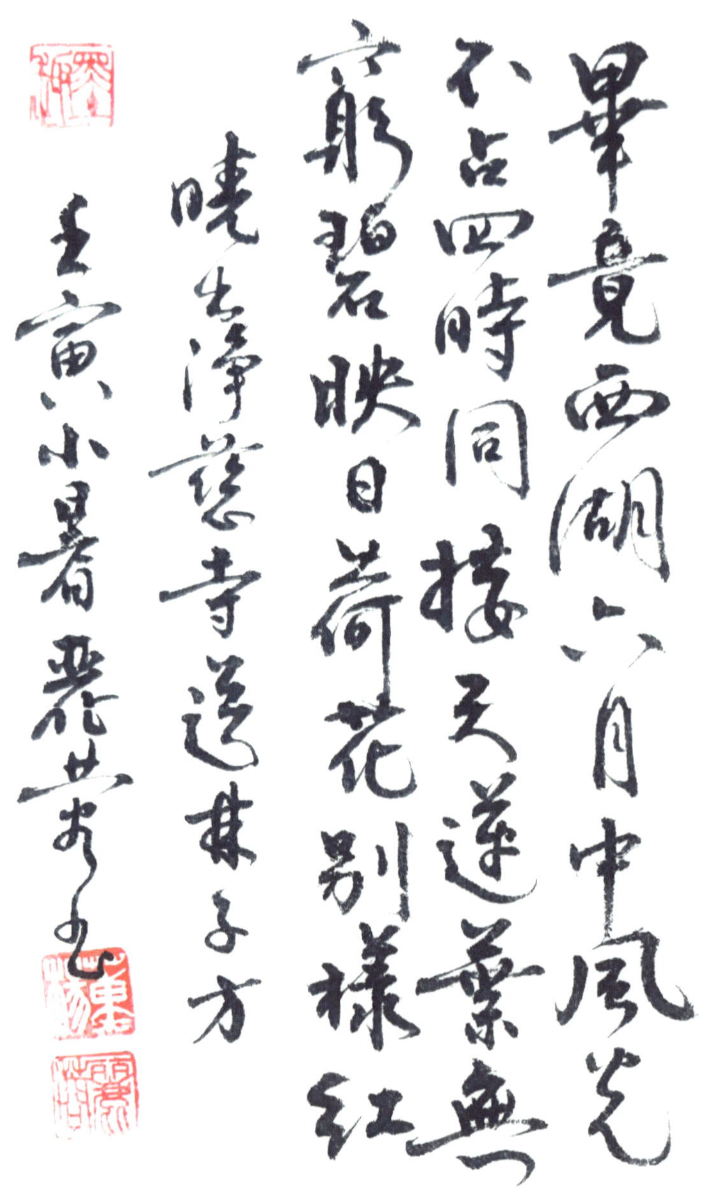

詩意節氣

小暑

Chapter 12
Fierce Summer Heat

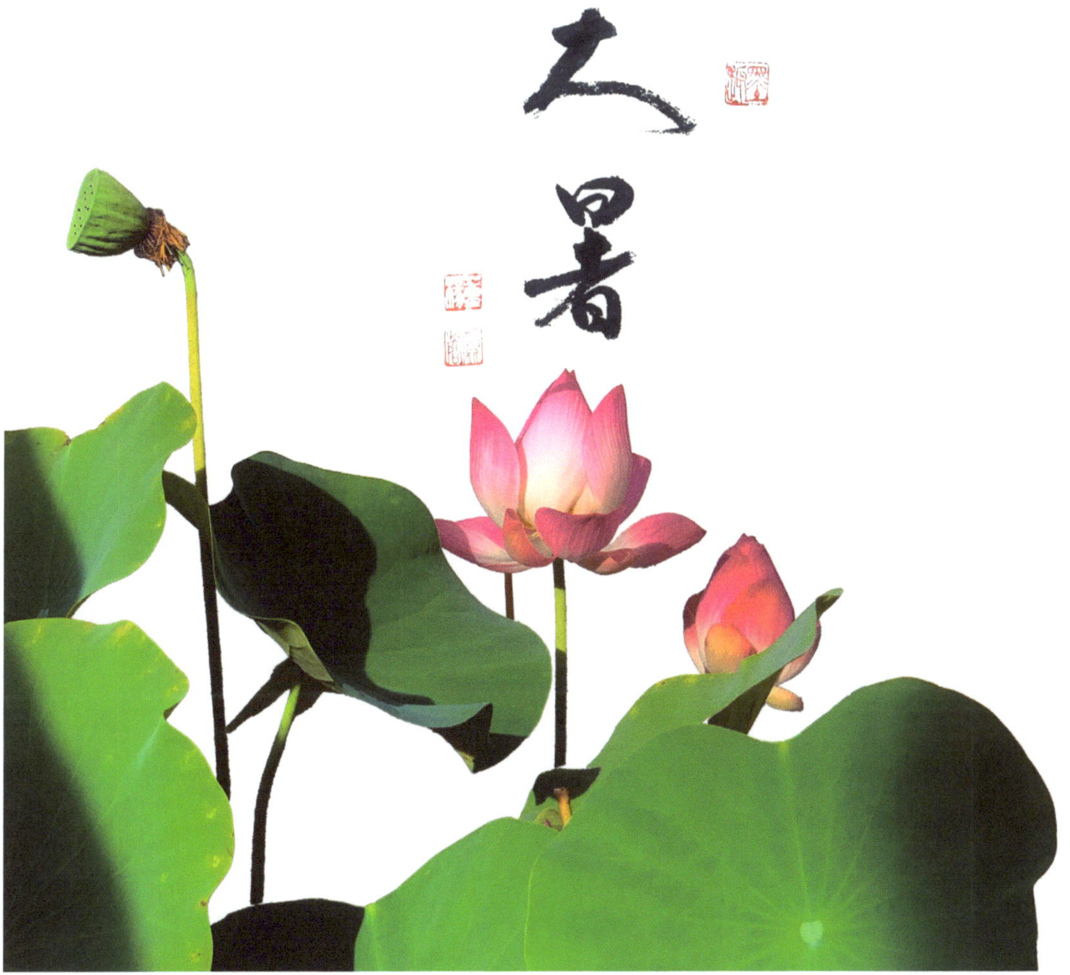

In the Northern Hemisphere, many records indicate that the hottest time of year is late July and early August. No wonder the Chinese call the 15-or-16-day solar term from late July to early August "Dashu," which means "fierce summer heat."

在北半球，許多記錄都顯示，一年最熱的時期是七月下旬到八月上旬。難怪中國人稱之為大暑。

The solar term with fierce summer heat starts when the sun reaches 120 degrees of the ecliptic drawn by ancient Chinese astronomers, or when the Earth arrives at 120 degrees of the celestial orbit redrawn by modern Chinese scientists to present the 24 solar terms. This day may be July 22, July 23, or July 24.

大暑時節始於古人所謂太陽到達黃經一百二十度的日子，亦即現代科學家按照地球繞太陽軌道所重畫的橢圓形二十四節氣圖表上，地球運轉到一百二十度之時。這一天可能是陽曆七月二十二日、二十三日，或二十四日。

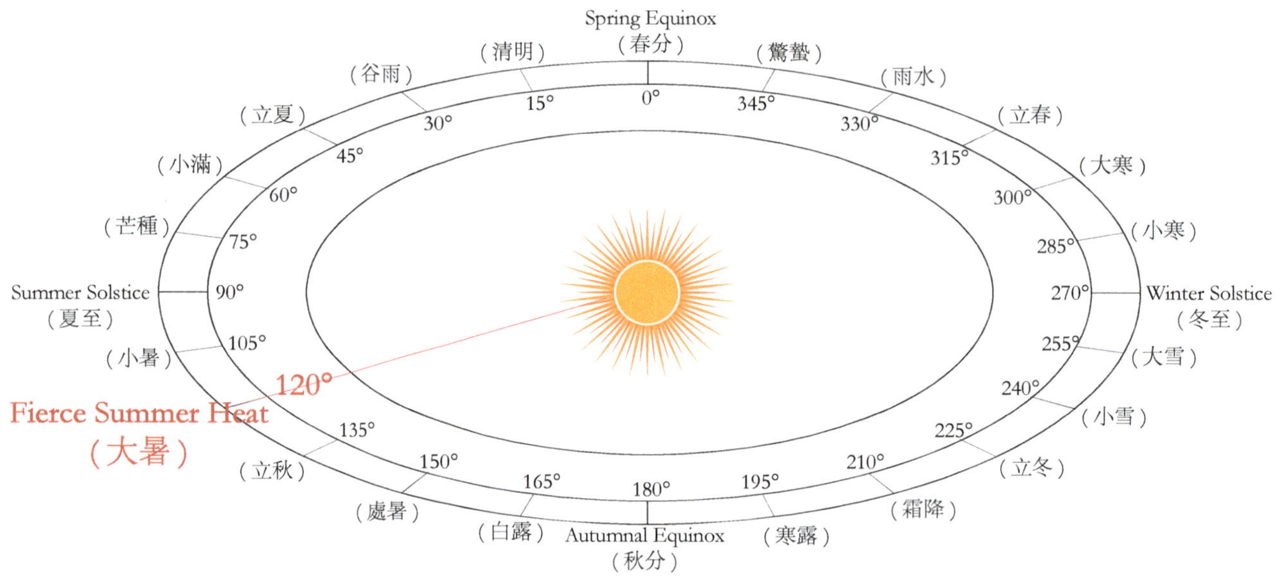

Like the other 23 solar terms, this one can be divided into three parts. Each part is five or six days long. The first part is when fireflies fly out of withering grass. The second part is when soil becomes soggy. The third part is when heavy downpours frequently occur.

如同另外二十三個節氣，大暑節氣可分為三候，每一候五或六天。大暑一候腐草為螢，二候土潤溽暑，三候大雨時行。

Rain or shine, the hot weather makes it unpleasant to do outdoor activities. Then indoor plants can provide a dose of nature. Better yet, plants naturally release water vapor. When an indoor plant does that, it will moisturize and cool the air.

無論晴雨，太熱的天氣不宜出門。這時候，室內盆栽可以提供一點大自然的氣息。況且，植物皆會釋放水蒸氣，當盆栽放出水蒸氣時，室內空氣會增加溼度而變涼。

Another cooling idea is to eat water-rich foods, which can help reduce body heat. Sushi is a good example, as rice and seafood generally have a high water content. Alternatively, for pasta lovers, this is a good time of year to indulge in clam linguini for clams' high water content. Clams are also low in calories and fat, but filled with vitamins, minerals, and protein.

另一個消暑方法是食用含水量較高的食物，那會有助於身體散熱。日本壽司是

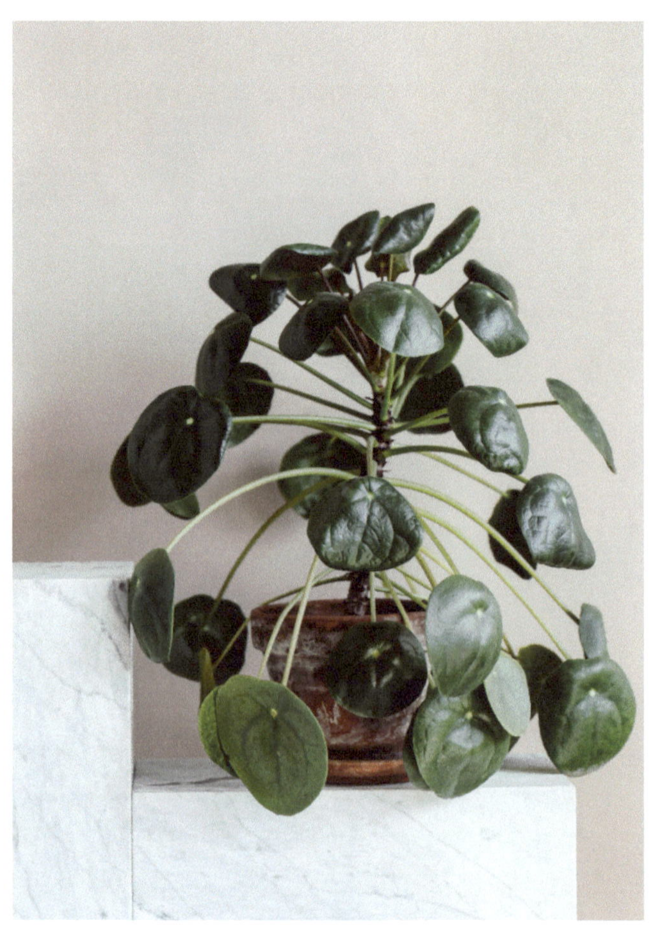

個好例子，因為米飯和海鮮含水量都很高。至於愛吃義大利麵之人，則可以選擇蛤蜊麵，因為蛤蜊含水量很高，而熱量很低，又富含維生素、礦物質，以及蛋白質。

Clams go well with squash as well as squash-like vegetables in Chinese cuisine, such as loofah gourds and white gourds. Chinese people often stir-fry clams with slices of loofah gourd.
如果做中餐，蛤蜊適合搭配瓜類。華人常做絲瓜炒蛤蜊。

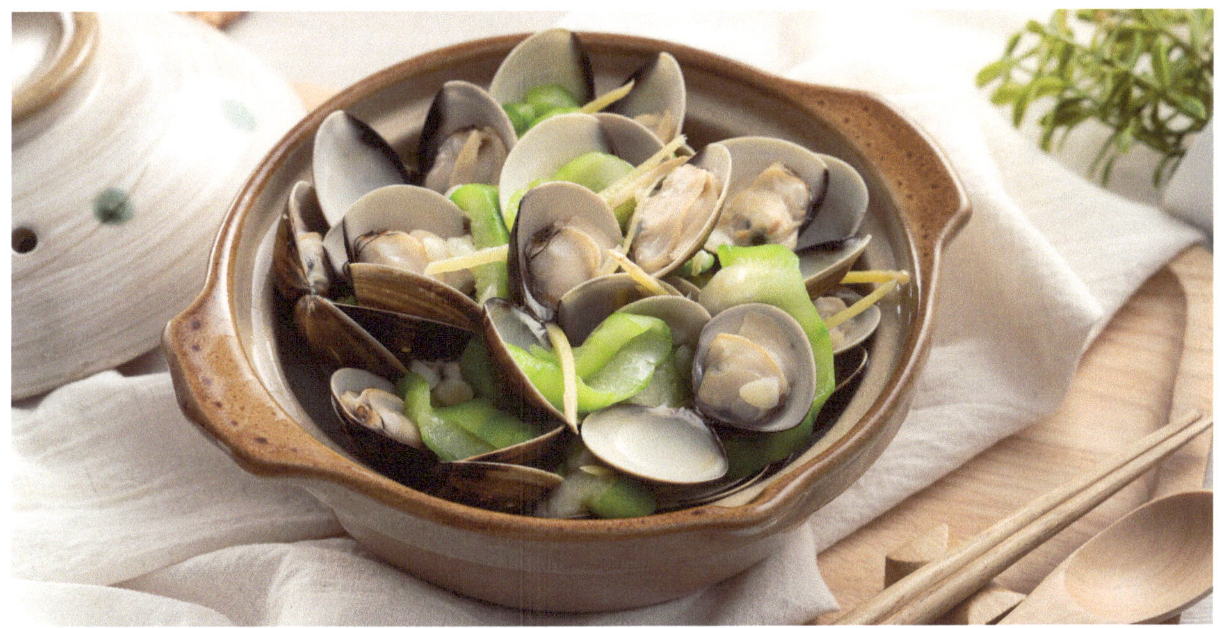

After a summer meal, how about a homemade pineapple ice pop for dessert? Simply insert popsicle sticks into pineapple slices, put them in a box, and freeze them. They will become all-natural ice pops.
夏日餐後，來一根鳳梨冰棒如何？只消把一根根冰棒棍子插進一片片鳳梨，裝盒放進冷凍櫃，就會做出純天然的冰棒了。

Hopefully, these cooling ideas can help reduce the use of air conditioning and save a considerable amount of energy. Imagine how humans used to live without air conditioners! They survived the hottest time of year, too.
盼望這些消暑方法有助於減少冷氣用量、節約能源。想像一下古人沒有冷氣如何過日子！他們也活過了大暑時節啊！

On the next page is a classical Chinese poem that metaphorically depicts scorching summer heat during the hottest solar term.
下一頁的絕句就善用比喻，淋漓盡致寫出了大暑的酷熱。

大暑　Fierce Summer Heat

Author：　Zhao, Yuan 趙元 (birth & death years unknown)
Translator：　Crystal Tai

旱雲飛火燎長空 Dry clouds fly with heat burning across the sky like fire;
白日渾如墮甑中 Daytime seems to be cooking in the steamer.
不到廣寒冰雪窟 If we cannot go to the ice cave on the moon,
扇頭能有幾多風 How many cool breezes can a fan bring in the stifling summer?

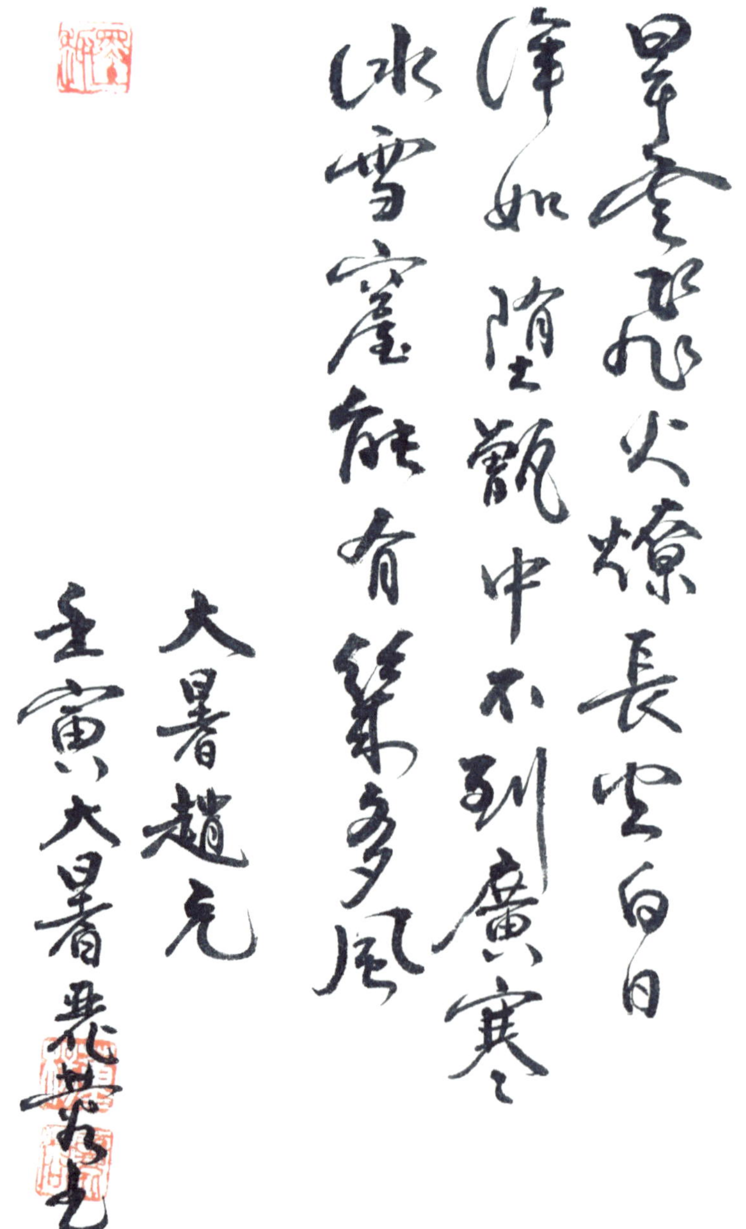

Chapter 13
First Signs of Autumn

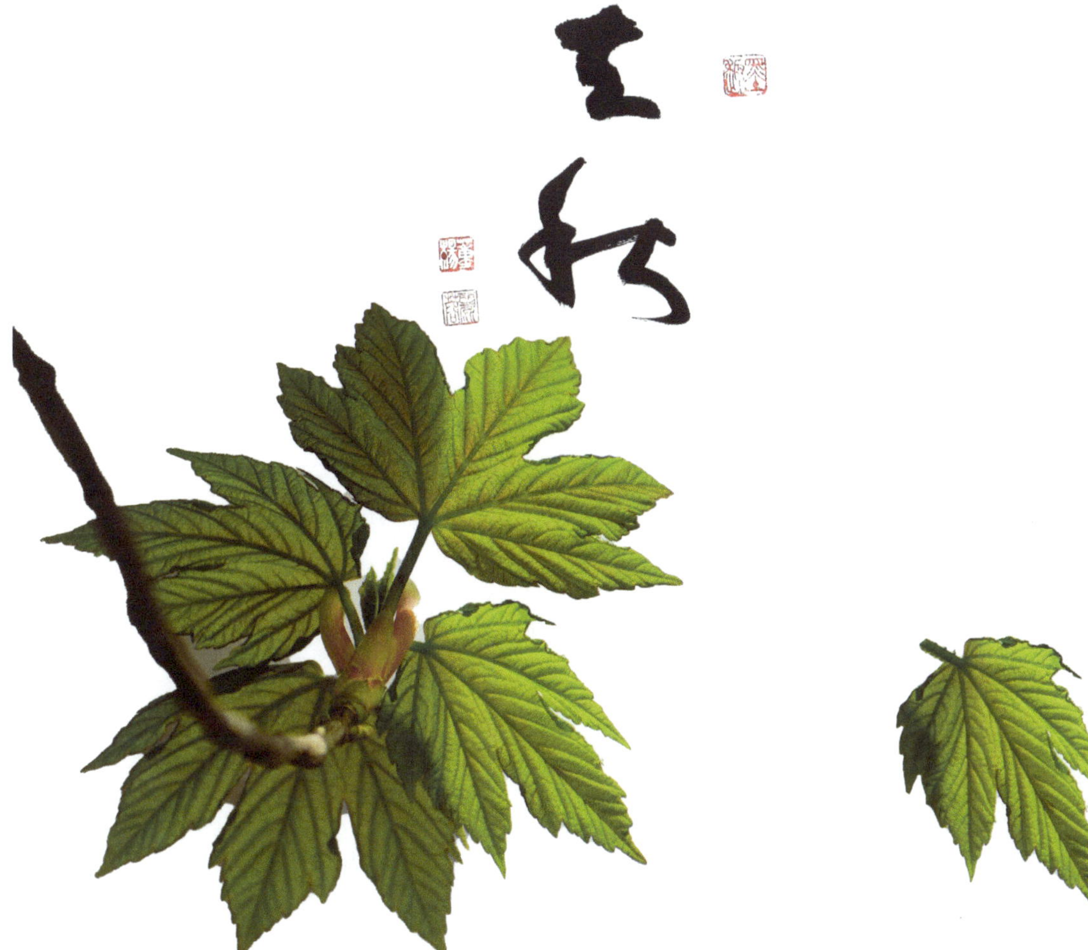

In China, sycamore trees generally start to shed their leaves in early to mid August. This is a very subtle phenomenon, but ancient Chinese scholars noticed it and wrote about it. They called it "*yi ye zhi qiu,*" which means "from one falling leaf, we can tell autumn is coming."
中國的梧桐樹通常都在陽曆八月上旬到中旬之間開始落葉。這是很細微的現象，但中國古代學者注意到了，也付諸筆墨，稱之為"一葉知秋"。

Ancient Chinese astronomers defined the beginning of autumn as when the sun reaches 135 degrees of the ecliptic they had discovered. That is exactly when the Earth arrives at 135 degrees of the celestial orbit redrawn by modern Chinese scientists to present the 24 solar terms. This day may be Aug 7, Aug 8, or Aug 9. It is called Liqiu in Chinese, which can be translated as "the first signs of autumn" in English.
中國古代天文學家定義秋天始於太陽到達黃經一百三十五度的日子，那也就是現代科學家按照地球繞太陽軌道所重畫的橢圓形二十四節氣圖表上，地球運轉到一百三十五度之時。這一天可能是陽曆八月七日、八月八日，或八月九日，中文名稱是立秋，可以英譯為早秋跡象初始。

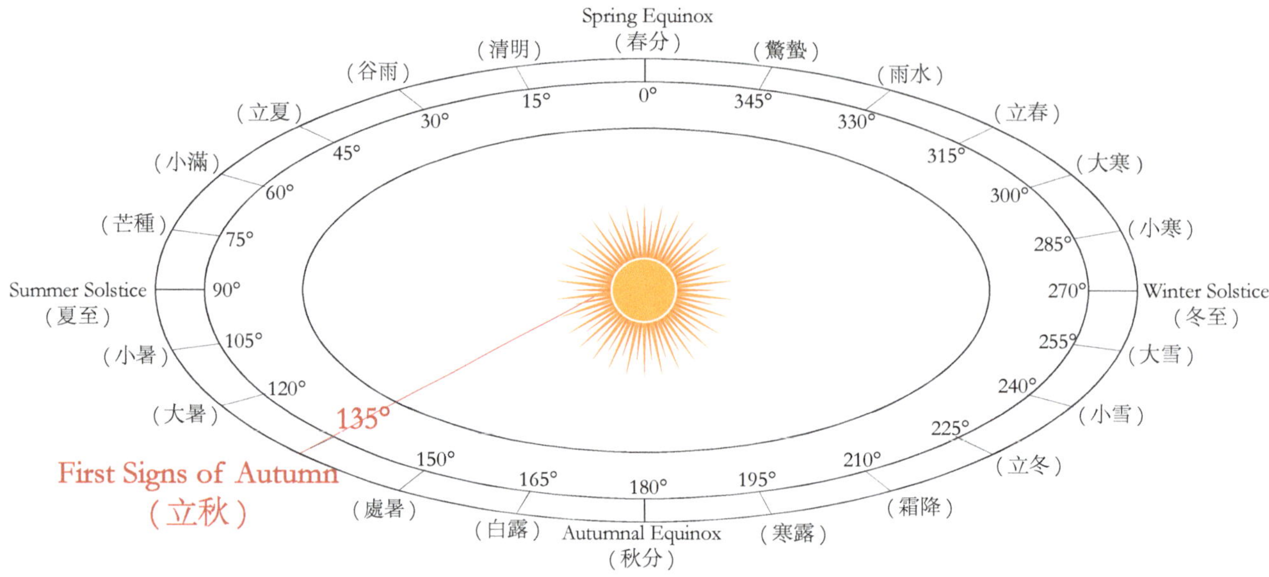

A 15-or-16-day solar term starts with the day that shows the first signs of autumn. Like the other 23 solar terms, this one can be divided into three parts. Each part is five or six days long. The first part of the solar term with the first signs of autumn is when cool breezes arrive. The second part is when white dew first appears. The third part of the solar term is when cicadas feel cold and cry loudly.

從立秋日開始的十五或十六天是立秋節氣。如同另外二十三個節氣，立秋可分為三候。每一候五或六天。立秋一候涼風至，二候白露生，三候寒蟬鳴。

Cicadas are definitely more sensitive to temperature changes than humans. In August, it still feels very hot to people in the Northern Hemisphere. That explains why Chinese medicine practitioners encourage people to eat eggplants during this time of year. Eggplants, which happen to be in season in August, can reduce body heat, according to Chinese medicinal classics.[1] Modern science has apparently confirmed that, because eggplants have a high water content. In addition, eggplants are a great source of vitamins and minerals. They contain a little protein, too. Vegans can stir-fry eggplant slices with string beans for more protein.

秋蟬對於溫度變化比人類敏感。在陽曆八月份，北半球居民都還覺得很熱。因此，中醫提倡在立秋吃茄子。茄子剛好在陽曆八月當令。根據中醫典籍記載，茄子能清熱。現代科學已經予以證實，因為茄子含水量很高。此外，茄子也富含維生素與礦物質，還有一點蛋白質。素食者可用茄子燒四季豆來獲取更多蛋白質。

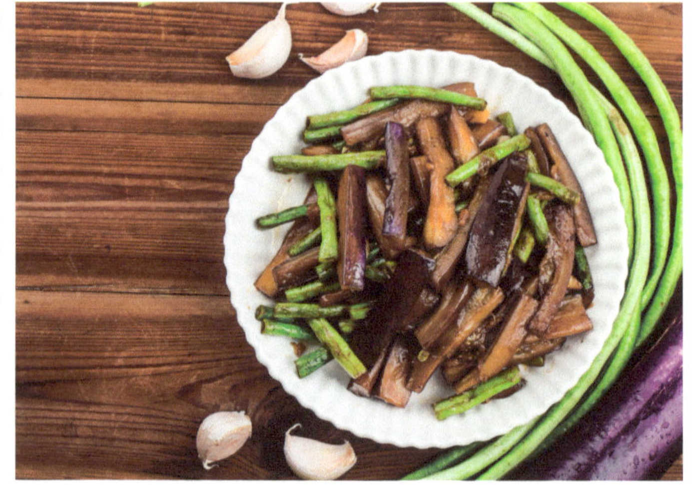

1　Chinese Medicine News. "Eggplants in Season." (Chinese edition). Traditional Chinese Medicine Bureau of Guangdong Province. http://szyyj.gd.gov.cn/zyyfw/ysbj/content/post_3330710.html

After the healthy main course, how about a fruit salad with in-season grapes for dessert? Although grapes can be imported, the local grape season generally starts in August in the temperate zone of the Northern Hemisphere, where August is also the month when vineyards are harvesting sparkling wine grapes, which are usually harvested first in order to get refreshing acidity in the sparkling wines.

健康的正餐之後，何妨拿當季葡萄來做一道水果沙拉作為甜點？雖然葡萄可以進口，但在北半球溫帶大多數地區，當地的食用葡萄產季通常始於陽曆八月。陽曆八月也是汽泡酒葡萄採收時節。汽泡酒葡萄在製酒葡萄之中最早收成，因為酸度能給汽泡酒清爽的口感。

August also coincides with the peak bloom period of epiphyllum, commonly known as orchid cacti. What's most special about these potted plants is that they only bloom at night. Their white flowers look dreamy and mysterious in darkness.

陽曆八月也是曇花的巔峰期。曇花最特別的是只在夜晚開花，在黑暗中開出夢幻而神秘的白花。

An epiphyllum viewing night is usually cool and breezy, making it easy to believe autumn has arrived, despite the hot weather during the day. Given the high temperatures in August, it is hard to blame modern astronomers and meteorologists for calling it a summer month. However, putting the first solar term of fall in August is a humbler approach, which goes way beyond how humans feel and pays attention to what all other creatures do.

觀賞曇花的黑夜通常涼爽而有微風，讓人容易相信秋天已來臨，儘管白日天氣依然炎熱。由於陽曆八月氣溫很高，實在難以責怪現代天文學家和氣象學家定義陽曆八月為夏季月份。不過，將立秋放在陽曆八月是比較謙卑的做法，等於超越了人類本身的感受，關注着其餘所有生物的行為。

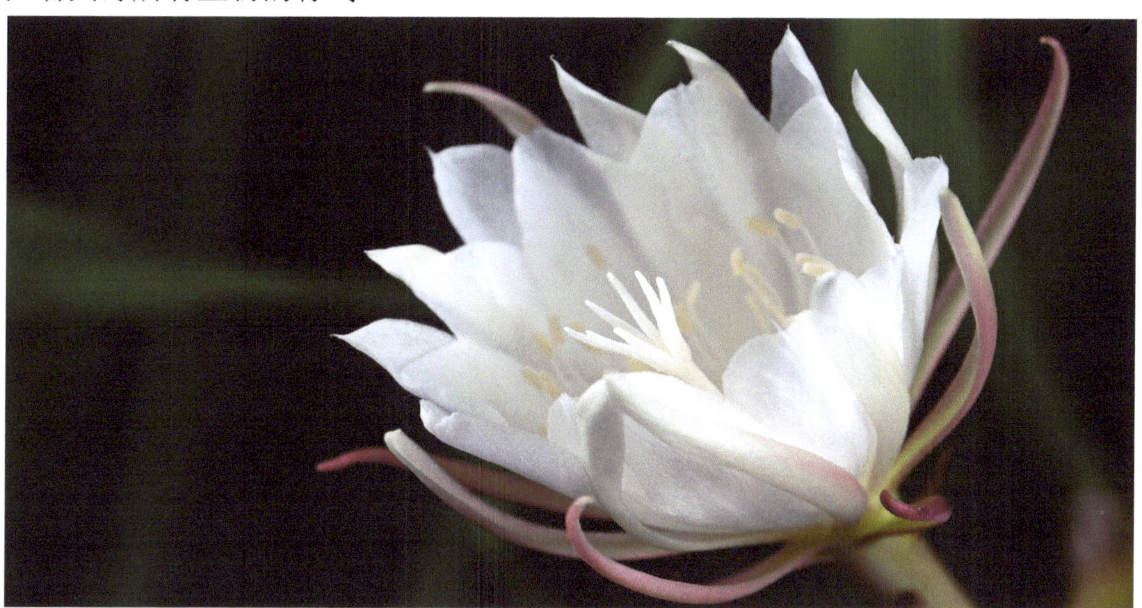

At the end of this chapter is a classical Chinese poem that adeptly demonstrates such keen observations of other creatures.

下一頁的古詩就表現了對於萬物的敏銳觀察。

早秋客舍 Traveling in Early Fall

Author: Du, Mu 杜牧 (803-852)
Translator: Crystal Tai

風吹一片葉 A falling leaf swirls in a gust of wind swiftly;
萬物已驚秋 All creatures are startled to realize that autumn has arrived suddenly.
獨夜他鄉淚 I'm shedding tears while spending the night as an out-of-towner alone;
年年為客愁 Being a wanderer year after year is my perpetual melancholy.
別離何處盡 Where will separated families get together finally?
搖落幾時休 When will fall foliage stop falling annually?
不及磻溪叟 I cannot compare with that elderly hermit sitting by the creek;
身閑長自由 He is never busy and always carefree.

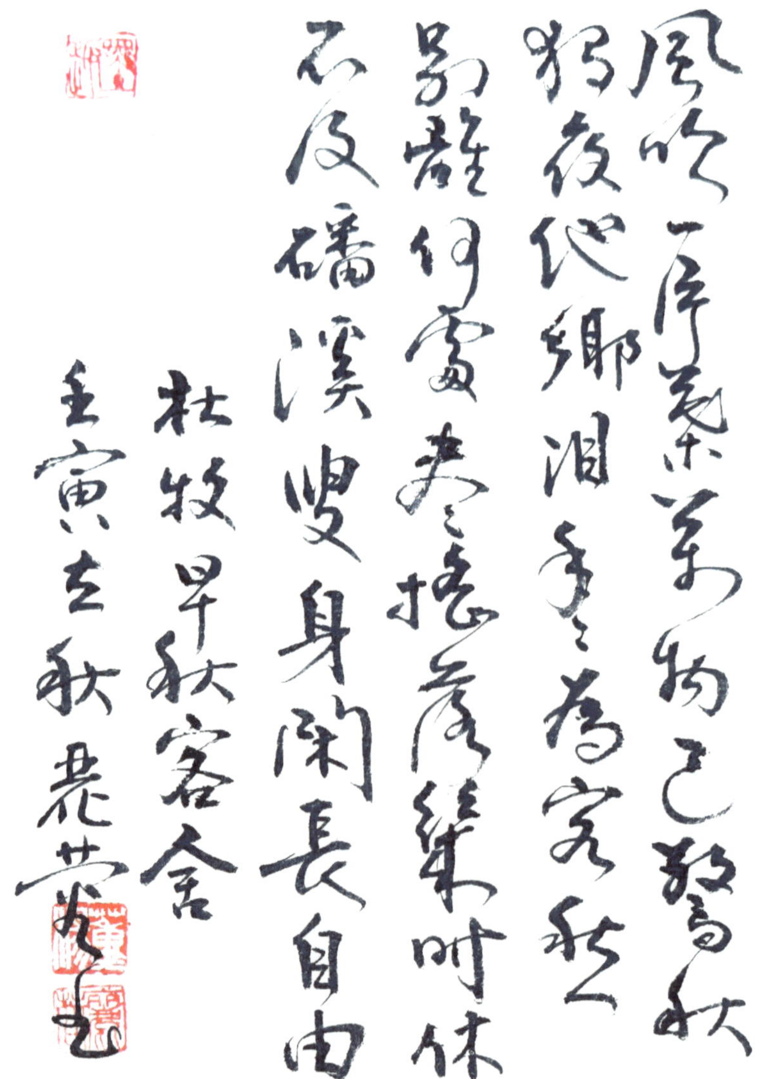

Chapter 14
Last Remnant of Summer Heat

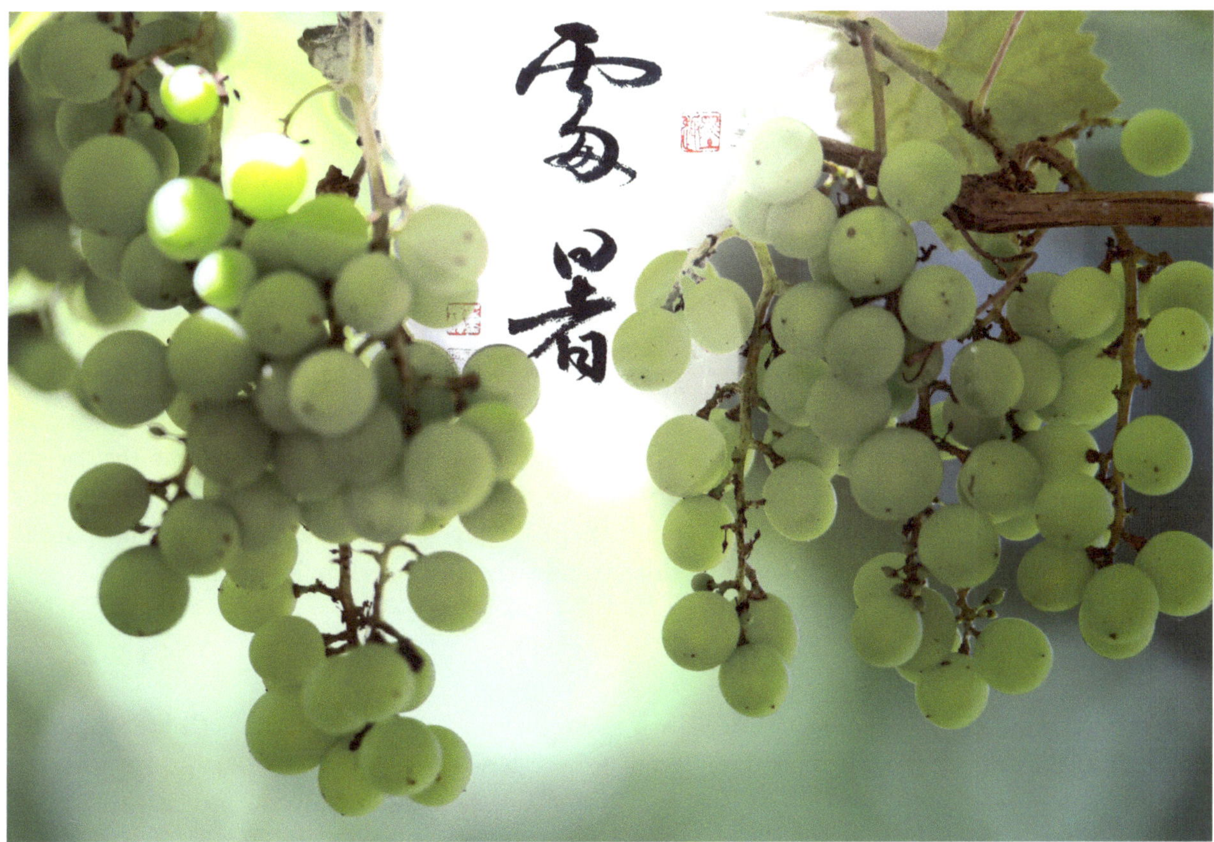

Late August is a great time of year to visit vineyards in the temperate zone of the Northern Hemisphere, where white wine grapes are being harvested, but some of them have not been harvested yet. Meanwhile, many vines are still laden with massive clusters of red wine grapes. Daylight is still pretty long, too, and daytime weather is still hot. However, some cool breezes indicate that summer heat is ending.

陽曆八月下旬在北半球溫帶是造訪葡萄園的好時節。此時白酒葡萄已在採收之中，但尚未收成完畢。同時，葡萄藤上都掛滿了紅酒葡萄。白晝依然很長，白天也還很熱。不過，有些涼風顯示暑熱正要結束。

This time of year belongs to a Chinese solar term called Chushu, which means "the last remnant of summer heat." The solar term starts when the sun reaches 150 degrees of the ecliptic drawn by ancient Chinese astronomers, or when the Earth arrives at 150 degrees of the celestial orbit redrawn by modern Chinese scientists to present the 24 solar terms. It may be Aug 22, Aug 23, or Aug 24.

每年此時屬於一個名叫處暑的節氣，意指殘留而將盡的暑熱。處暑節氣始於太陽到達黃經一百五十度的日子，亦即現代科學家按照地球繞太陽軌道所重畫的橢圓形二十四節氣圖表上，地球運轉到一百五十度之時。這可能是陽曆八月二十二，二十三，或二十四日。

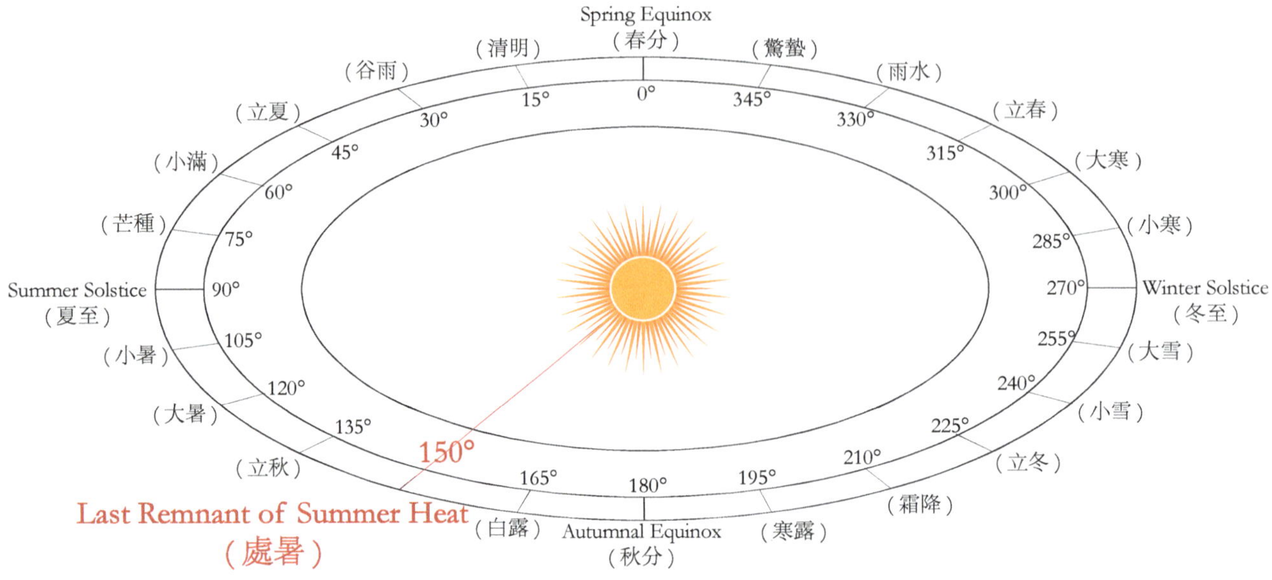

Like the other 23 solar terms, this one can be divided into three parts. Each part is five or six days long. The first part of the solar term with the remnant of summer heat is when eagles aggressively search for birds in order to catch them before they migrate. The second part is when heaven and earth become quiet. The third part is when rice and millet are harvested.

如同另外二十三個節氣，處暑節氣可分為三候，每一候五或六天。一候鷹乃祭鳥，二候天地始肅，三候禾乃登。

Rice is a staple food in Chinese culture. In late August and early September, Chinese people often choose to eat duck with their rice, because there tends to be dry heat during this time of year and duck meat has a moisturizing effect, based on traditional Chinese medical theories.[1] There is even a duck dish particularly created for the solar term from late August to early September. It is steamed duck with sliced lily bulbs, which have a high water content. Vegans can stir-fry sliced lily bulbs with snow peas instead.

米飯是華人的主食。在陽曆八月底九月初，華人常吃鴨肉來配飯，因為這段時期天氣乾熱，而鴨肉能夠潤燥。甚至有一道鴨肉佳肴名叫處暑鴨，就是清蒸百合鴨肉。百合含水量很高。素食者可用百合來炒雪豆。

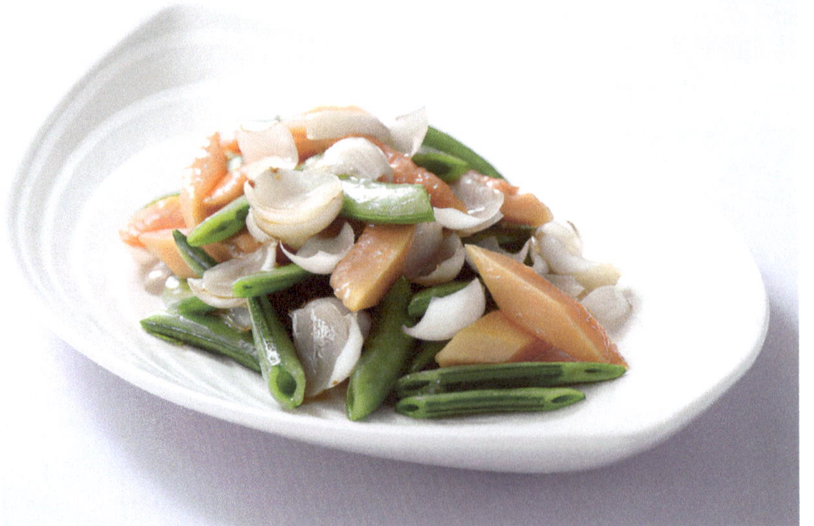

1   Guangdong Chinese Medicine Net. "It Is the Number One Meat in Autumn." (Chinese edition). Traditional Chinese Medicine Bureau of Guangdong Province. http://szyyj.gd.gov.cn/zyyfw/ysbj/content/post_4005967.html

Frozen lily bulbs can be found at Chinese markets in the US. So are frozen lotus roots, which are another hydrating and nutritious vegetable in Chinese cuisine.
冷凍百合在美國的華人超市有售。冷凍蓮藕亦然。蓮藕也是既能補水又有營養的蔬菜。

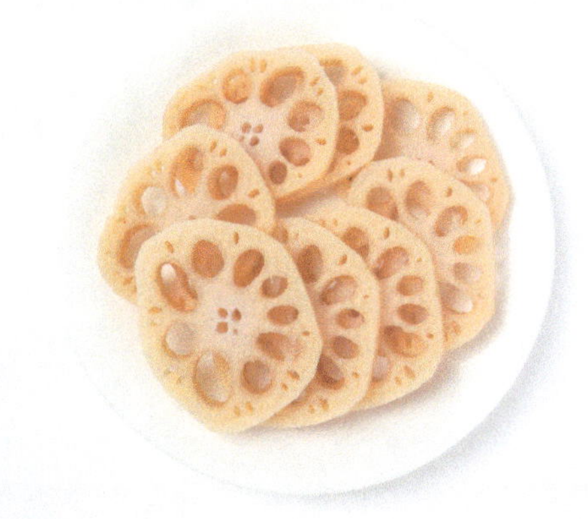

Fresh lotus roots happen to be in season in late August and early September, because they are usually picked after the end of the year's lotus flower season. While lotus flowers have faded away, a flower species of the genus Hibiscus comes into bloom colorfully. Commonly known as the cotton rose or the Confederate rose, these hibiscus shrubs are not aquatic plants, but they prefer damp soil and generally grow near water.
新鮮蓮藕恰好在八月底九月初上市，因為蓮藕的採摘總在荷花季過後。在荷花凋零時，木芙蓉繽紛綻放。雖然木芙蓉不是水生植物，卻偏愛潮溼土壤而長在水邊。

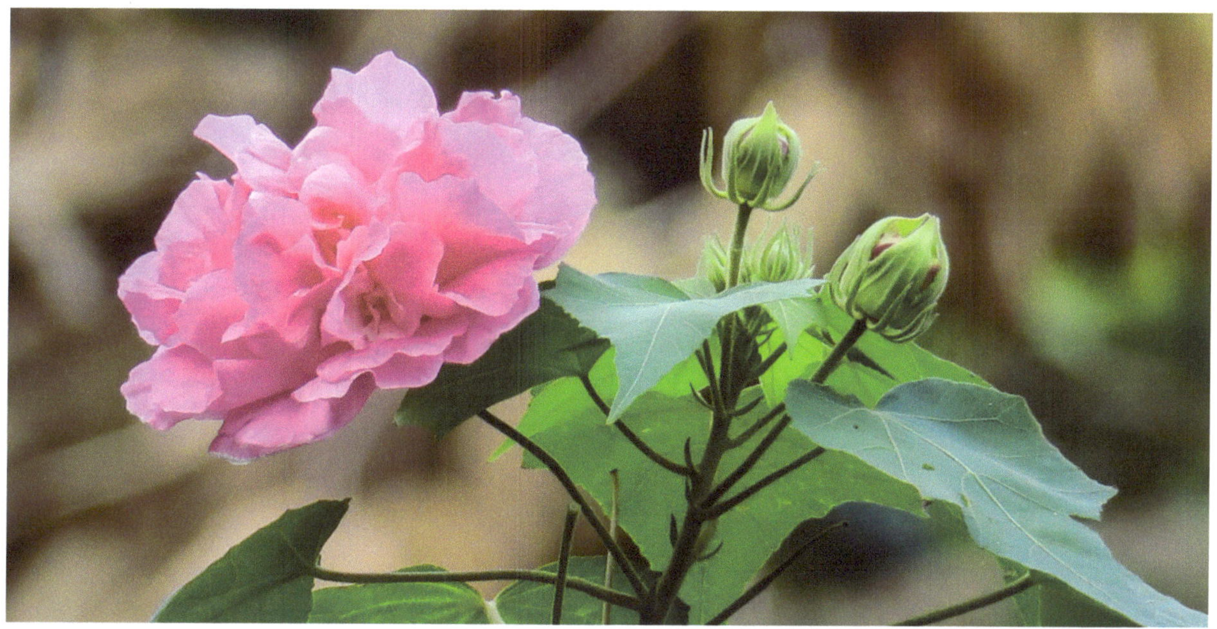

Apparently, the solar term from late August to early September is quite a busy time of year in nature.
顯然，處暑是大自然相當忙碌的時節。

At the end of this chapter is a classical Chinese poem that comprehensively conveys the juxtaposition of natural phenomena during this solar term.
下一頁的律詩就逐一呈現着處暑節氣甚為繁忙的各種自然景象。

處暑七月中
Last Remnant of Summer Heat in the Seventh Lunar Month (Which Overlaps with August)

Author：Yuan, Zhen 元稹 (779-831)
Translator： Crystal Tai

向來鷹祭鳥 Hawks prey on birds as always.
漸覺白藏深 It's when the senses of autumn run deeper.
葉下空驚吹 Falling leaves feel startled while getting blown away;
天高不見心 Heaven's heart is invisible while being hidden higher.
氣收禾黍熟 Natural forces taper off with mature crops
風靜草蟲吟 Cool breezes calm down with insects' murmur.
緩酌樽中酒 I slowly drink a goblet of wine
容調膝上琴 While adjusting the strings of my zither.

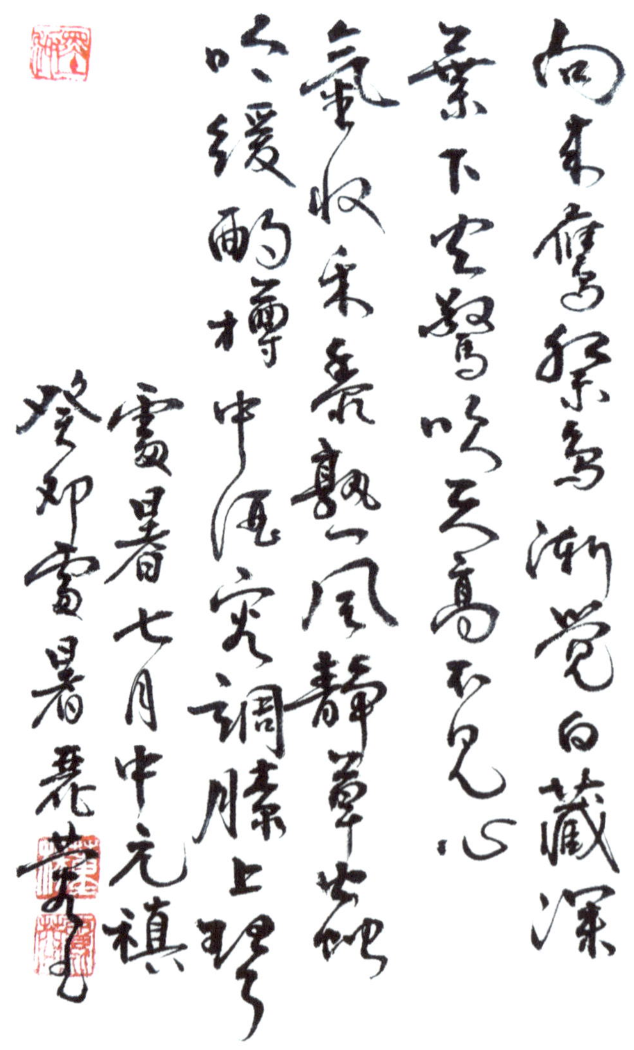

Chapter 15
White Dew

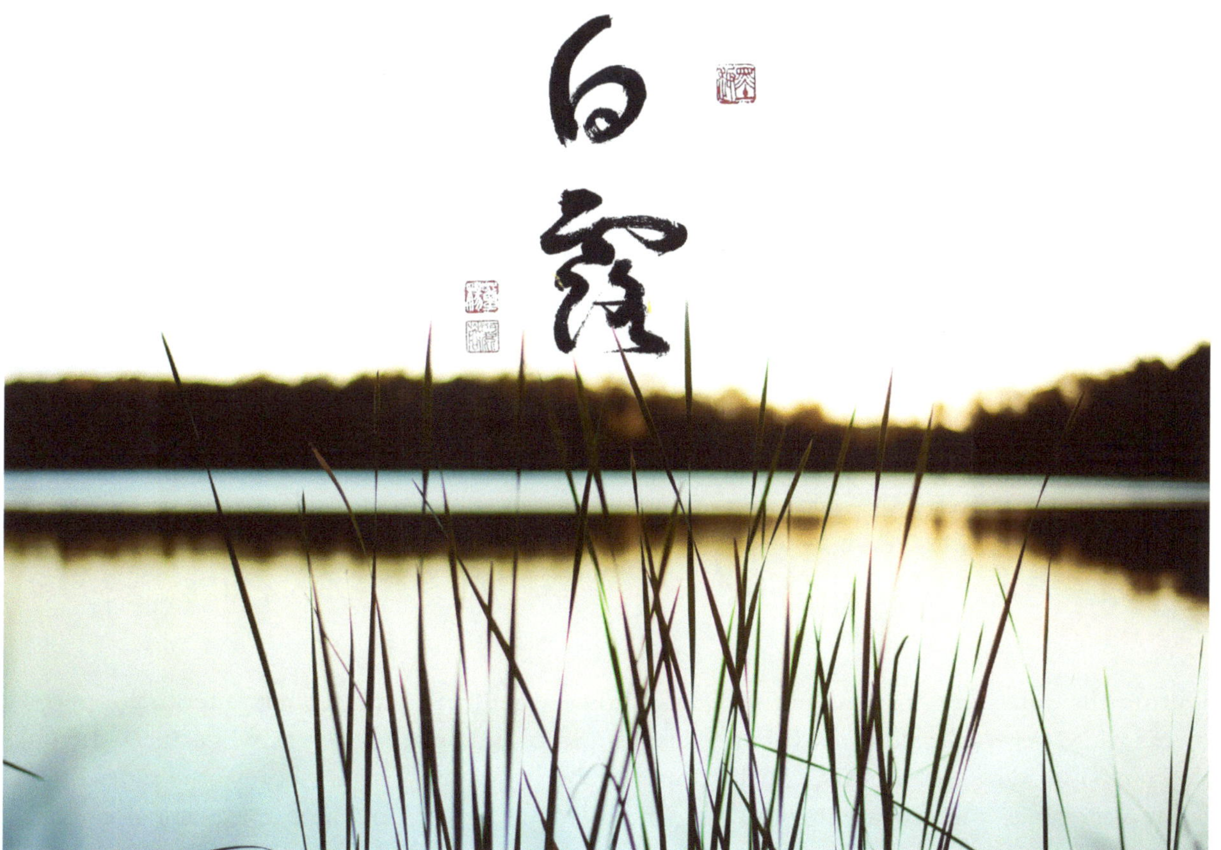

There is a temperature called the dew point, at which water vapor in the air will begin to condense, turning into liquid water. That is how dew forms on surfaces, such as grass and leaves, which are not warmed by the heat radiated from the ground. In other words, the weather has to be cool enough for dew to show up. That explains why a 15-or-16-day solar term in September is called Bailu in Chinese, which means "white dew."

有一種氣溫稱為凝露點，能讓空氣中的水蒸氣凝結為液態的水。那就是露珠如何在未受地熱感染的草木上形成。換言之，天氣要夠涼才會有露珠。於是，陽曆九月份有一段十五天或十六天的節氣名叫白露。

Post-summer morning dew first appears when the sun reaches 165 degrees of the ecliptic drawn by ancient Chinese astronomers, or when the Earth arrives at 165 degrees of the celestial orbit redrawn by modern Chinese scientists to present the 24 solar terms. This day may be Sept 7, Sept 8, or Sept 9.

夏天過後的朝露最早出現於太陽到達黃經一百六十五度的日子，亦即現代科學家按照地球繞太陽軌道所重畫的橢圓形二十四節氣圖表上，地球運轉到一百六十五度之時。這一天可能是陽曆九月七日、九月八日，或九月九日。

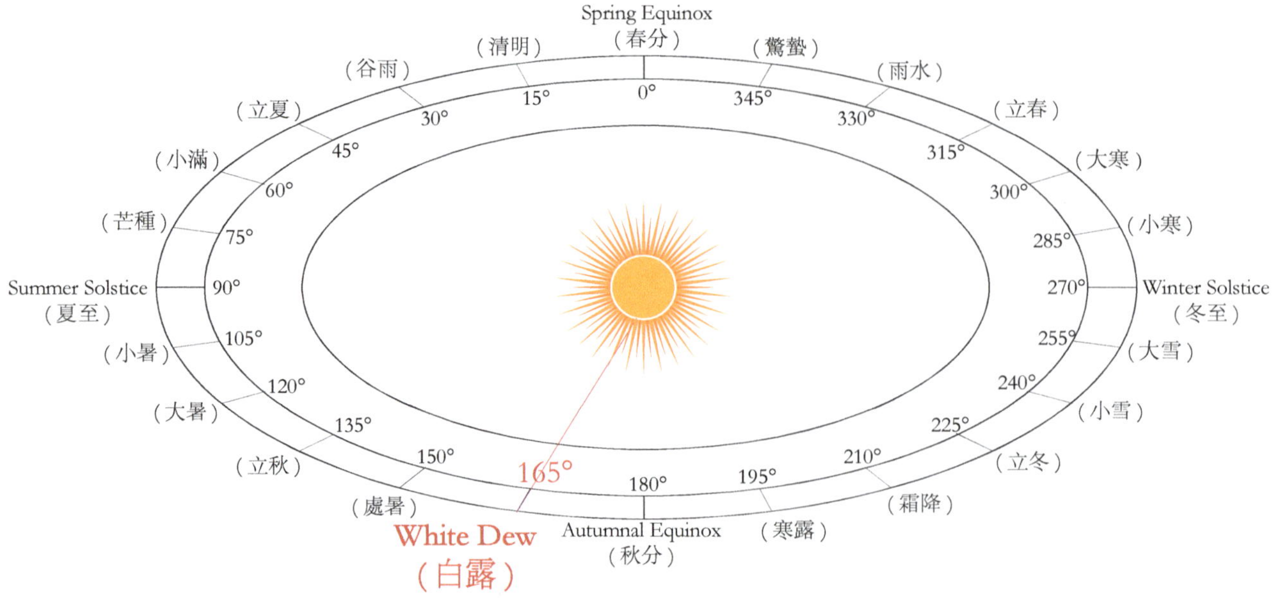

Like the other 23 solar terms, this one can be divided into three parts. Each part is five or six days long. The first part of the solar term named White Dew is when wild swans and wild geese migrate south. The second part is when swallows migrate south. The third part is when birds store food to get ready for colder weather.

如同另外二十三個節氣，白露節氣亦可分為三候，每一候五或六天。白露一候鴻雁來，二候玄鳥歸，三候群鳥養羞。

During the solar term named White Dew, Chinese medicine practitioners encourage people to eat white vegetables such as daikon radishes and cauliflower, as well as white fleshed fruits, definitely including Asian pears, which happen to be in season. This is because the nutrients of white vegetables and fruits enter the lung meridian, according to Chinese medicinal classics,[1] while sudden weather changes in September may irritate the respiratory system.

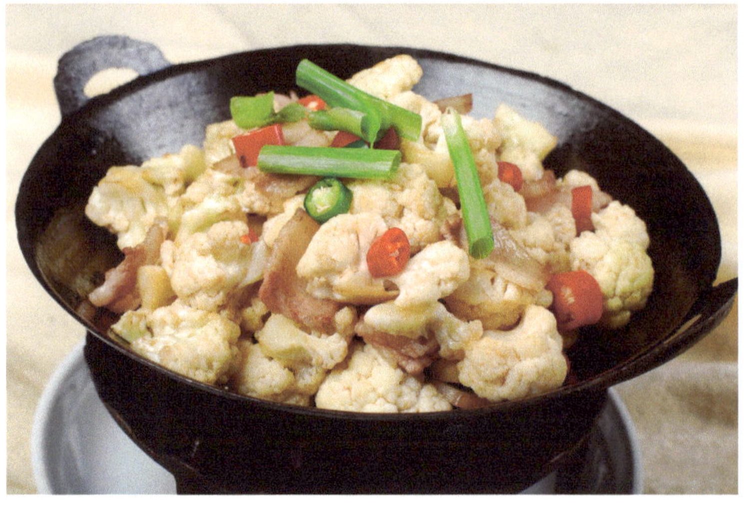

在白露節氣，中醫提倡多吃白蘿蔔、花椰菜等白色蔬菜，以及包括當令梨子在內的白肉水果。這是因為白色食物入肺經，而陽曆九月多變的天氣易損呼吸系統。

1   Chinese Medicine News. "Eight White Foods for Nourishing the Lungs" (Chinese edition). Traditional Chinese Medicine Bureau of Guangdong Province. http://szyyj.gd.gov.cn/zyyfw/ysbj/content/post_4246683.html#:~:text=%E7%99%BD%E8%89%B2%EF%BC%8C%E5%9C%A8%E4%B8%AD%E5%8C%BB%E4%BA%94%E8%A1%8C%E4%B8%AD,%E6%98%93%E5%8F%97%E7%87%A5%E9%82%AA%E4%BC%A4%E5%AE%B3%E3%80%82a

To nourish the lung meridian, Chinese people often cook pork bone soup or fish soup with daikon radishes during this time of year. Crucian carp soup with daikon radishes is especially delicious and nutritious.

為了潤肺，華人在白露時節常用白蘿蔔煮排骨湯或魚湯。蘿蔔鯽魚湯尤其既美味又營養。

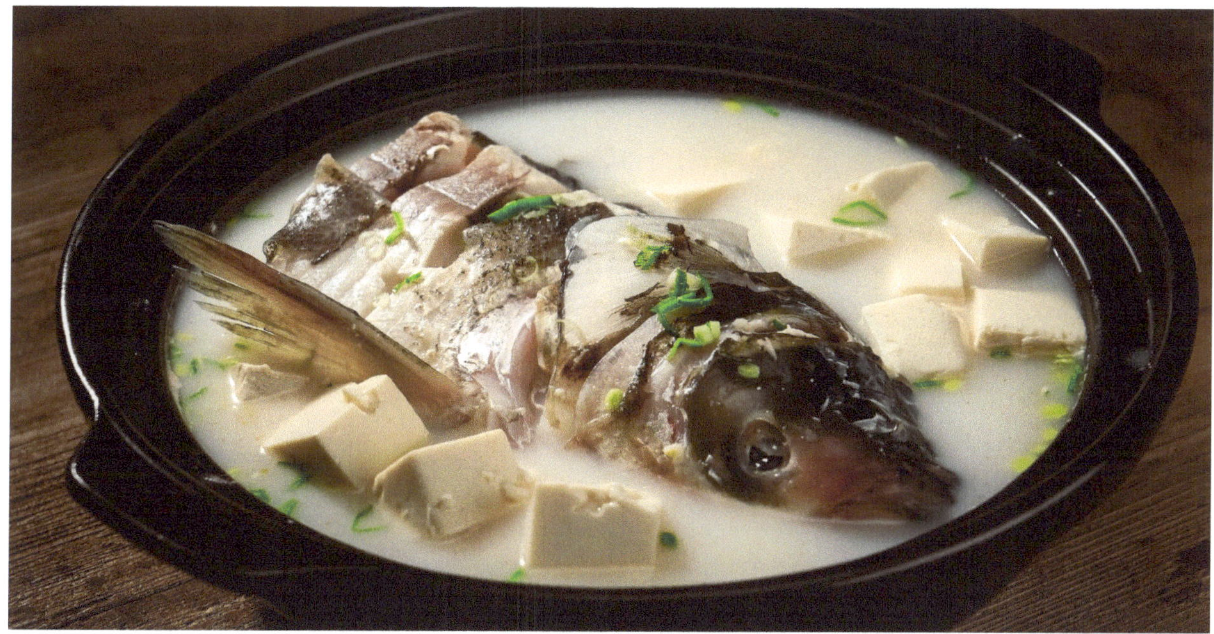

After a lung nourishing meal, how about dessert? During the solar term from early to mid September, moon cakes are always available at Chinese markets, because the Moon Festival, which marks the full moon closest to the autumnal equinox, falls either in this solar term or in the next one.

享用過潤肺餐之後，可吃月餅當甜點。月餅在白露時節總是已上市，因為中秋節總在白露節氣或下個節氣。

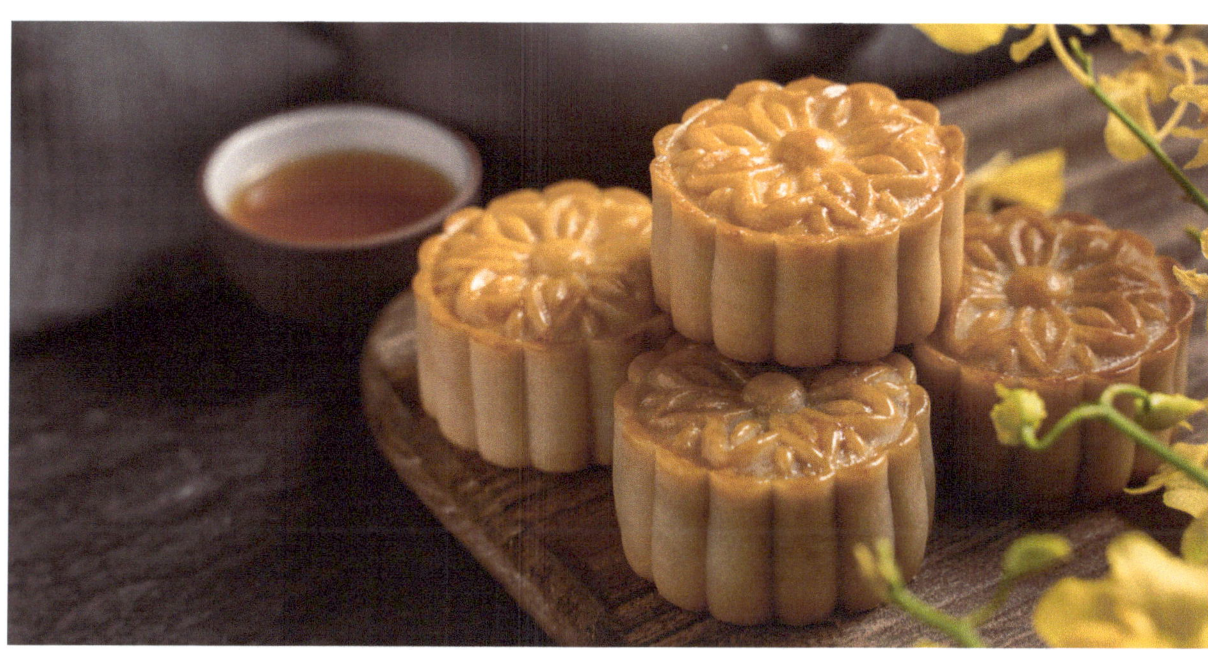

Both of these solar terms are good for bird watching near water in the temperate zone of the Northern Hemisphere. No wonder classical Chinese poems often describe taking a walk along the river during this time of year. At the end of this chapter is one of the oldest examples.

白露和下個節氣都是到水邊觀鳥的好時節。難怪中國古典文學常有描述河濱漫步的詩篇。以下就展示最古老的這類作品之一。

《詩經》蒹葭篇 The Reeds – from *The Book of Songs*

Author: Anonymous
Translator: Crystal Tai

蒹葭蒼蒼	Lush, lush are the reeds by the water.
白露為霜	White dew appears like frost with splendor.
所謂伊人	More dewy is that young lady
在水一方	On the other side of the river.
溯洄從之	I'm going upstream to follow her.
道阻且長	The rocky journey gets increasingly longer.
溯游從之	I'm going downstream to follow her.
宛在水中央	She seems to be in the middle of the river.
蒹葭萋萋	Grassy, grassy are the reeds by the inlet.
白露未晞	White dew has not dried yet.
所謂伊人	More dewy is that young lady
在水之湄	On the curved shore of the inlet.
溯洄從之	I'm going upstream to follow her.
道阻且躋	The rocky way gets increasingly wet.
溯游從之	I'm going downstream to follow her.
宛在水中坻	She seems to be on an islet in the inlet.
蒹葭采采	Lively, lively are the reeds along the shoreline.
白露未已	White dew has not lost its shine.
所謂伊人	More dewy is that young lady
在水之涘	On the sandy edge of the shoreline.
溯洄從之	I'm going upstream to follow her.
道阻且右	The rocky route gets increasingly unfine.
溯游從之	I'm going downstream to follow her.
宛在水中沚	She seems to be on an isle near the shoreline.

蒹葭蒼蒼　白露為霜　所謂佳人
在水一方　溯洄從之　道阻且長
溯游從之　宛在水中央
蒹葭萋萋　白露未晞　所謂伊人
在水之湄　溯洄從之　道阻且躋
溯游從之　宛在水中坻
蒹葭采采　白露未已　所謂伊人
在水之涘　溯洄從之　道阻且右
溯游從之　宛在水中沚

詩經蒹葭

癸卯白露花甲之年

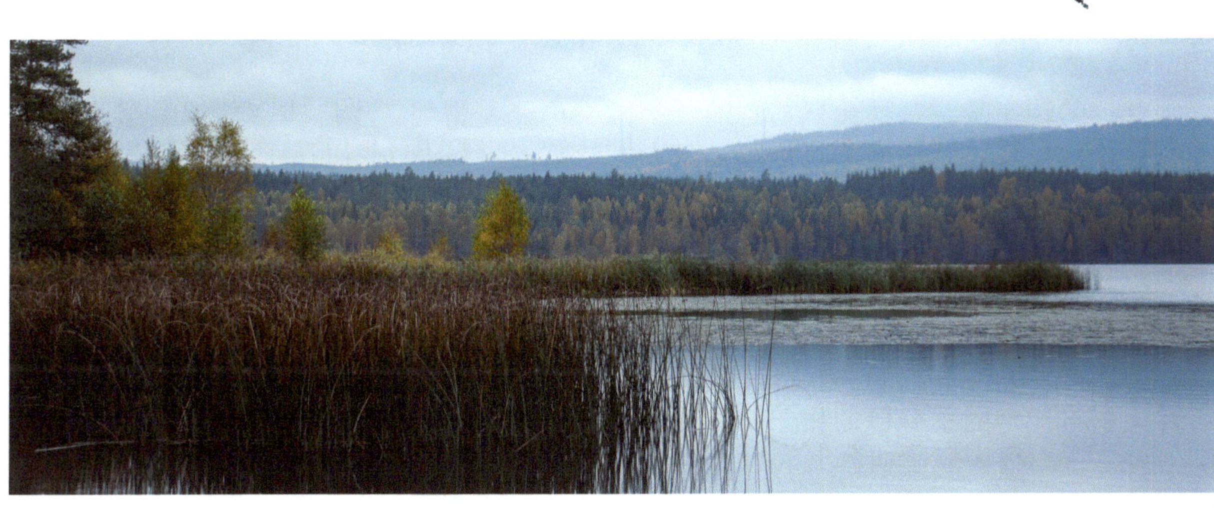

Chapter 16
Autumnal Equinox

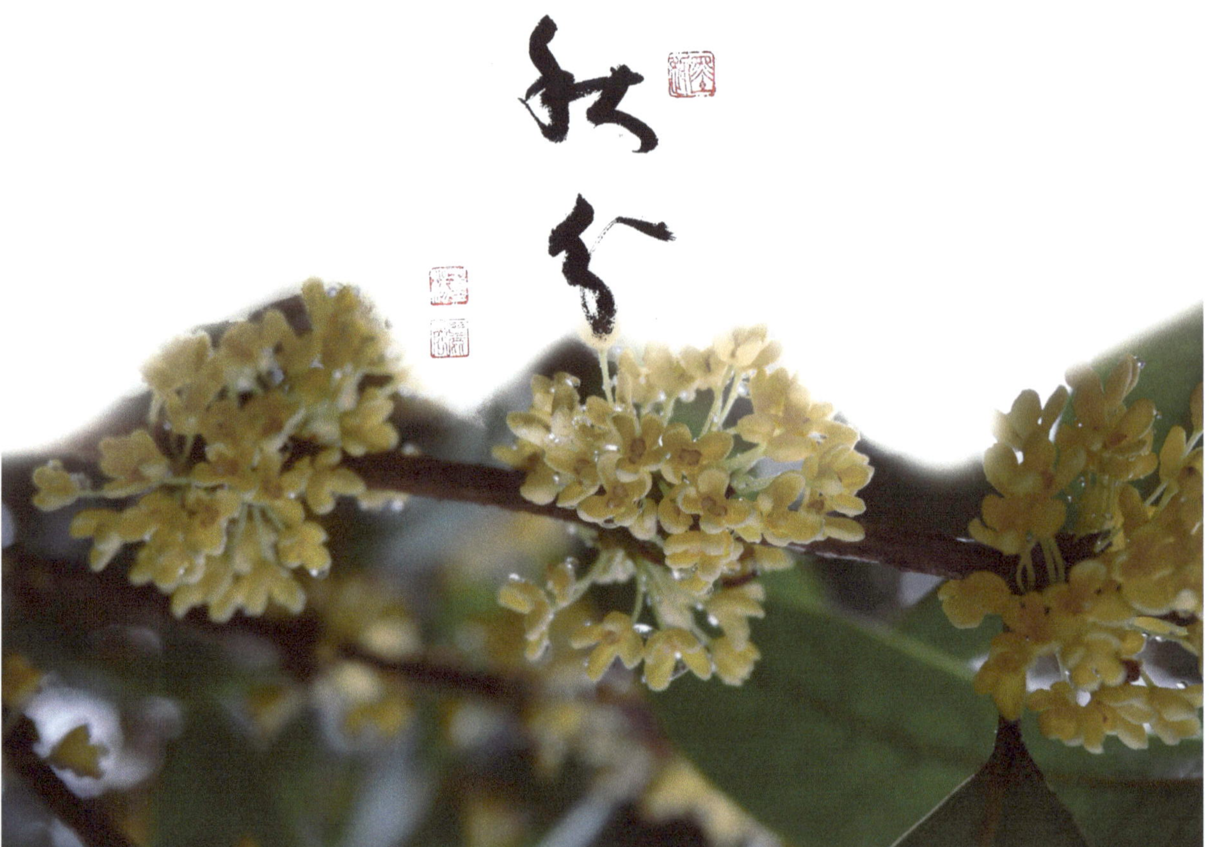

詩意節氣

It is interesting that rain doesn't come with thunder during the fall foliage season. Ancient Chinese meteorologists observed that thunder disappears after the autumnal equinox, which is when the sun reaches 180 degrees of the ecliptic drawn by ancient Chinese astronomers, or when the Earth arrives at 180 degrees of the celestial orbit redrawn by modern Chinese scientists to present the 24 solar terms. This day may be Sept 22, Sept 23, or Sept 24. The autumnal equinox is called Qiufen in Chinese, in which *qiu* means "autumn" and *fen* "divided in half."

有個有趣的現象是，在秋葉飄零時節，秋雨不再伴着雷聲。中國古代氣象學家觀察到了雷聲在秋分之後就消失了。秋分是太陽到達黃經一百八十度的日子，亦即現代科學家按照地球繞太陽軌道所重畫的橢圓形二十四節氣圖表上，地球運轉到一百八十度之時。這一天可能是陽曆九月二十二日、二十三日，或二十四日。

The East and the West share the same autumnal equinox. However, there is a 15-or-16-day solar term that starts with the autumnal equinox and is also called Qiufen in Chinese. Like the other 23 solar terms, this one can be divided into three parts. Each part is five or six days long.

秋分

東方與西方制定的秋分日期相同。然而秋分日之後，在中國還有一個同名的節氣。如同另外二十三個節氣，秋分節氣可分為三候。每一候五或六天。

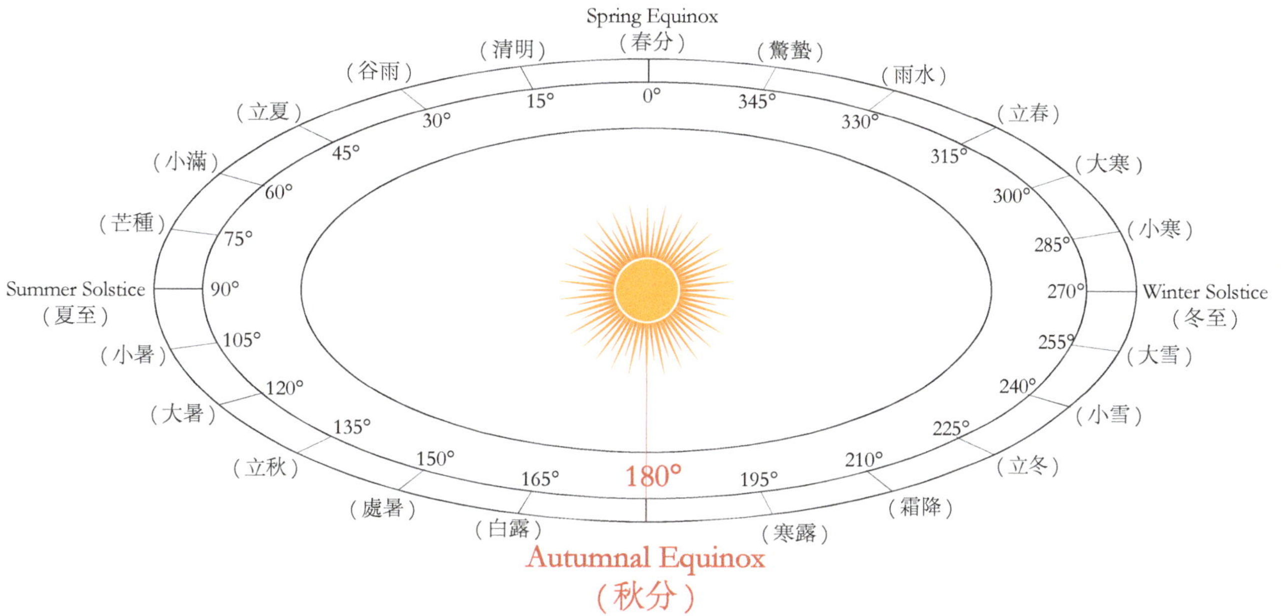

The first part of the solar term following the autumnal equinox is when thunder vanishes on rainy days, as stated earlier. The second part is when insects start to hide at home. The third part is when freshwater bodies are gradually drying up.

秋分一候雷始收聲，二候蟄蟲坯戶，三候水始涸。

The solar term following the autumnal equinox is when to enjoy fresh pomegranates and pomelos. The pomelo is the largest citrus fruit and the principal ancestor of the grapefruit. It tastes more refreshing than grapefruit, without the slight bitterness. It is extremely high in vitamin C. It also contains several other vitamins and minerals.

秋分是享用新鮮石榴和柚子的時節。柚子是最大的柑橘類水果，也是葡萄柚的祖先，比葡萄柚爽口，並富含維生素 C，也含有別的維生素與礦物質。

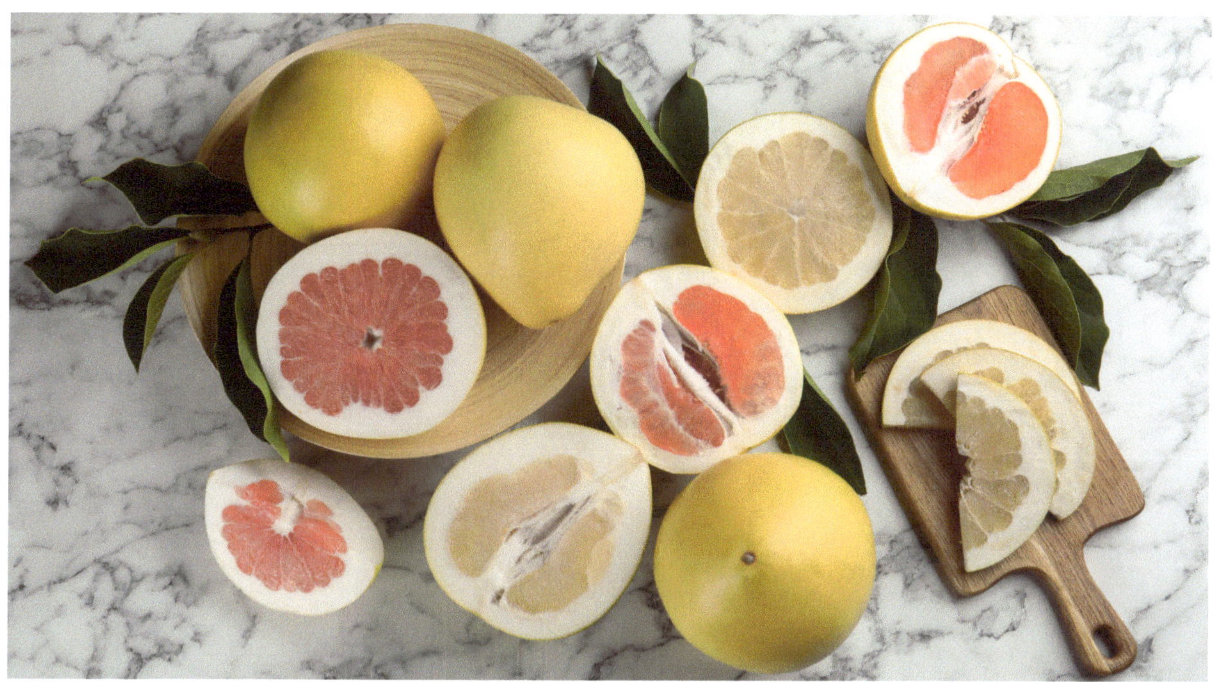

While fresh pomelos are in season, osmanthus flowers reach peak bloom. Osmanthus flowers are not as commonly seen in the West as they are in the East. They sweeten the autumn air in East Asia.
柚子上市時也是桂花巔峰期。桂花在西方比較少見，但在東亞的秋天飄香。

The Chinese take advantage of fragrant osmanthus flowers as a flavoring ingredient while cooking. For instance, osmanthus flower sauce is in a duck dish called *guihua ya*, which means "osmanthus flower flavored duck."
桂花是中國食物常用的香料。有一道名菜叫做桂花鴨。

Osmanthus flower sauce is often added to moon cake fillings as well. As mentioned in Chapter 15, the Moon Festival marks the full moon closest to the autumnal equinox. The Asian holiday comes either before or after the autumnal equinox. It may sometimes fall in this post-autumnal-equinox solar term.
桂花也常用於月餅餡料。如同本書第十五章所述，中秋節是最靠近秋分的滿月當天。那就總在秋分前後，有時候在秋分節氣。

Aside from moon cakes, there are other desserts that frequently get flavored by osmanthus flowers, including sweetened lotus roots stuffed with glutinous rice, sprinkled with osmanthus flowers, available at Shanghai-style restaurants not only in China but also in America.
除了月餅以外，別的甜點也經常含有桂花。例如桂花糯米糖藕，在美國的上海餐館也有。

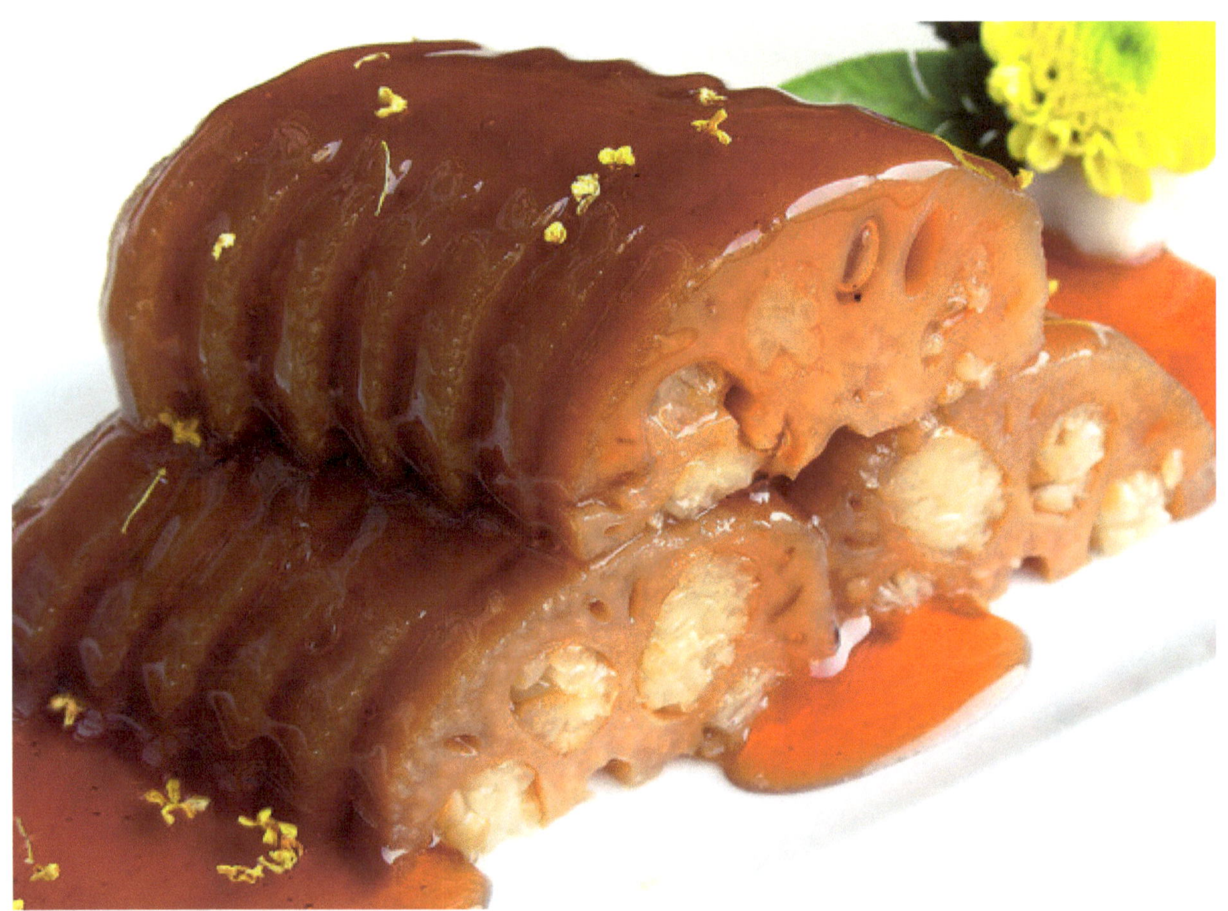

Another example was allegedly former US president Bill Clinton's favorite when he and his wife visited Shanghai. Named *guihua gao* in Chinese, it is rice cakes sprinkled with osmanthus flowers.
另外還有一道上海點心名叫桂花糕，據說是美國前總統柯林頓訪問上海期間最愛吃的甜品。

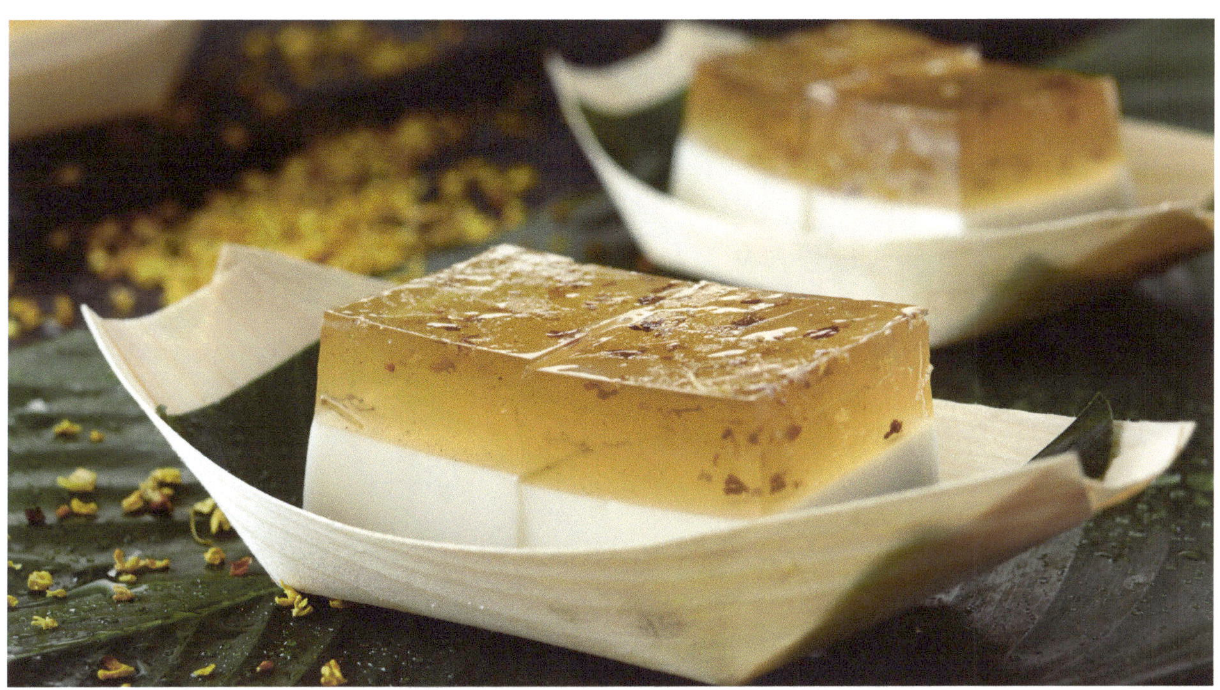

Evidently, osmanthus flowers have universal appeal. They are timeless, too. Countless Chinese poets have written about them.
顯然，桂花具有國際性的魅力。桂花也超越時代。歷代無數中國詩人描寫過桂花。

At the end of this chapter is a classical Chinese poem that metaphorically mysterizes the spellbinding scent of osmanthus flowers.
下一頁的桂花絕句尤其特別出色，以暗喻的筆法為桂香的魔力憑添神秘感。

詠桂 In Praise of Osmanthus

Author: Yang, Wanli 楊萬里 (1127-1206)
Translator: Crystal Tai

不是人間種　Osmanthus did not originate from the earthly world,
移從月裡來　But from the moon as a transplant.
廣寒香一點　With a sweet swish of the magic wand from the moon palace,
吹得滿山開　The moon goddess makes hillside trees burst into bloom, all fragrant.

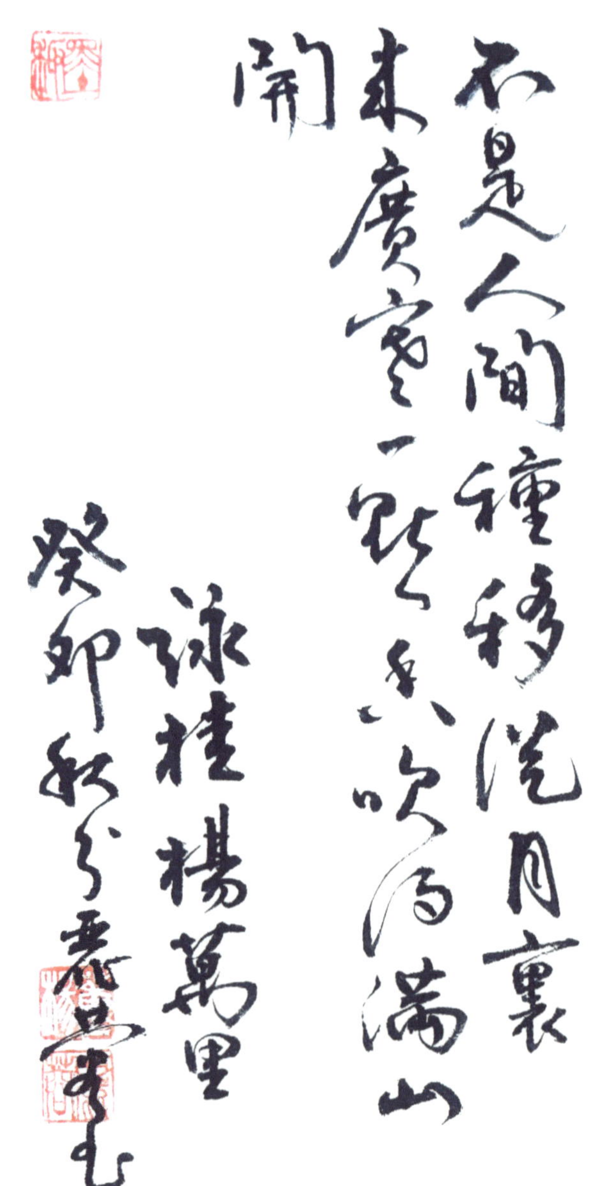

Chapter 17
Cold Dew

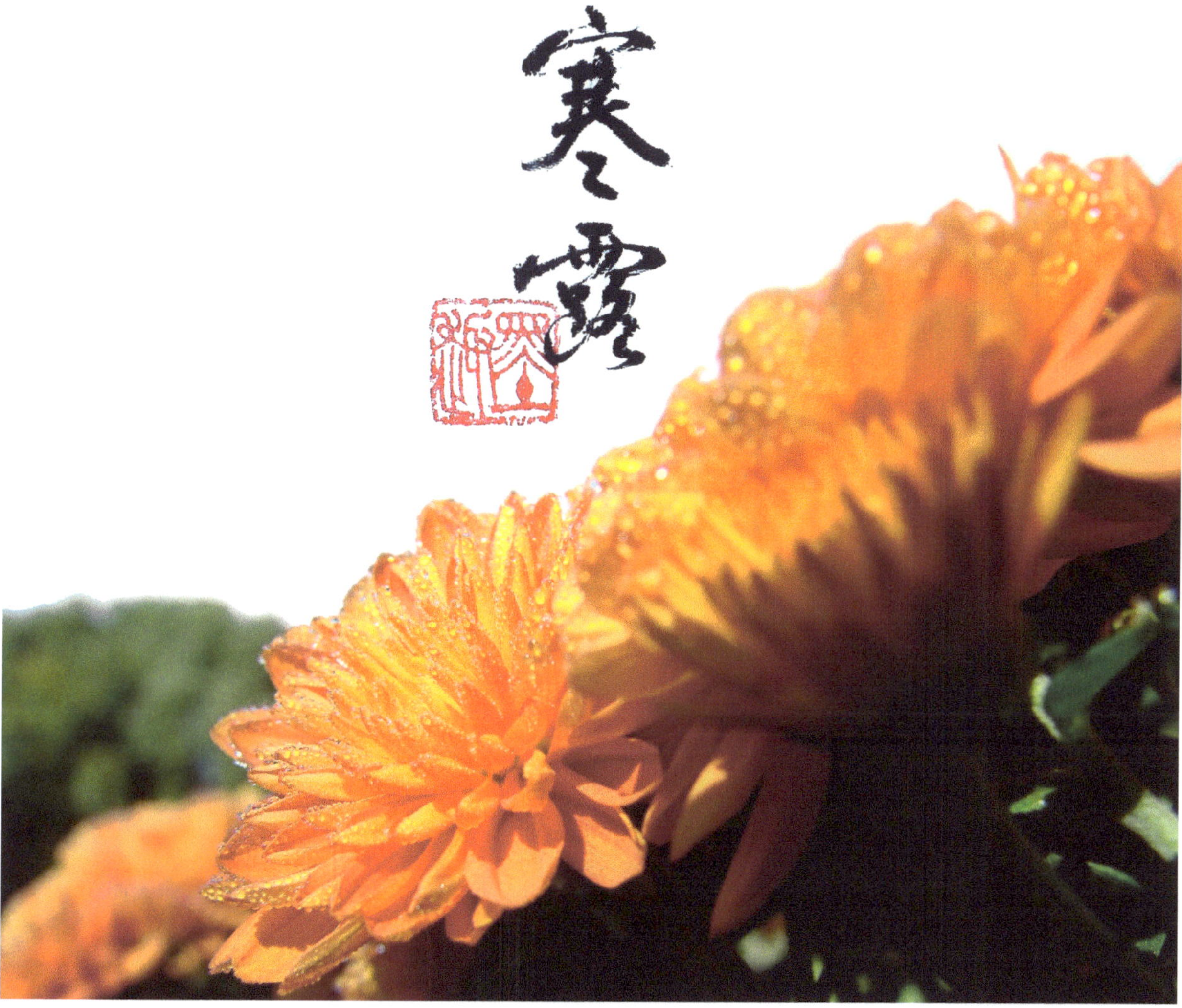

In the temperate zone of the Northern Hemisphere, dewy grass begins to feel a little cold to those taking a walk in the morning in October. That explains why a 15-or-16-day solar term in October is called Hanlu in Chinese, which means "cold dew."

在北半球溫帶，凝露的草地在陽曆十月開始讓散步之人感到寒意。因此，陽曆十月有個十五或十六天的節氣稱為寒露。

This 15-or-16-day period starts when the sun reaches 195 degrees of the ecliptic drawn by ancient Chinese astronomers, or when the Earth arrives at 195 degrees of the celestial orbit redrawn by modern Chinese scientists to present the 24 solar terms. It may be Oct 7, Oct 8, or Oct 9.

寒露節氣始於太陽到達黃經一百九十五度的日子，亦即現代科學家按照地球繞太陽軌道所重畫的橢圓形二十四節氣圖表上，地球運轉到一百九十五度之時。這可能是陽曆十月七日、十月八日，或十月九日。

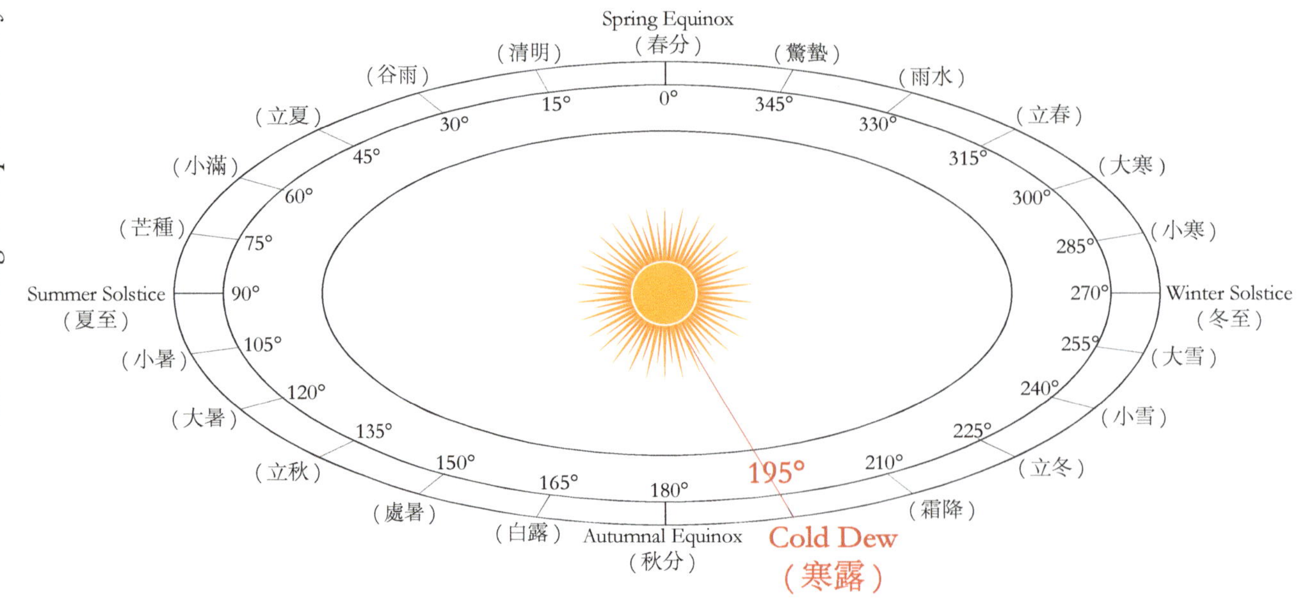

Like the other 23 solar terms, this one can be divided into three parts. Each part is five or six days long. The first part of the solar term named Cold Dew is when wild swans and wild geese arrive one after another like guests. The second part is when small birds disappear and clams appear. The third part is when yellow chrysanthemums come into bloom.

如同另外二十三個節氣，寒露節氣可分為三候，每一候五或六天。寒露一候鴻雁來賓；二候雀入大水為蛤；三候菊有黃華。

Equally notable is a traditional holiday that is almost always observed within this solar term. The holiday is called Chongyang, which means "double *yang*" in Chinese. As explained in Chapters 3, 4, and 10, *yang* represents the active forces of the universe in Chinese culture. Ancient Chinese considered number nine a strong digit that could exemplify *yang*, so they made the holiday on the ninth of the ninth lunar month the Double Yang Festival, which usually falls in early or mid October.

同樣值得注意的是，重陽節幾乎都在寒露時節。重陽的意思是雙重之陽。正如本書第三、四、十等章節所述，陽是宇宙間主動的力量。中國古人認為九是一個很強的數字，可代表陽，就將陰曆九月初九定名為重陽節。重陽節通常在陽曆十月上旬或中旬。

Interestingly, the Double Yang Festival is a day dedicated to hiking. According to folklore, there was a man named Huanjing, and he had a teacher who could see the future. One day his teacher told him, "A disaster will happen to you and your family. Your whole family can only avoid it by going to a high place on the ninth of the ninth lunar month." Huanjing followed the advice, and his whole family did survive the crisis. Decades later, he became a centenarian. That explains why the Double Yang Festival is also known as Senior Citizen's Day.

有趣的是，重陽節是登山的日子。依據傳說，曾有一個名叫桓景的男子師從一位能夠未卜先知的智者。某一天他的老師告訴他：" 大難將至。你跟你的家人必須在九月初九到高處去，才可能避禍。" 結果，桓景遵從老師指示，他一家人就確實免禍了。數十年後，桓景成為人瑞。因此，重陽節又名敬老節。

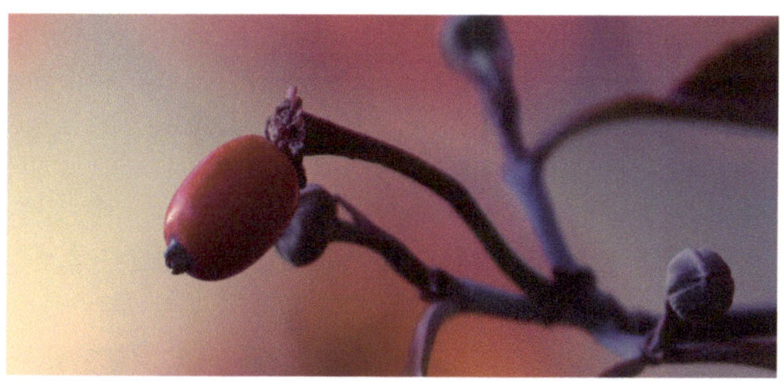

On this day, Chinese people used to wear dogwood headpieces or corsages while hiking. This custom is fading, but some Chinese people still use dogwood as an insect repellent.
中國古人總在重陽節佩戴茱萸。此一習俗已式微，但現代有些華人還用茱萸來驅蟲。

Another tradition of the Double Yang Festival is to eat a special type of rice cake, which is often filled with nuts and dried fruit. Since the Chinese word for cake, *gao*, sounds exactly the same as the Chinese word for height, Double Yang rice cakes symbolize height. No wonder a Double Yang cake sometimes comes with a little flag standing on top. The flag is a symbol of height as well.

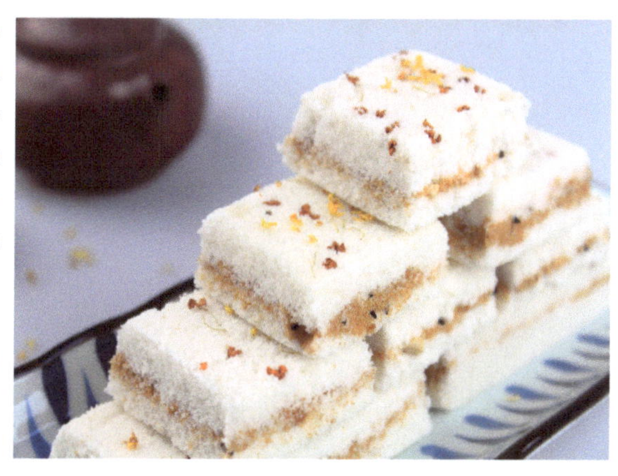

另一個重陽節傳統是吃重陽糕。由於“糕”和“高”同音，重陽糕象徵高升。難怪重陽糕上面有時候插着小旗子，那也代表着高度。

While having Double Yang cakes for a picnic, the Chinese call the Double Yang festival the day to say good-bye to greenery, because this is the last solar term of the year to still see some green leaves on deciduous trees. In the temperate zone of the Northern Hemisphere, deciduous trees will completely change colors during the next solar term. However, chrysanthemum flowers will stay in bloom through the next solar term and perhaps even the following one.
重陽節不僅是能帶重陽糕去野餐的一天，也是辭青的日子，因為寒露是一年之內落葉喬木還有綠葉的最後一個節氣。在北半球溫帶，落葉喬木的樹葉皆會在下個節氣變色。然而，菊花到下個節氣還會照樣綻放，甚至到再下一個節氣或許還能開花。

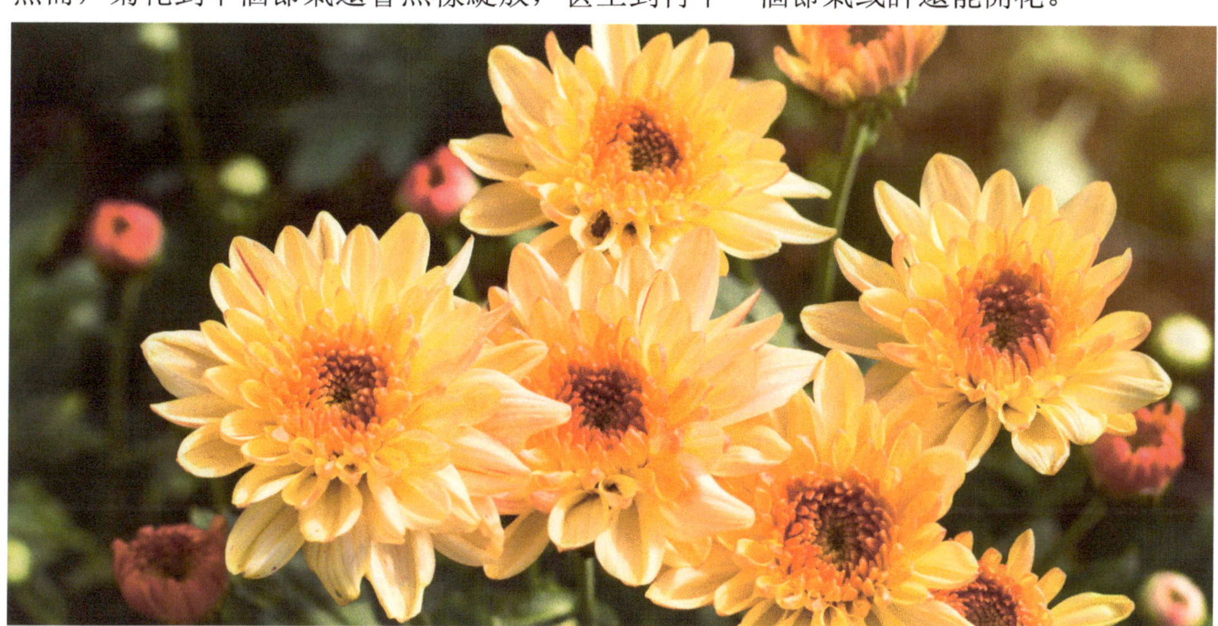

Speaking of chrysanthemums, there was a Chinese tradition to host a chrysanthemum viewing party during this solar term at a garden where people would drink chrysanthemum wine and eat crab. One of the classic Chinese novels, *Dream of the Red Chamber*, includes an episode about a chrysanthemum viewing party, where everyone writes a poem on the spot.

談到菊花，中國古人會在寒露時節舉行賞菊會，讓與會人士在花園一邊喝菊花酒，一邊吃螃蟹。中國名著小說《紅樓夢》有一段描述賞菊會，其中每人都要當場做一首詠菊詩。

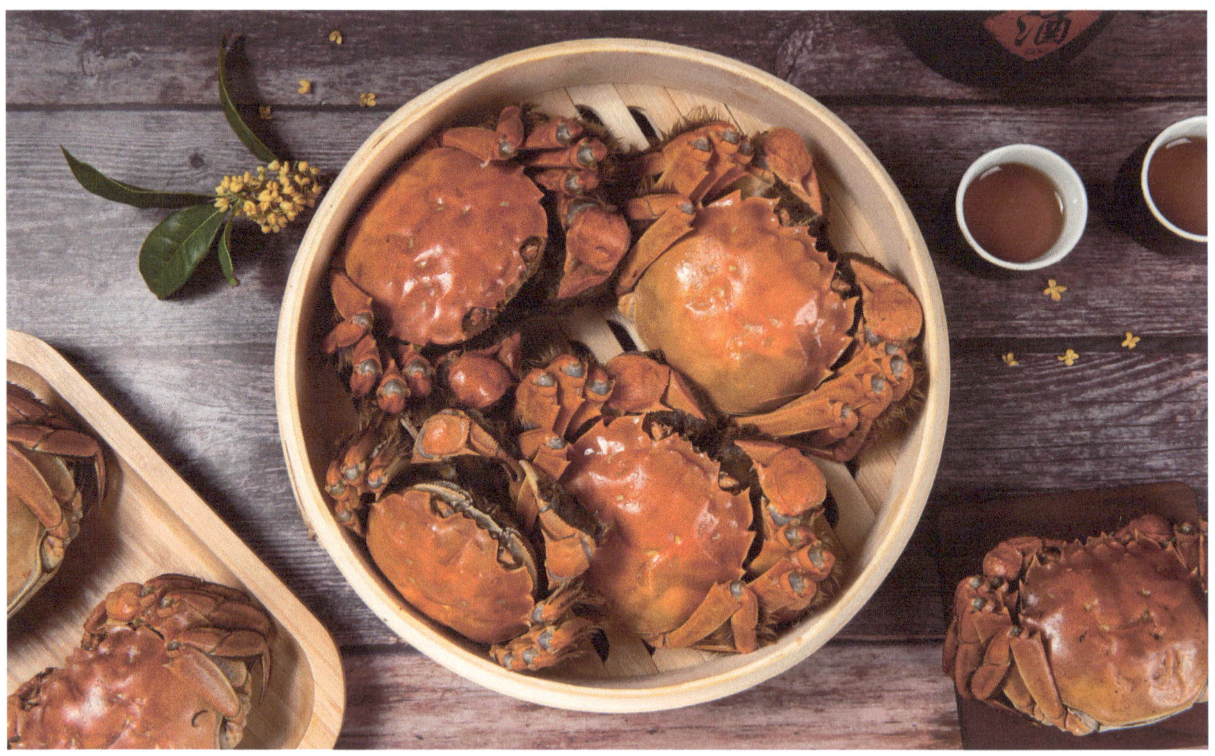

At the end of this chapter is the most brilliant poem from that chrysanthemum viewing party.

下一頁就在展示出於《紅樓夢》賞菊會的最佳詠菊詩。

詠菊詩 In Praise of Chrysanthemums

Author: Cao, Xueqin 曹雪芹 (1715-1763)
Translator: Crystal Tai

無奈詩魔昏曉侵
The Muse of lyric poetry keeps haunting me night and day,
繞籬倚石自沉音
Making me murmur while walking around the fence or leaning against a rock on my way.
毫端蘊秀臨霜寫
My writing brush depicts the beauty of chrysanthemums as I scribble by the frost-covered wooden window;
口角噙香對月吟
My open lips catch the fragrance of chrysanthemums when I chant to the moon-lit Milky Way:
滿紙自憐題素怨
A full page of self pity to express my regrets from the distant past;
片言誰解訴秋心
A brief phrase for which person to understand my feelings about this autumn day?
一從陶令評章後
Since Mayor Tao commented on chrysanthemums,
千古高風說到今
Their high resilience has always been admired and still is today.

Note: "Mayor Tao" in this poem refers to Tao Yuan-Ming (365-427). Please note that the Chinese name order puts the surname first. Tao once worked as a county magistrate (similar to today's mayor) before he resigned. Then he lived a hermit's life and became a distinguished writer for writing about hermithood.

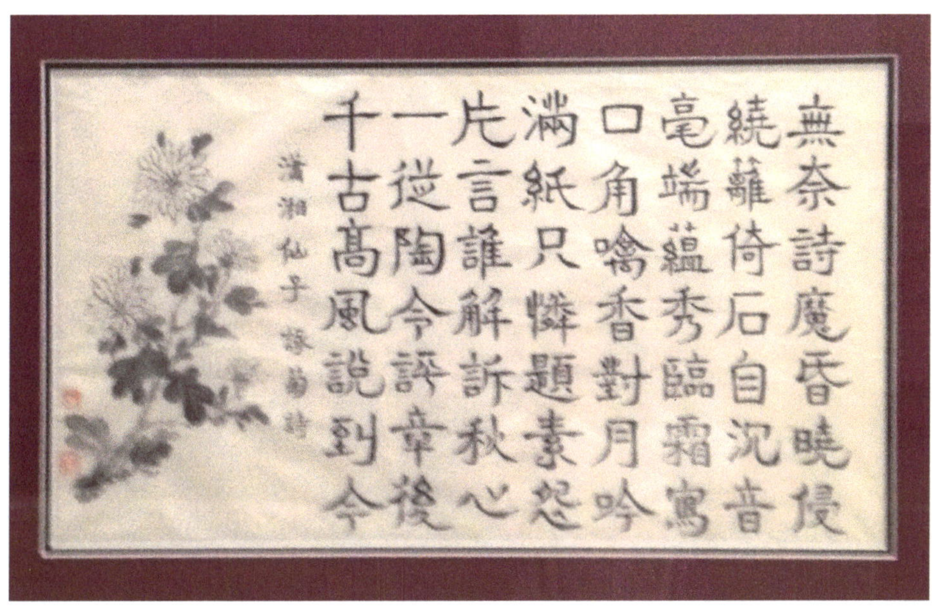

Chapter 18
Appearance of Frost

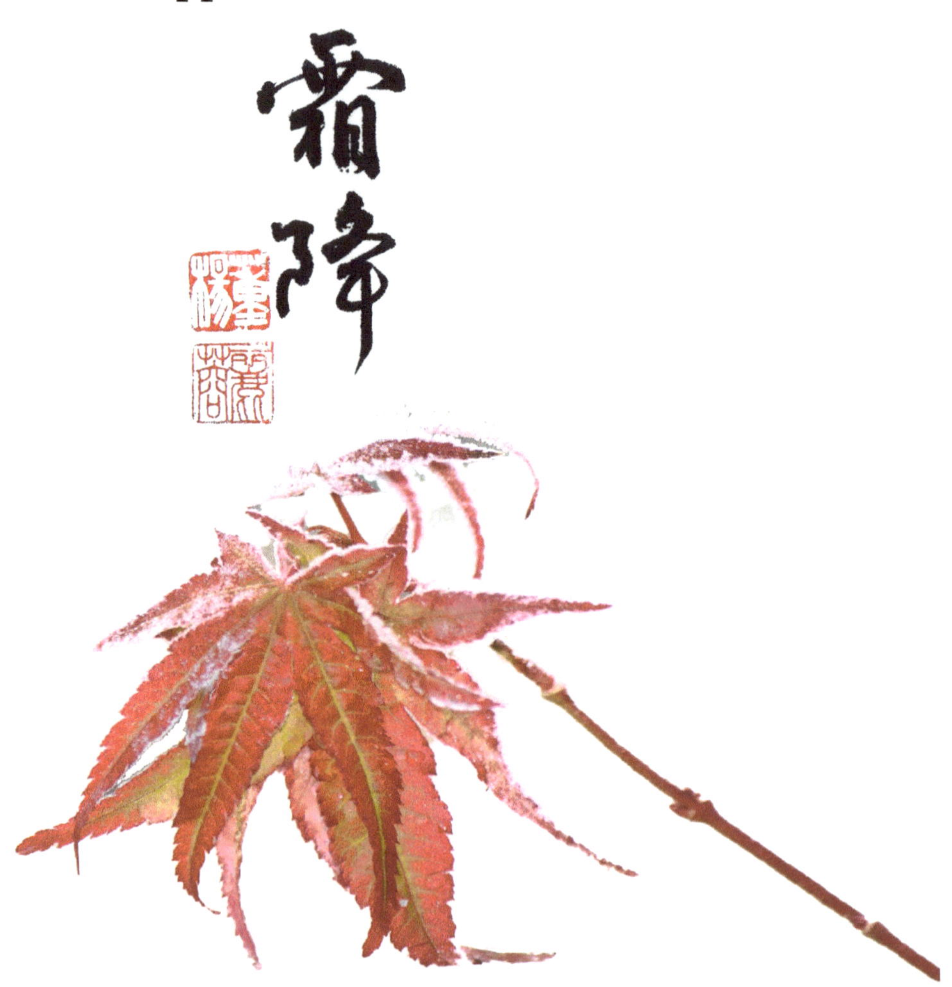

Late October is when fall foliage normally peaks in the temperate zone of the Northern Hemisphere, where frost appears around the same time. That explains why the Chinese call the 15-or-16-day solar term starting in late October "Shuangjiang", which means "the appearance of frost."

陽曆十月下旬在北半球溫帶是秋葉巔峰期，同時也開始降霜了。因此，十月下旬起始的節氣名叫霜降。

This 15-or-16-day solar term starts when the sun reaches 210 degrees of the ecliptic drawn by ancient Chinese astronomers, or when the Earth arrives at 210 degrees of the celestial orbit redrawn by modern Chinese scientists to present the 24 solar terms. This day may be Oct 22, Oct 23, or Oct 24.

寒露節氣始於太陽到達黃經二百一十度的日子，亦即現代科學家按照地球繞太陽軌道所重畫的橢圓形二十四節氣圖表上，地球運轉到二百一十度之時。這一天可能是陽曆十月二十二日、二十三日，或二十四日。

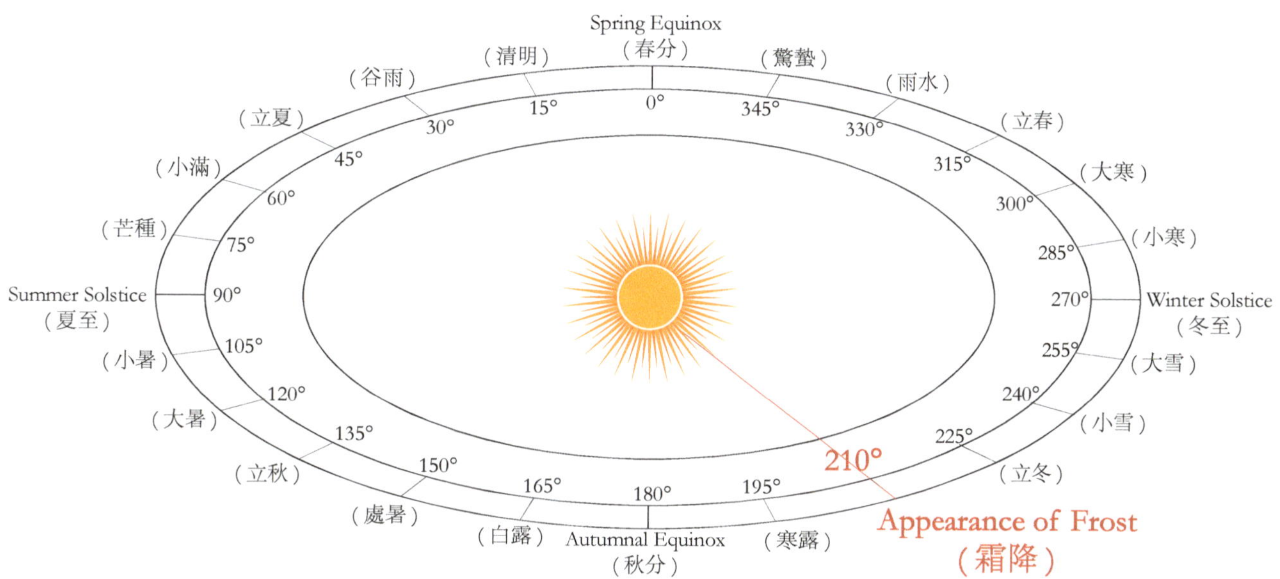

Like the other 23 solar terms, this one can be divided into three parts. Each part is five or six days long. The first part of the solar term coming with frost is when jackals go hunting most aggressively. The second part is when grasses all turn yellow and deciduous trees shed leaves. The third part is when cold-blooded creatures, including insects, begin to hibernate.

如同另外二十三個節氣，霜降節氣可分為三候。每一候五或六天。霜降一候豺乃祭獸；二候草木黃落；三候蜇蟲咸俯。

During this solar term, temperatures tend to drop rapidly, making it necessary to boost the immune system. There is a Chinese tradition to eat fresh persimmons as an immunity booster during the solar term coming with frost. Persimmons are rich in vitamins, minerals, and fiber. They happen to be in season during this time of year, and they always become sweeter after a frost.

在霜降時節，氣溫降低得很快，需要增強免疫系統，而在霜降時節吃新鮮柿子就有提高免疫力的功效。柿子富含維生素、礦物質，以及纖維。恰好柿子是霜降時節的當令水果，並且經過霜打之後更甜。

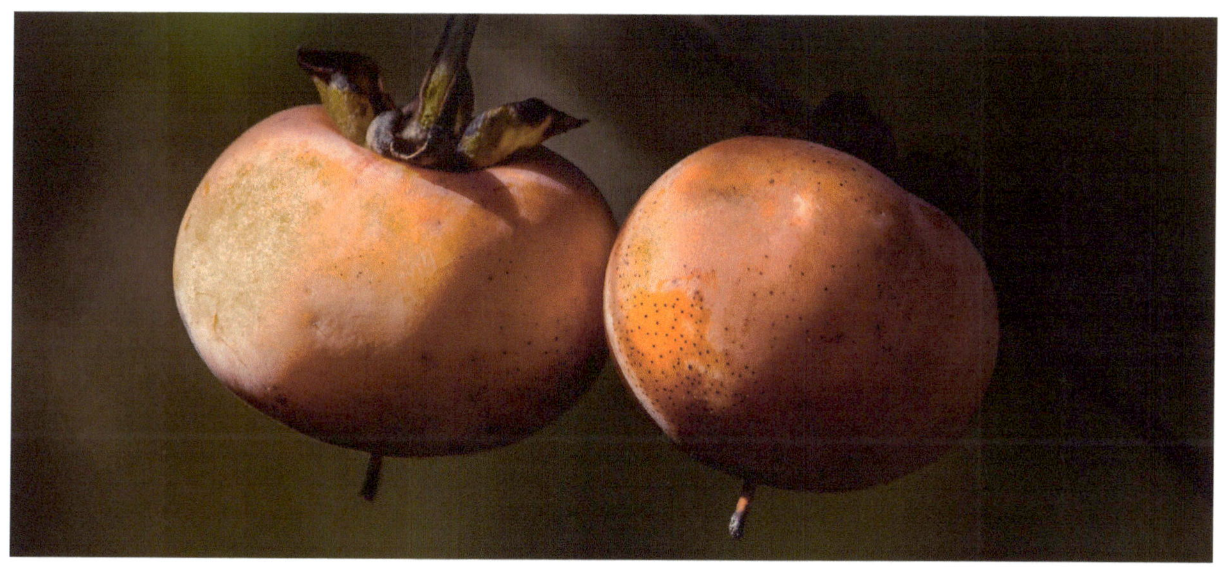

Other seasonal sources of vitamins and minerals include chestnuts and pumpkins. Many street vendors in China sell sugared chestnuts as a snack in the fall. Chestnuts can also be incorporated into savory dishes, among which the most famous is slow cooked chicken with chestnuts. Vegans can use dried tofu to create a similar dish. Slow cooking will enable chestnuts to absorb the sauce, and then they will taste like heaven!

此外，栗子和南瓜也是當季的維生素和礦物質來源。秋天有很多小販出售糖炒栗子。栗子也適合入菜。最有名的是栗子燒雞肉。素食者可以改用栗子燒豆乾。慢燉能讓栗子吸收醬汁而入味，簡直好比天堂美食！

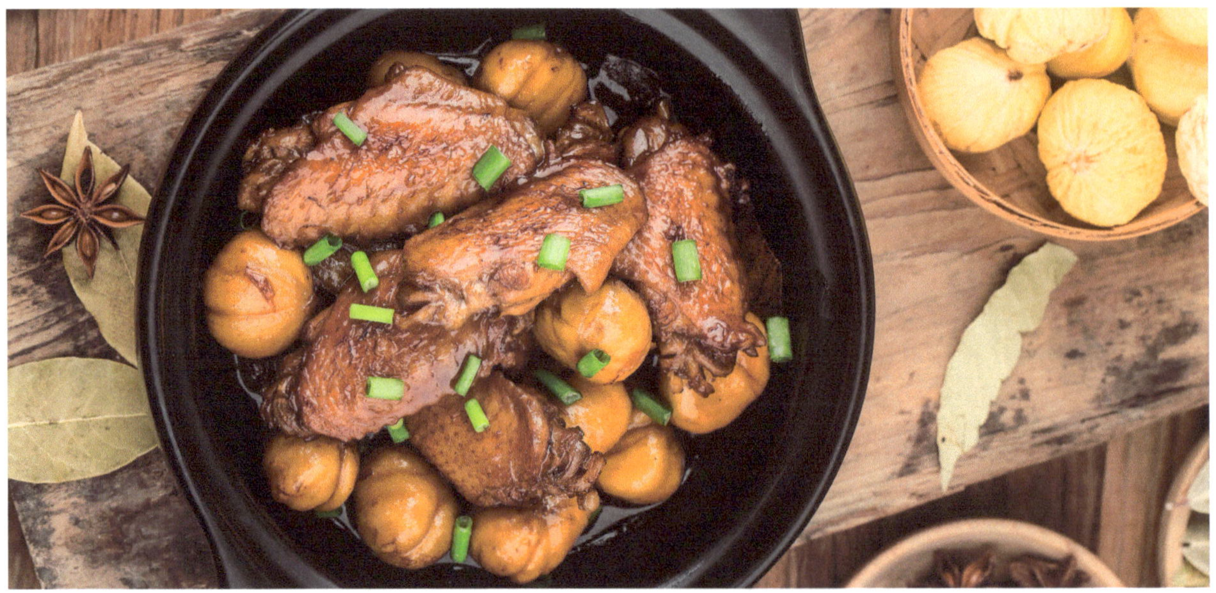

Likewise, steaming can make pumpkin absolutely yummy. Chinese people often steam breaded pork ribs or diced chicken in a gutted pumpkin. Vegans can put tofu instead of meat in the gutted pumpkin.

另外，蒸熟的南瓜也很可口。挖空的南瓜常讓人用來做南瓜粉蒸排骨，南瓜粉蒸雞肉，或素食的南瓜豆腐盅。

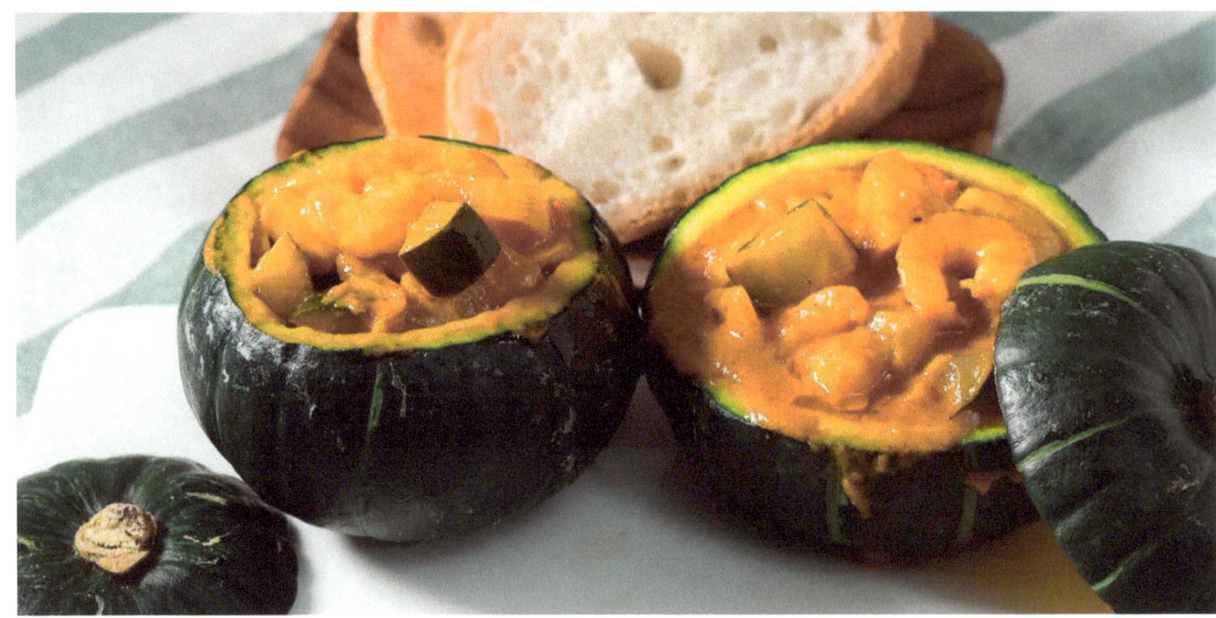

After your immunity boosting meal, how about a small persimmon cake for dessert? Osmanthus flower sauce can be added to persimmon cakes to make them smell as sweet as they taste.
吃完了有助於免疫力的一餐，來一個柿子糕當甜點如何？柿子糕配上桂花醬，更是又甜又香。

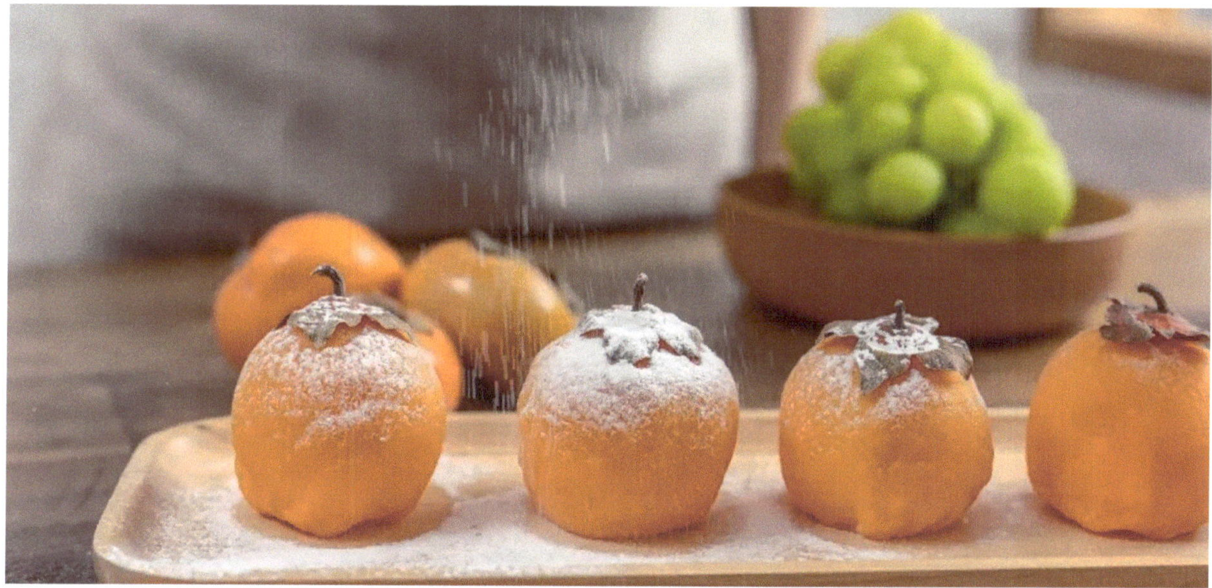

While there is still plenty of osmanthus flower sauce, osmanthus flowers are nearly all gone during the solar term from late October to early November. Given ubiquitous frost in the temperate zone of the Northern Hemisphere during this solar term, it is when every creature quiets down.
雖然霜降時節照樣有很多桂花醬，桂花可在這段時期大多凋謝了。這是北半球溫帶到處降霜之時，所有生物都逐漸靜下來。

At the end of this chapter is a classical Chinese poem widely popular for skillfully capturing this time of year's serene essence.
下一頁的絕句廣為流傳，正由於巧妙捕捉了霜降時節的寧靜本質。

楓橋夜泊 Stopping by the Maple Bridge

Author：Zhang, Ji 張繼 (unknown birth year - 779)
Translator：Crystal Tai

月落烏啼霜滿天 The moon sets while a raven's call pierces the frosty skyline;
江楓漁火對愁眠 Riverside maple trees and fishermen's lamps accompany me as I repine.
姑蘇城外寒山寺 The Cold Mountain Temple stands outside of Suzhou City.
夜半鐘聲到客船 A midnight bell sends sound waves to the passenger boat of mine.

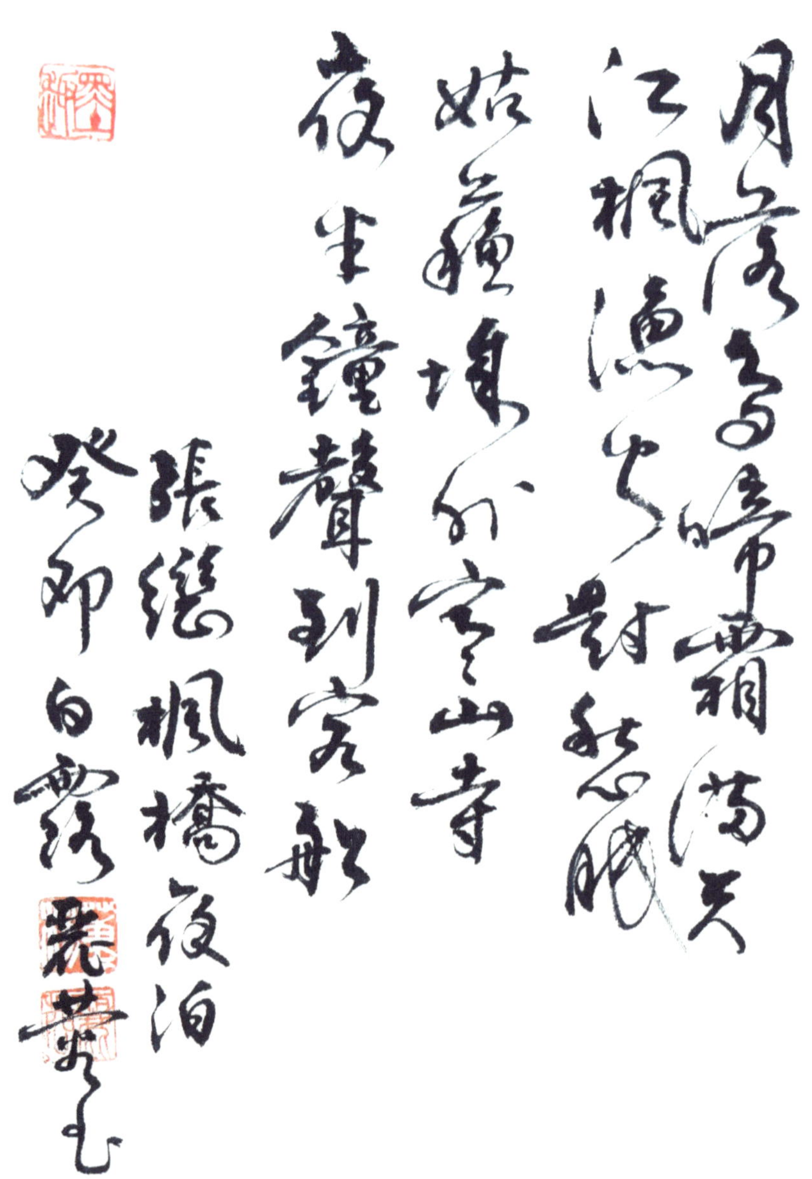

Chapter 19
First Signs of Winter

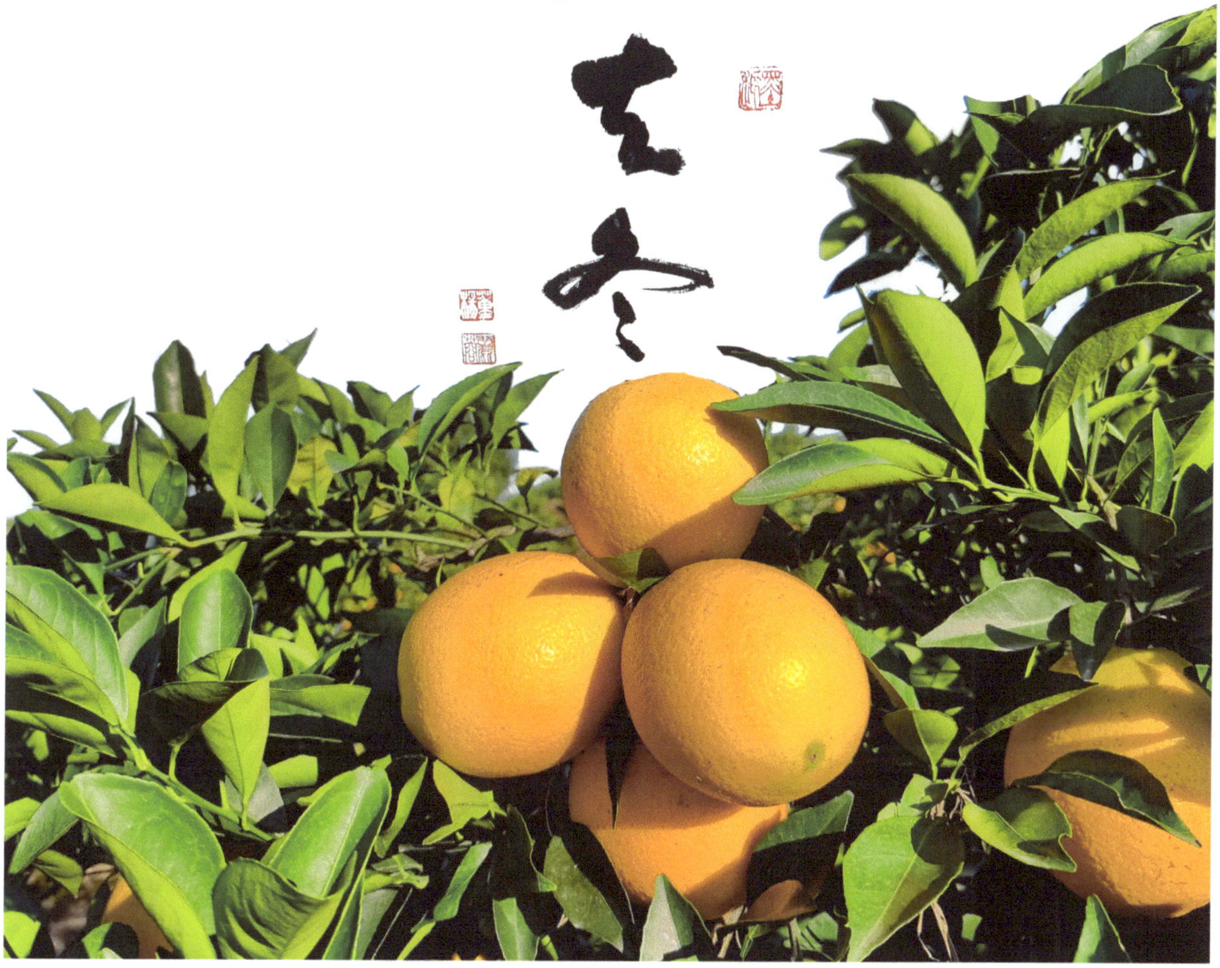

November is the perfect month to bake an orange pound cake for afternoon tea in the Northern Hemisphere. During this time of year, oranges are ready for harvest, and cooling temperatures make people crave cake fresh out of the oven. November is also when ice starts forming in the temperate zone of the Northern Hemisphere. That explains why a Chinese solar term in November is called Lidong, which indicates "the first signs of winter."

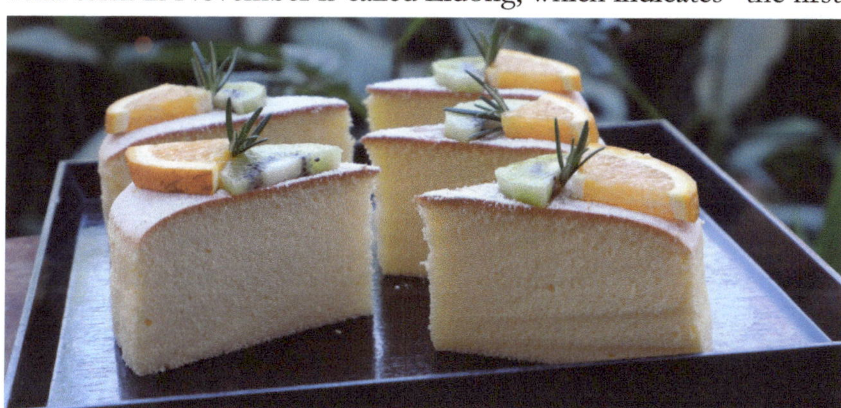

陽曆十一月在北半球是最適合烤香橙磅蛋糕來配下午茶的月份。每年此時，柳橙正值採收期，天氣又涼到讓人想吃剛出爐的蛋糕。陽曆十一月也是北半球溫帶的淡水開始結冰之時。因此，陽曆十一月有個節氣稱為立冬。

This is the first solar term of winter. It begins when the sun reaches 225 degrees of the ecliptic drawn by ancient Chinese astronomers, or when the Earth arrives at 225 degrees of the celestial orbit redrawn by modern Chinese scientists to present the 24 solar terms. It may be Nov 6, Nov 7, or Nov 8.

立冬節氣始於太陽到達黃經二百二十五度的日子，亦即現代科學家按照地球繞太陽軌道所重畫的橢圓形二十四節氣圖表上，地球運轉到二百二十五度之時。這可能是陽曆十一月六日、十一月七日，或十一月八日。

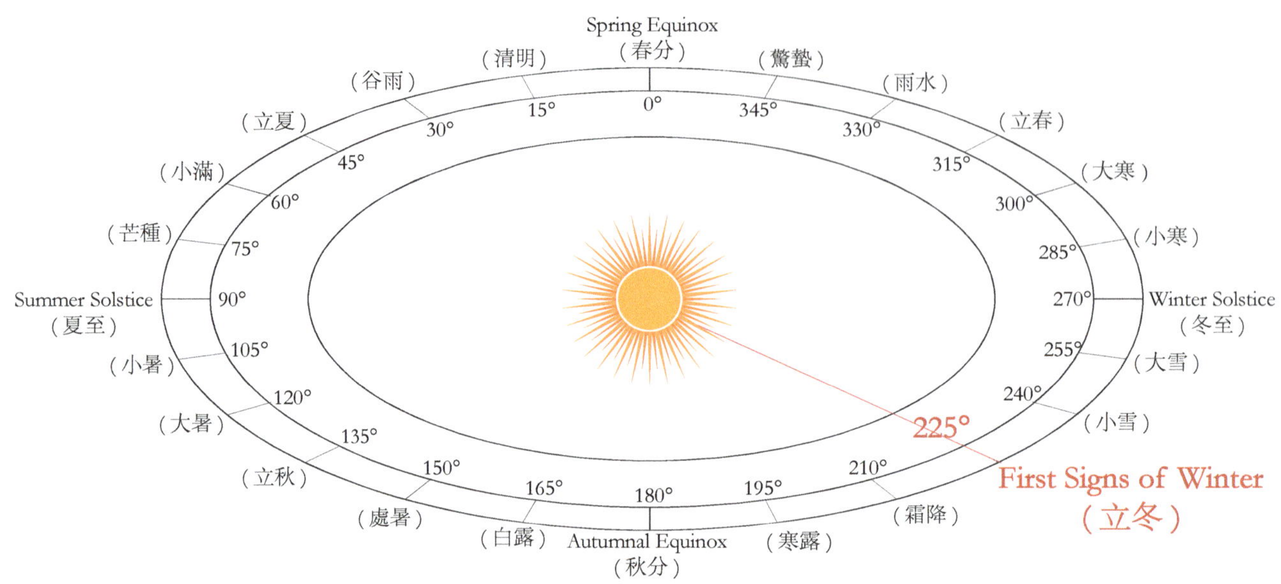

Like the other 23 solar terms, this one can be divided into three parts. Each part is five or six days long. The first part of the solar term with the first signs of winter is when ice starts forming on the surfaces of freshwater bodies. The second part is when the ground begins to freeze. The third part is when big birds disappear and large clams appear.

如同另外二十三個節氣，立冬節氣可分為三候，每一候五或六天。立冬一候水始冰，二候地始凍，三候雉入大水為蜃。

When the solar term with the first signs of winter begins, people in northern China often cook dumplings, which can warm up the body when the weather gets colder. In central and southern China, people prefer hot pot, which is similar to fondue but without cheese. Many Chinese restaurants in big cities of the United States also serve hot pot.

立冬來臨時，北方人常煮餃子，因為吃餃子能暖身。在華中和華南則流行立冬吃火鍋。中國火鍋很像瑞士火鍋，只是不含奶酪。美國有很多中國餐館也供應火鍋。

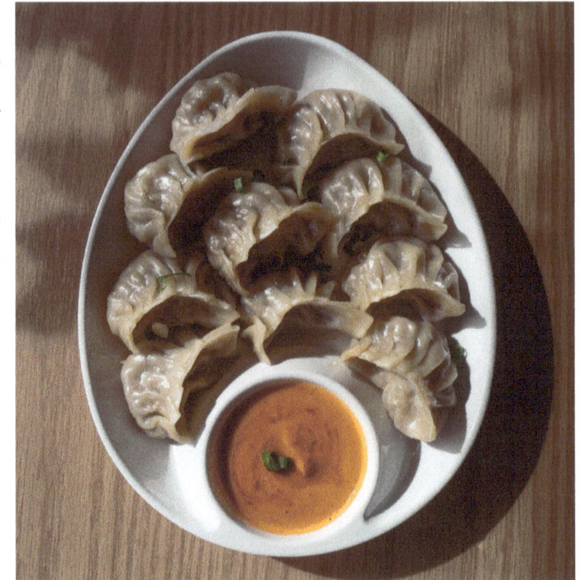

There can be a variety of ingredients in the hot pot. Certain Chinese herbs may be added to the hot pot, too. Speaking of herbal medicine, Chinese medical professionals encourage people to eat black foods when initial signs of winter appear. This is because, according to Chinese medicinal classics, the nutrients of black foods will enter the kidney meridian and nourish the kidneys[1], which work harder in cold weather.

火鍋材料花樣很多，包括某些藥材。談到草藥，中醫提倡在立冬多吃黑色食物。這是因為，依據中醫理論，黑色食物的養份入腎經，可以滋養在冬天特別辛苦的腎臟。

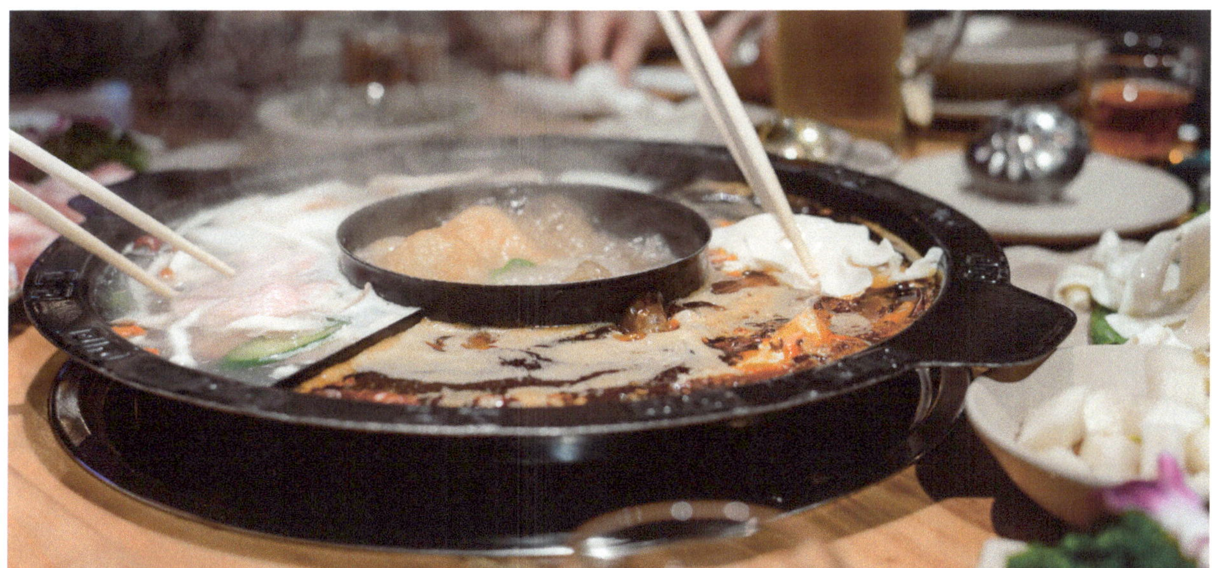

Among black foods, fermented black beans can be used as a seasoning. They are available at Chinese markets in the United States and even on Amazon. Steamed fish with fermented black beans would be yummy and healthy.

在黑色食物之中，黑豆豉可作調味料，在美國的中國超市甚至亞馬遜網站都有售。豆豉清蒸魚會是既美味又健康的佳肴。

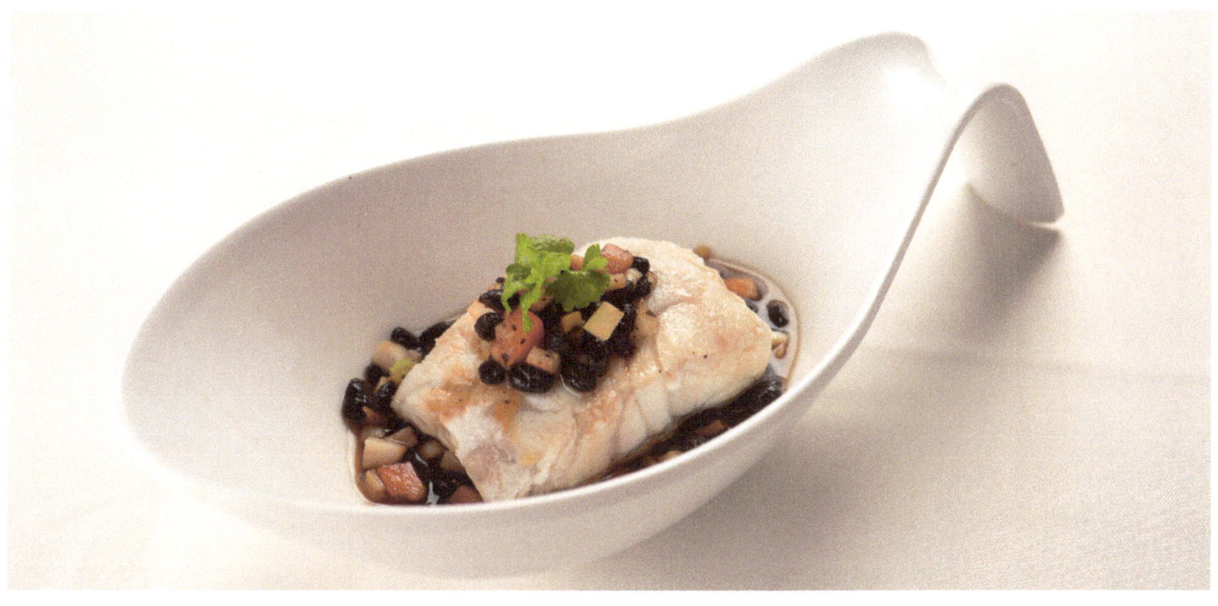

1   Nutrition News. "Eat More Black Foods in Winter for the Kidneys" (Chinese edition). Yu-An Clinic, Dec 29, 2016. http://www.styuantang.com/Home/ArticleDetail/23

For dessert, how about a creamy slice of orange souffle cheesecake? After all, this is orange harvest season!

至於餐後甜點，滑潤可口的香橙舒芙蕾起司蛋糕如何？畢竟，這是柳橙豐收時節！

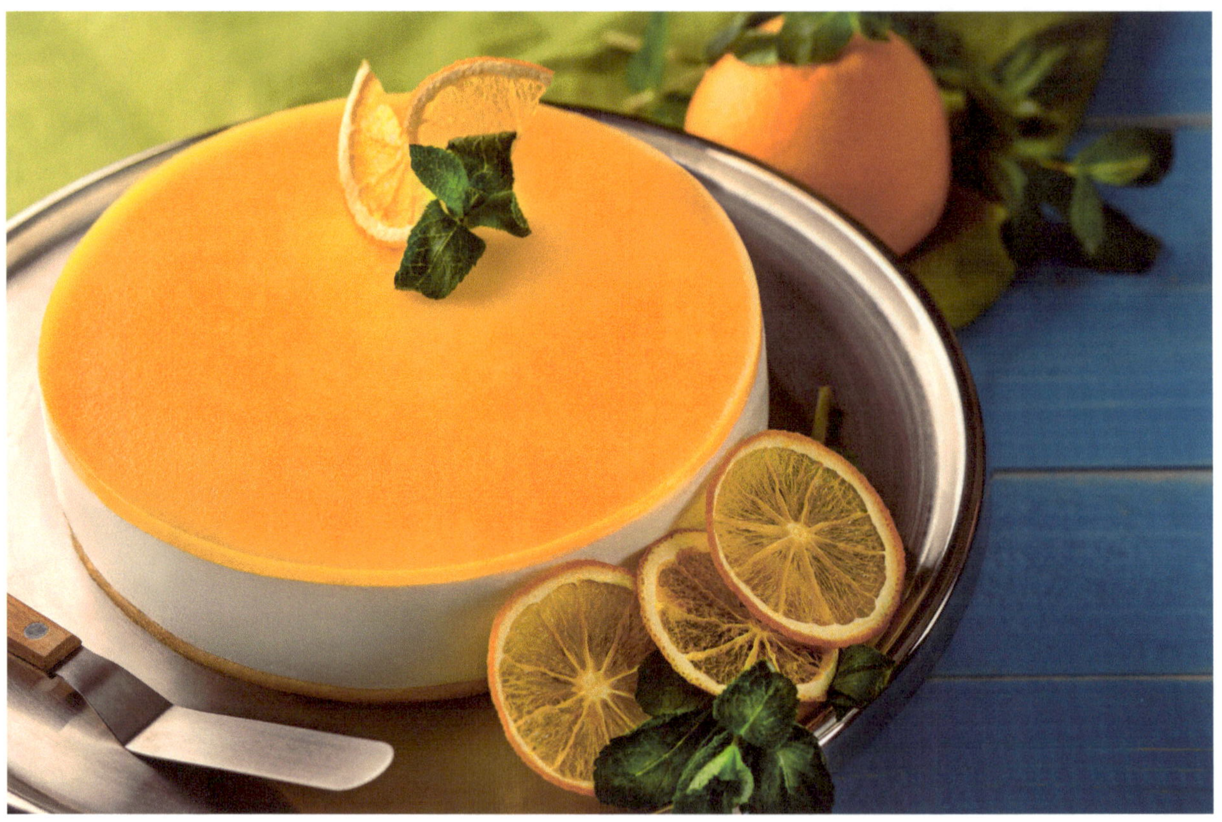

At the end of this chapter is a classical Chinese poem that refreshingly raves about orange harvest as well as other early signs of winter. The last two lines of the poem have become a famous quote.

下一頁的絕句就是以清新的筆法讚美柳橙豐收等立冬景象。此詩後兩句已成為名言。

贈劉景文 To My Friend Liu Jingwen

Author: Su, Dongpo 蘇東坡 (1037-1101)
Translator: Crystal Tai

荷葉已無擎雨蓋 Lotus has wilted, without umbrella-shaped leaves spreading out;
菊殘猶有傲霜枝 Chrysanthemums have withered, with frost-resistant branches stretching around.
一年好景君須記 The best time of year for you to keep in mind, however,
最是橙黃橘綠時 It's when yellow oranges and green tangerines abound.

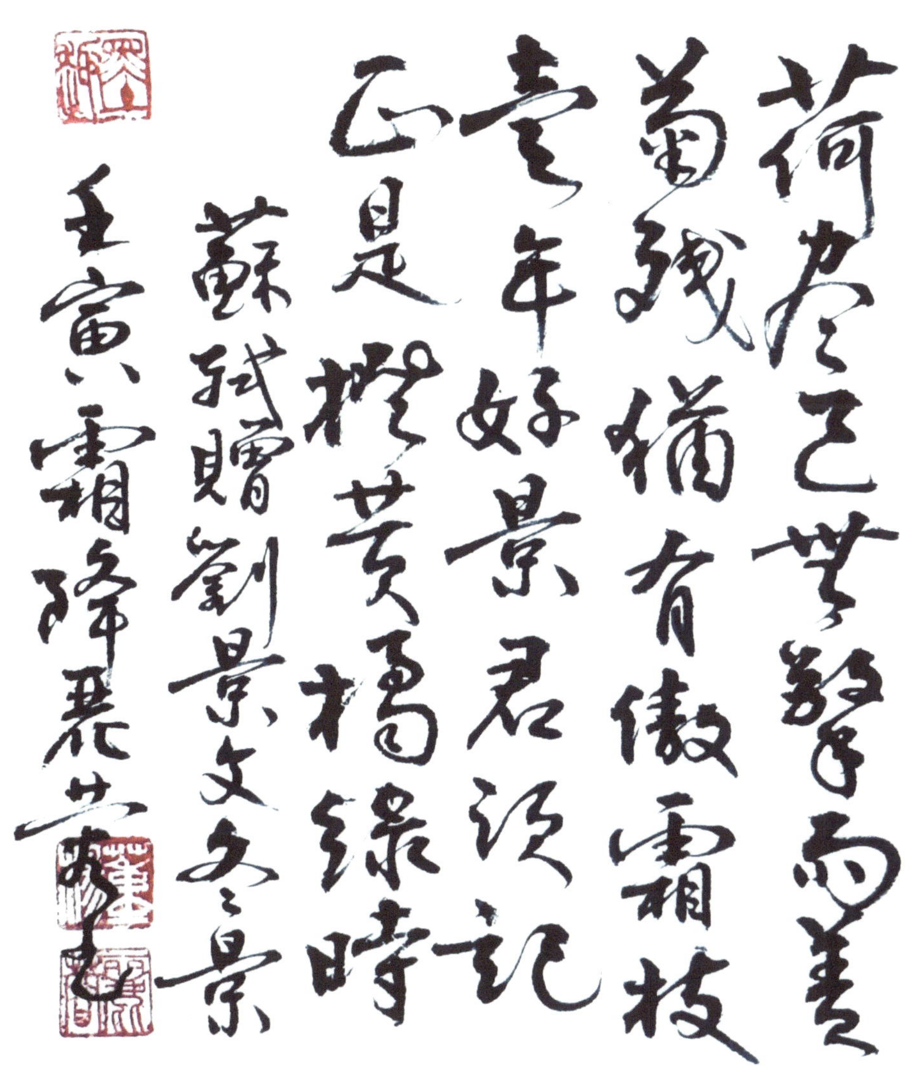

Chapter 20
Light Snow

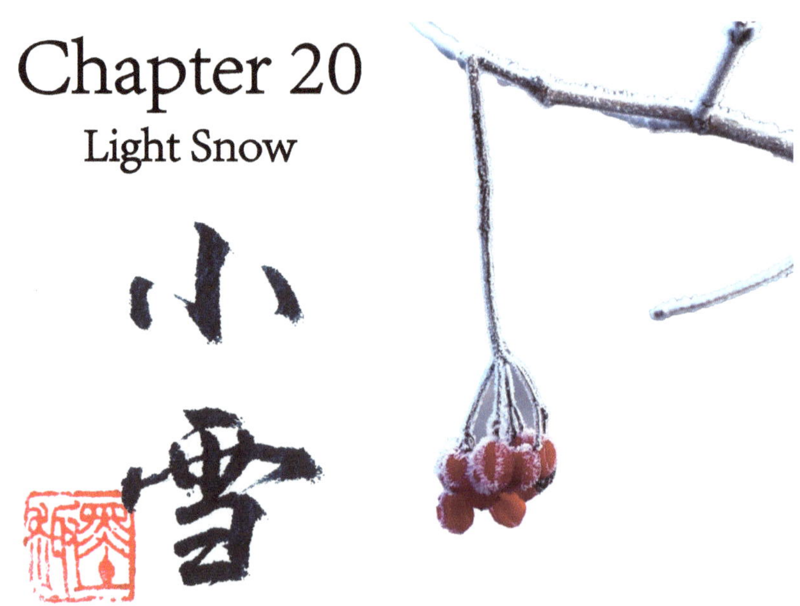

When does the temperature drop to the point at which rain first turns into snow in the temperate zone of the Northern Hemisphere annually? According to the time-tested observations of ancient Chinese meteorologists, it should be in late November.

在北半球溫帶，每年何時氣溫降到雨化為雪呢？依據古中國歷代氣象學家已通過時間考驗的觀察，這應在陽曆十一月下旬。

To be exact, snow will replace rain after the sun reaches 240 degrees of the ecliptic drawn by ancient Chinese astronomers, or after the Earth arrives at 240 degrees of the celestial orbit redrawn by modern Chinese scientists to present the 24 solar terms. The turning point may occur on Nov 22, Nov 23, or Nov 24.

較為精確的說法是，雪取代雨始於太陽到達黃經二百四十度的日子，亦即現代科學家按照地球繞太陽軌道所重畫的橢圓形二十四節氣圖表上，地球運轉到二百四十度之時。此一轉捩點可能在陽曆十一月二十二日、二十三日、或二十四日。

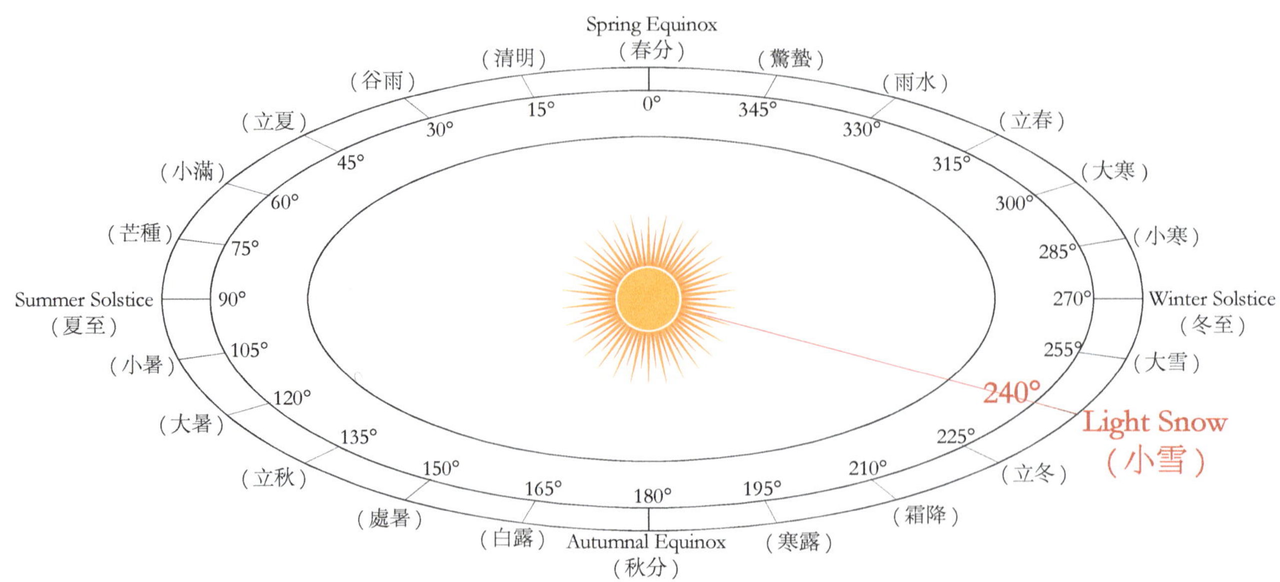

Starting from this day, there is a 15-or-16-day solar term called Xiaoxue in Chinese, in which *xiao* means "small or a little," and *xue* is snow.

從這一天起，為時共有十五或十六天的節氣稱為小雪。小是意指一點點。

Like the other 23 solar terms, the solar term with light snow can be divided into three parts. Each part is five or six days long. The first part of this solar term is when rainbows disappear. The second part is when warm air vanishes into the sky and cold air comes down to the ground. The third part is when everything freezes to present a wintry landscape.

小雪如同另外二十三個節氣，可分為三候。每一候五或六天。小雪一候虹藏不見；二候天氣上升地氣下降；三候閉塞而成冬。

During this time of year, there used to be a universal tradition of preserving vegetables. Nowadays fresh vegetables are available in winter, but pickled vegetables contain probiotics and therefore have health benefits. The only problem with them is their high sodium content. Soaking them in water and then draining them can help remove some salt.

每年此時，世界各地曾有腌製蔬菜的傳統。現代人則在冬天也買得到新鮮蔬菜，但是腌漬蔬菜含有益生菌，有助於保健。腌漬蔬菜唯一的問題只是含鹽量太高。泡水可以去掉腌漬蔬菜之中一些鹽份。

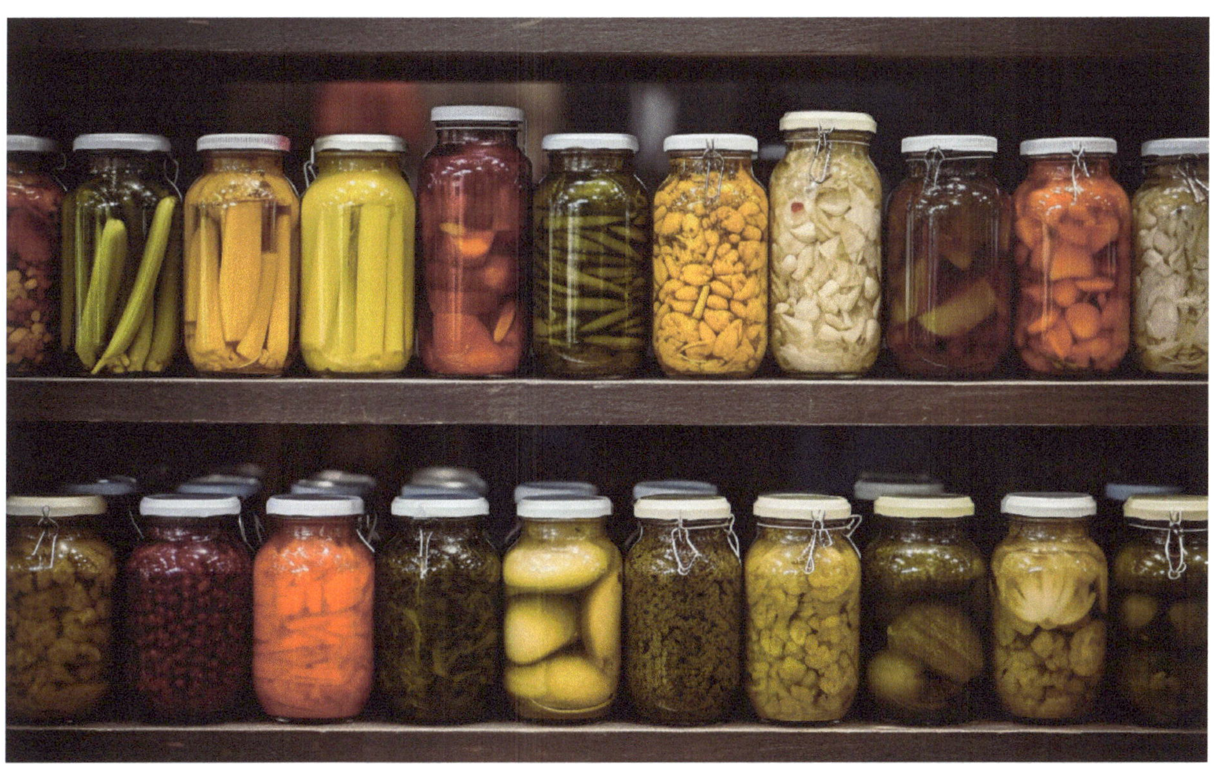

Among pickled vegetables, Chinese sauerkraut looks like German sauerkraut and may appeal to Westerners. It can be chopped very fine and used as a filling for steamed buns. Better yet, Chinese sauerkraut can make a fish soup taste fantastic. This type of fish soup is available at many authentic Chinese restaurants in the United States.

在腌漬蔬菜之中，中國酸菜類似德國酸菜，或許合乎西方人口味。切碎的中國酸菜常作包子餡。酸菜魚也很棒，在美國一些道地的中餐館能吃得到。

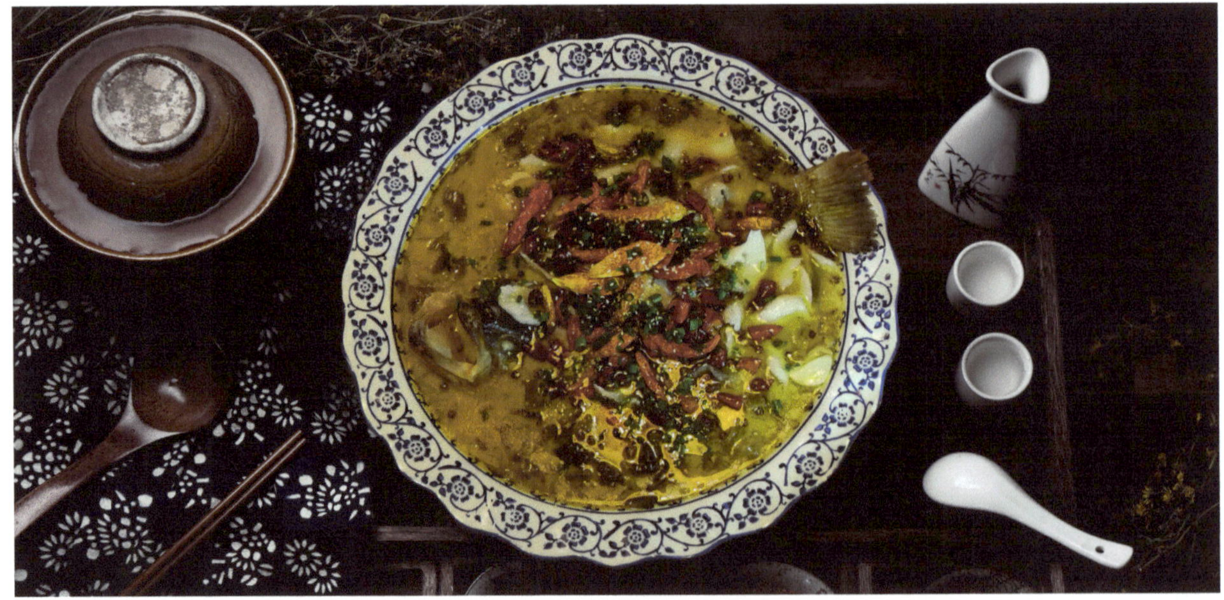

Speaking of fish, the solar term from late November to early December is conventionally the time of year to produce dried fish. Dried anchovies can be a great source of calcium, especially when stir-fried with dried tofu, which is high in calcium as well. However, dried anchovies are often found to contain heavy metals nowadays because of ocean pollution.[1] They should no longer be consumed frequently in winter or any other season.

談到魚類，小雪通常是曬魚乾的時期。小魚乾是良好鈣質來源，尤其與豆乾同炒，更加補鈣。然而由於海洋污染，目前的小魚乾往往含有重金屬，不宜在冬天或任何別的季節經常食用。

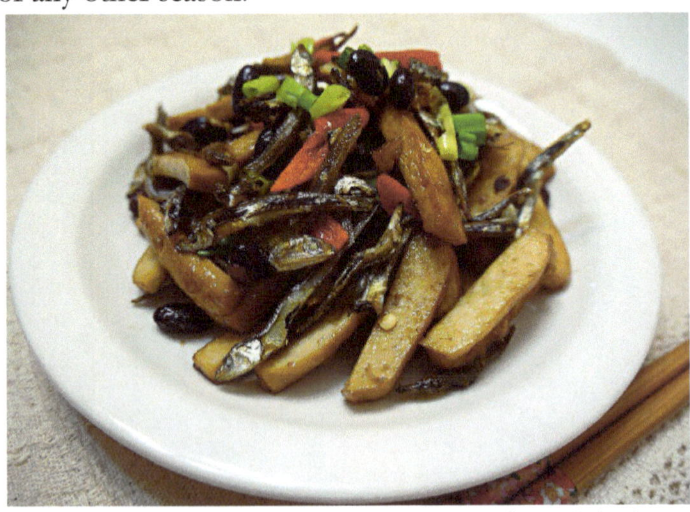

During the solar term that marks the first snowfall of the season, the snowy days tend to be pleasant, without piles of snow affecting traffic on the road. This is a terrific time to watch snowflakes gently falling.

在小雪時節，下雪天往往令人愉悅，尚無影響路上交通的積雪。這是觀賞雪花輕輕飄落的好時光。

At the end of this chapter is a classical Chinese poem that lightheartedly portrays light snow.
下一頁就有一首輕快描摹小雪的古詩。

1　Storelli, M.M. et al. "Occurrence of Heavy Metals (Hg, Cd, and Pb) and Polychlorinated Biphenyls in Salted Anchovies." Journal of Food Protection, May 2011. https://www.sciencedirect.com/science/article/pii/S0362028X22110124

清平樂 A Song of Serenity, Peace, and Joy

Author: Li, Po 李白 (701-762) or Yuan, Tao 袁綯 (birth & death years unknown)
Translator: Crystal Tai

畫堂晨起 An early morning in the polished hall,
來報雪花墜 A servant brings me the news of a snowfall.
高卷簾櫳看佳瑞 I raise the curtains high to see the auspicious scene outside the window.
皓色遠迷庭砌 Through the garden, a spread of white color blurs all.
盛氣光引爐煙 The glare of snowy air inspires fire in the stove;
素草寒生玉佩 The chill of white grass resembles jade with a glow.
應是天上狂醉 It must be drunk gods in heaven
亂把白雲揉碎 Wildly shredding clouds into snow.

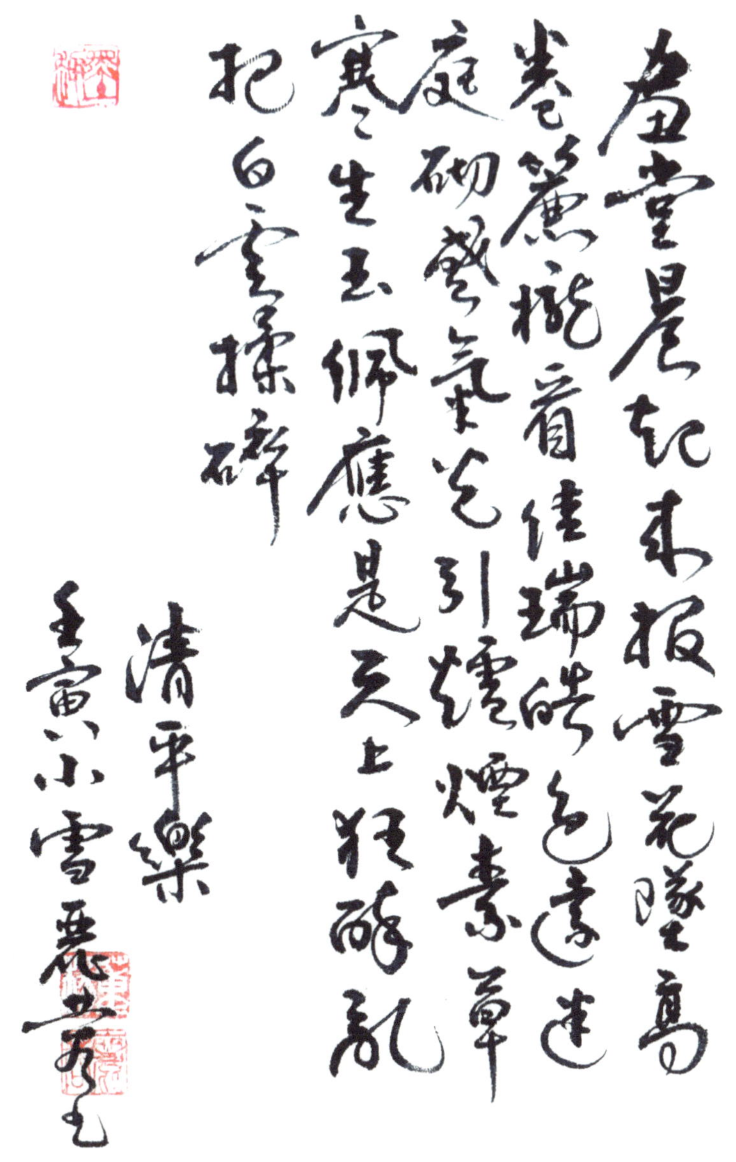

Chapter 21
Heavy Snow

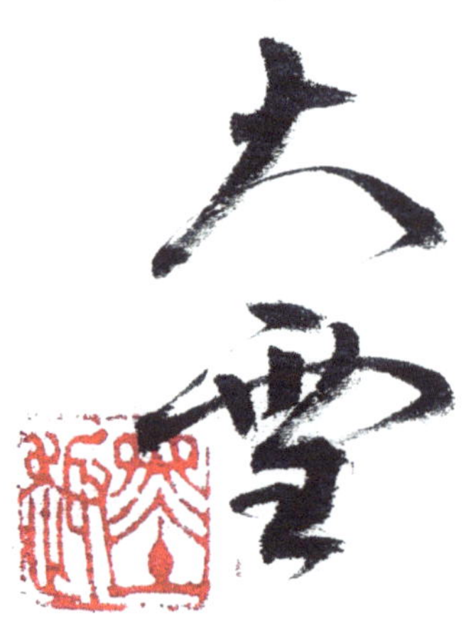

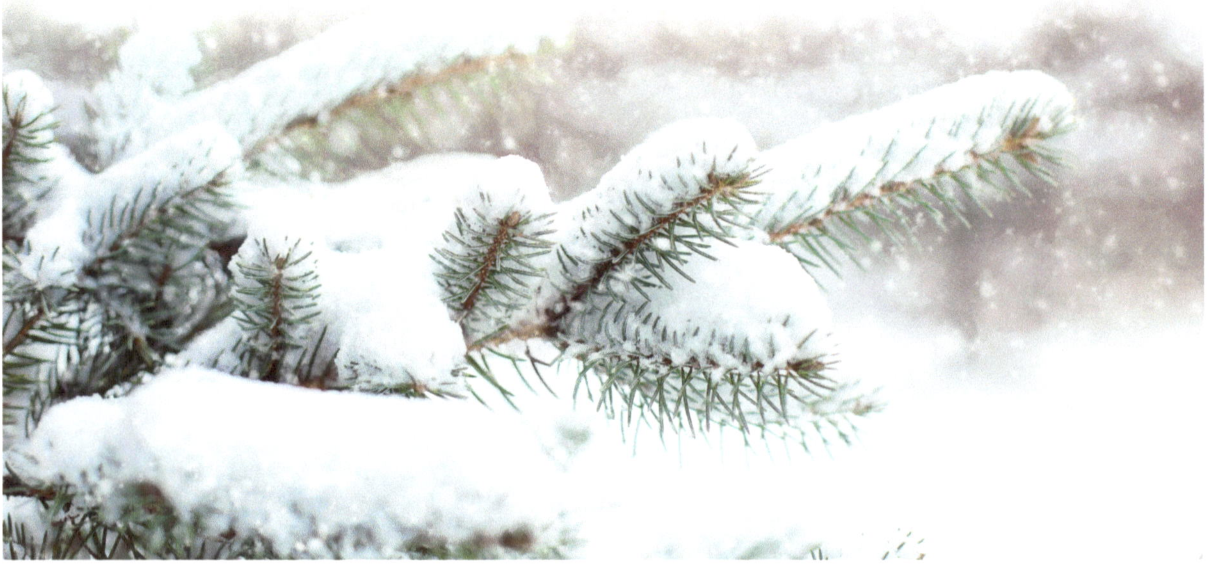

It takes heavy snow to build a snowman, so people usually do it in December in the temperate zone of the Northern Hemisphere. Interestingly, there is a 15-or-16-day solar term in December that is called Daxue in Chinese, which means "heavy snow."
如果要堆雪人，總要有很厚的積雪才行，因此北半球溫帶居民都在陽曆十二月堆雪人。有趣的是，陽曆十二月有一段十五或十六天的節氣，稱為大雪。

This solar term coming with heavy snow starts when the sun reaches 255 degrees of the ecliptic drawn by ancient Chinese astronomers, or when the Earth arrives at 255 degrees of the celestial orbit redrawn by modern Chinese scientists to present the 24 solar terms. This day may be Dec 6, Dec 7, or Dec 8.
大雪節氣始於太陽到達黃經二百五十五度的日子，亦即現代科學家按照地球繞太陽軌道所重畫的橢圓形二十四節氣圖表上，地球運轉到二百五十五度之時。這一天可能是陽曆十二月六日、十二月七日，或十二月八日。

大雪

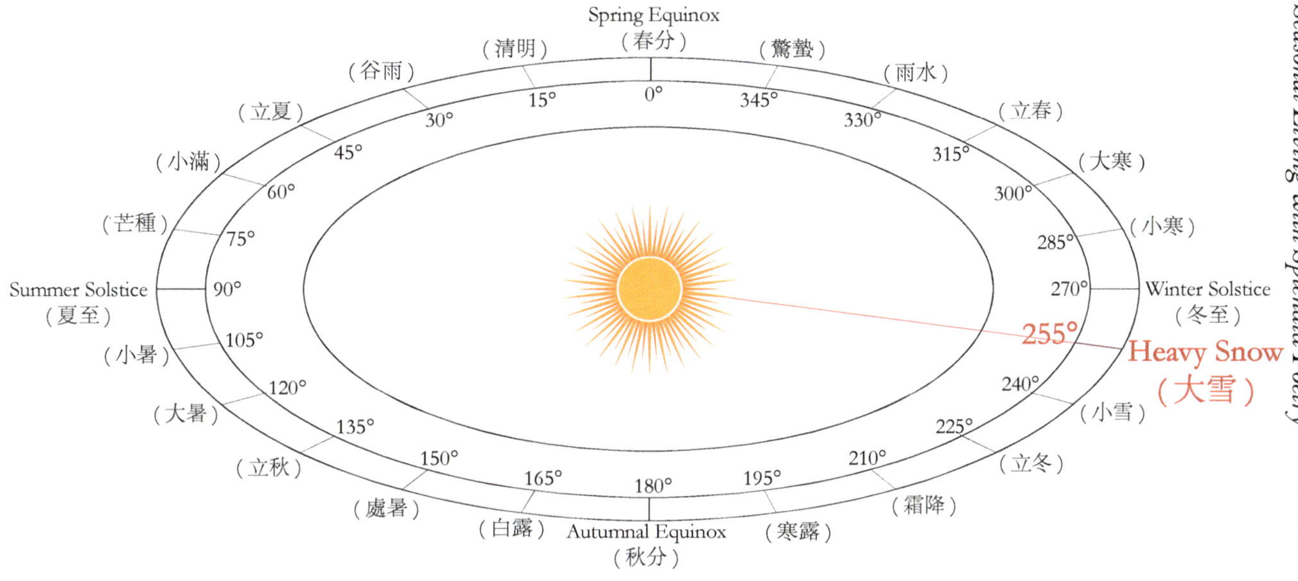

Like the other 23 solar terms, this one can be divided into three parts. Each part is five or six days long. The first part of the solar term with heavy snow is when wild roosters stop crowing. The second part is when the mating season of tigers begins. The third part is when a certain type of orchid called *li-ting* in Chinese starts sprouting. Amazingly, the earth is still alive under heavy snow!

如同另外二十三個節氣，大雪節氣可分為三候。每一候五或六天。大雪一候鶡鴠不鳴；二候虎始交；三候荔挺出。 驚人的是，厚厚積雪下面的大地依然在孕育生命！

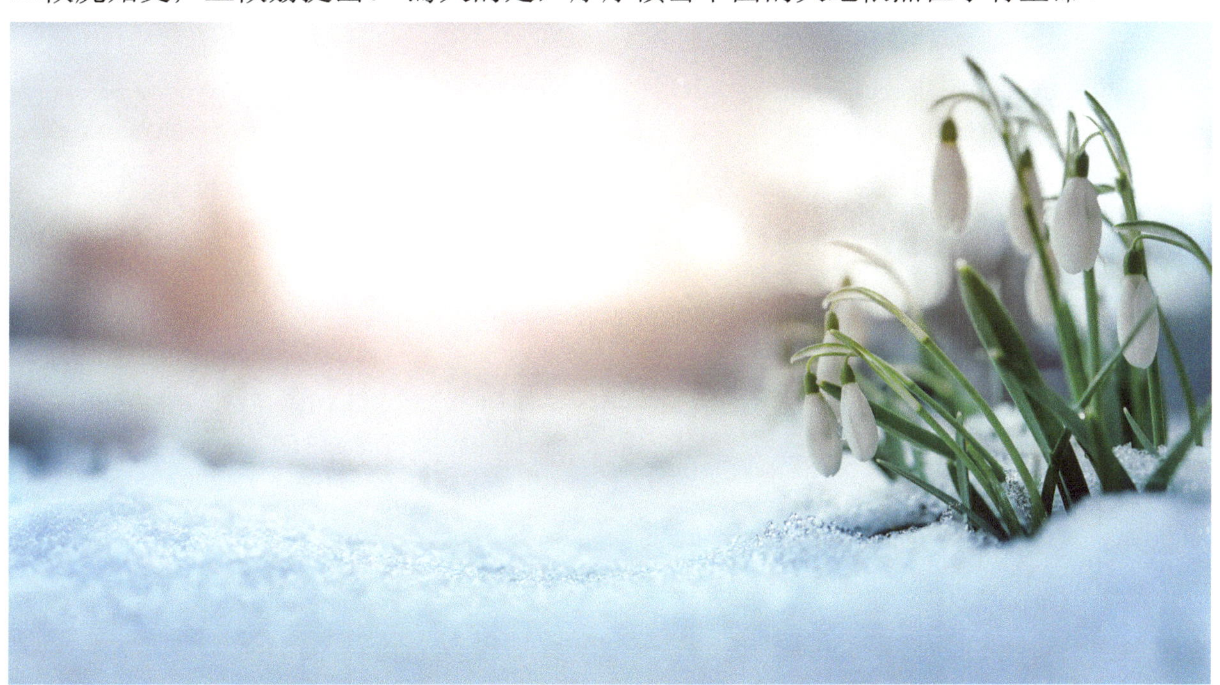

Culturally, Chinese people have always welcomed snow. There is a Chinese proverb that goes, "Auspicious snow promises an abundant harvest in the next year."

中國文化總是歡迎降雪。有句中文名言：" 瑞雪兆豐年。"

In fact, snow really can serve as a fertilizer. Snow contains nitrogen,[1] which it collects while falling through the atmosphere to nourish the soil. Better yet, when the ground is frozen, a blanket of snow works like a layer of protective mulch. The insulative properties of snow can protect both the soil and the plants from harmful winds and freezing temperatures.

事實上，雪真能作為肥料，因為含有氮。雪在降落過程中從空氣吸收氮氣，飄落下來滋養泥土。更棒的是，大地凍結時，積雪像毯子一樣具有隔離作用，可以保護泥土和植物不受寒風與低溫侵害。

When farmland is covered with snow, farmers naturally take a break. In the past, this was universally the time of year to preserve meat and make sausage for winter consumption. Nowadays people can eat processed meats all year round and perhaps consume more processed meats while having traditional winter meals.

當農田積雪時，農民自然休假。過去這曾是世界各地人民腌肉類、灌香腸以過冬的時節。如今大眾一年到頭都能吃到加工肉類，而在冬天經常享用傳統熱食，加工肉類或許吃得更多。

However, meat processing such as curing or smoking can lead to the formation of potentially cancer-causing chemicals. In October 2015, the World Health Organization classified processed meats including ham, salami, pepperoni, sausages, beef jerky, and hot dogs as Group 1 carcinogens. The so-called Group 1 represents the most dangerous group.[2]

加工肉類的過程會產生致癌物質。世界衛生組織已在西元 2015 年十月將包括火腿、各式香腸、牛肉乾、熱狗等加工肉類列為第一組致癌物，亦即最危險的一組。

Researchers discovered that each 50-gram (1.8-ounce) portion of processed meat eaten daily increased the risk of colorectal cancer by 18%. They found three chemicals in processed meats that can cause colorectal cancer. One is a natural pigment in red meat. The others develop or are added during the production of processed meats. No wonder the World Health Organization placed processed meats in the same category as cigarettes.

研究人員發現，每五十克加工肉類攝取量增加百分之十八的大腸癌罹患率。他們找到了加工肉類之中三種致癌成份，其中之一是紅肉的天然色素，另外兩種是化學添加物。難怪世界衛生組織將加工肉類與香煙歸於同樣有害的類別。

The same report places fresh red meat in Group 2A, which means "probably carcinogenic to humans." Eating red meat is particularly linked to pancreatic and prostate cancer.

同一篇報告將新鮮紅肉列入 2A 組，意思是很有可能致癌。食用紅肉特別容易導致胰臟癌和前列腺癌。

1 Liu, Lin et al. "Effects of Seasonal Snow Cover on Soil Nitrogen Transformation in Alpine Ecosystem: a Review." National Library of Medicine, Aug 22, 2011. https://pubmed.ncbi.nlm.nih.gov/22097387/

2 Bouvard, Veronique et al. "Carcinogenicity of Consumption of Red & Processed Meat." The Lancet Oncology. Oct 26, 2015. https://www.thelancet.com/journals/lanonc/article/PIIS1470-2045%2815%2900444-1/fulltext

It has been years since the report was published, but many people are still unaware of it. Perhaps even lesser known is the fact that methane from cattle is 28 times more potent than carbon dioxide in warming the atmosphere.[1] It would be a great idea to share theses pieces of scientific information and cook vegan meat dishes.

那篇報告發表之後，已有好些年，但很多人卻並不知曉。或許更鮮為人知的是，牛所排出的廢氣污染空氣而引起暖化的程度比二氧化碳嚴重二十八倍。最好能夠傳播這些科學信息，並且用素肉代替紅肉。

Vegan meat products have a much longer history in the East than in the West, thanks to the prevalence of Buddhism in Asia. Chinese chefs are therefore good at creating plant-based cold cuts. For instance, thin slices of vegan braised pork can look very real and taste incredibly flavorful.

素肉在東方比在西方源遠流長，因為佛教風行於亞洲。中國廚師往往善於製作鹵味素肉。例如，薄片的素鹵豬肉可以做到望似真豬肉，味道也好得出人意表。

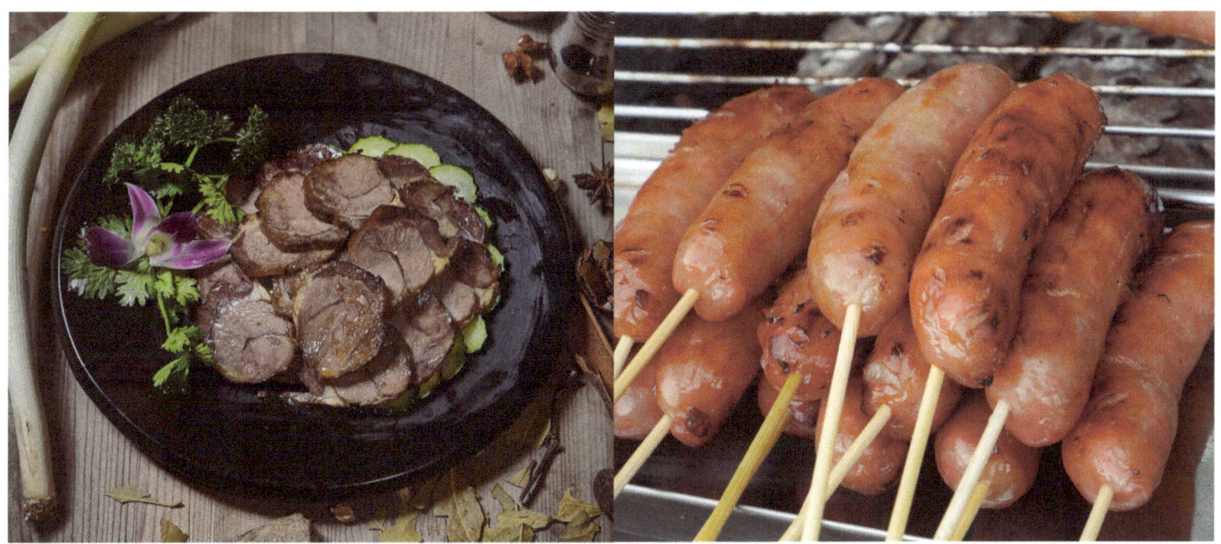

Imitation roasts and meatless sausages can easily replace real meat in holiday meals. They really should.

素肉和素香腸能夠很容易在節日餐會中取代真實肉類。確實理應這樣做才對。

Speaking of holidays, the holiday season is normally full of family gatherings and social events, but it may also be the best time for introspection. During off hours, heavy snow can bring serenity to the soul.

談到節日，節日頗多的陽曆年底往往是西方社會充滿家庭聚會和社交活動的時候，却也可以是自我內省的最佳時機。無須工作時，大雪能夠帶給靈魂一陣恬靜。

At the end of this chapter is a classical Chinese poem that compellingly conveys serene solitude in a wintry scene with heavy snow.

下一頁的曠古絕句就在傳神表達大雪冬景的空闊寂静。

1　Quinto, Amy. "Cows and Climate Change." UC Davis News. June 27, 2019. https://www.ucdavis.edu/food/news/making-cattle-more-sustainable

江雪 Snow on the River

Author: Liu, Zongyuan 柳宗元（773-819）
Translator: Crystal Tai

千山鳥飛絕 A thousand mountains stand with no flying birds to be found;
萬徑人蹤滅 Ten thousand paths remain with no venturing travelers to walk around.
孤舟蓑笠翁 An elderly man in a straw hat and raincoat sits in a canoe,
獨釣寒江雪 Fishing alone while cold snow continues to mound.

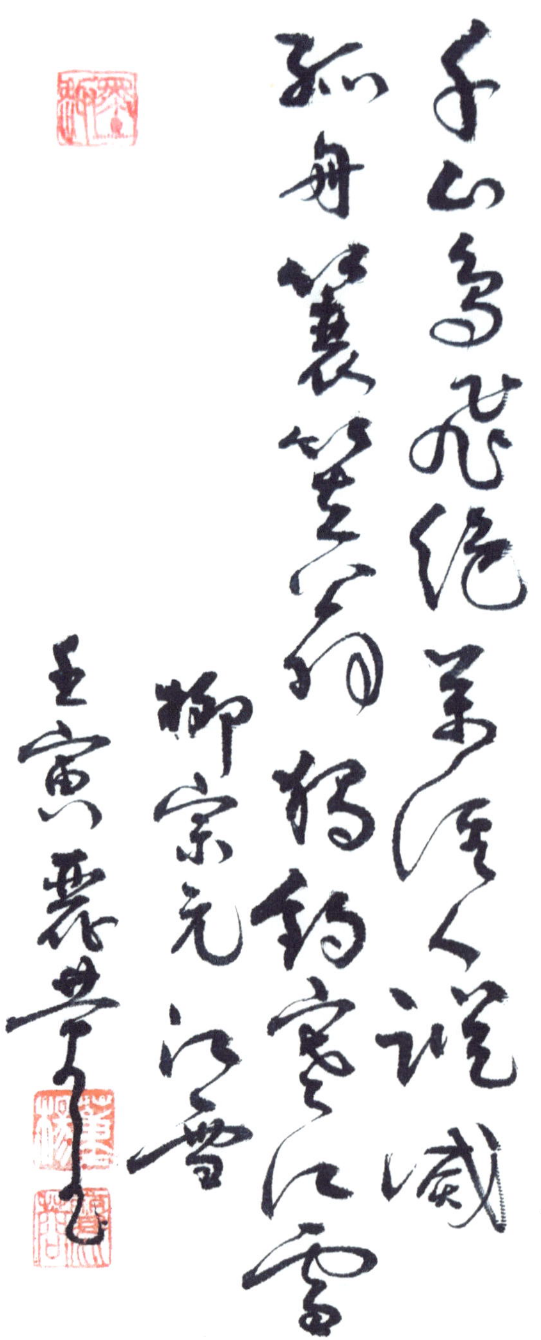

Chapter 22
Winter Solstice

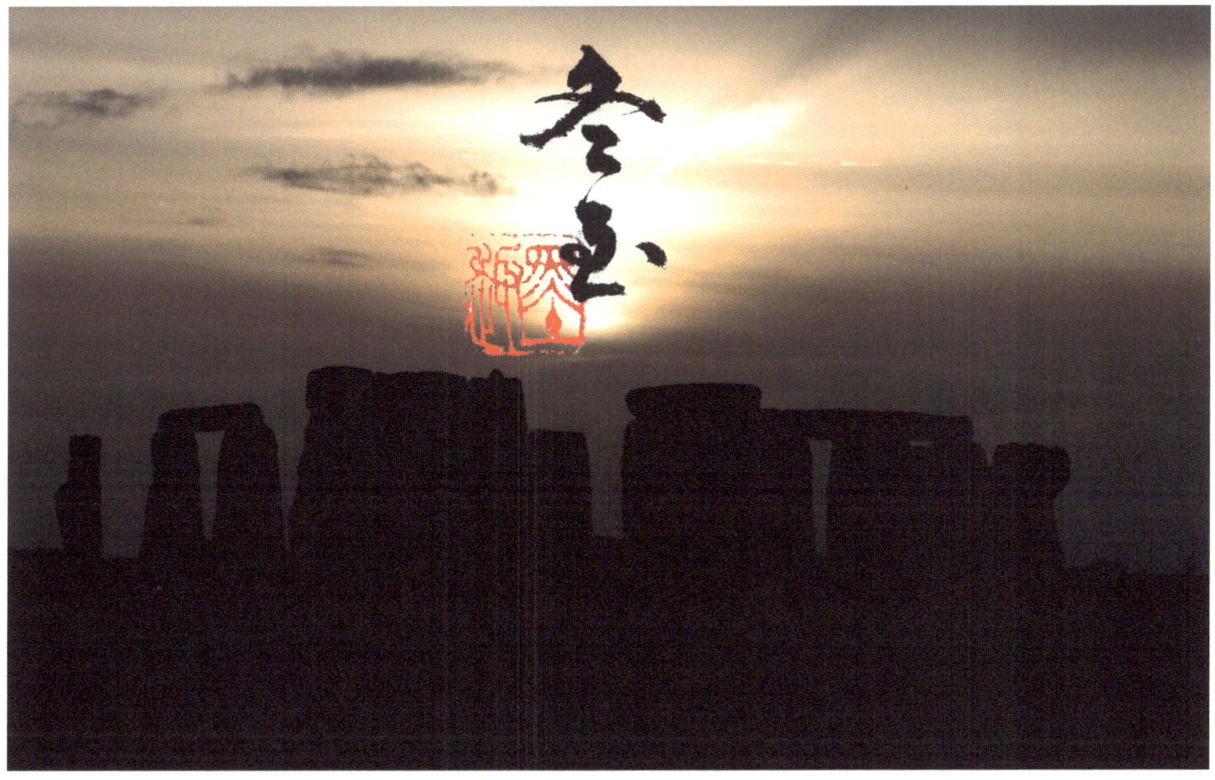

Stonehenge is a neolithic monument in England, as stated in Chapter 10. It contains stones that were set up to frame the sunset at the winter solstice, which comes with the longest night of the year.

如同本書第十章所述，英國的巨石陣是新石器時代的遺址。在冬至日，亦即一年中黑夜最長的日子，巨石陣的石柱會框住當天傍晚的夕陽。

The winter solstice is called Dongzhi in Chinese. The Chinese word *zhi* in Dongzhi has multiple meanings. It can mean "arrival" or "pinnacle." Some people therefore mistranslated Dongzhi into the arrival of winter. In fact, however, the ancient Chinese defined the winter solstice as the midpoint of winter for having the shortest daylight of the year. Dongzhi should be literally translated as the peak of winter.

冬至中文名稱的至字有多重意義，可以意指"來臨"或"極致"。有些人因此在英文之中把中文冬至的意思誤解成冬天降臨。事實上，中國古人將冬至視為冬天的中間點，因為冬至是白晝最短的一天。冬至的中文名稱應在英文之中講解為冬天的頂點才對。

詩意節氣

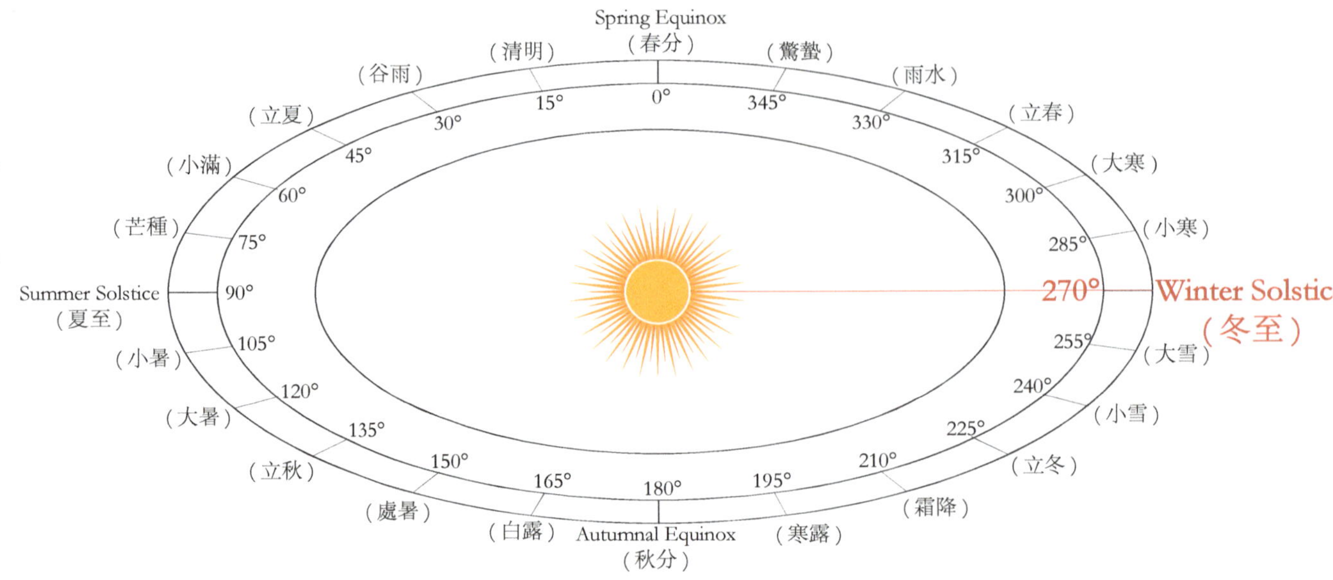

On the day of the winter solstice, people in northern China customarily eat dumplings. People in southern China have rice balls instead. The rice balls may have savory or sweet fillings. They are often served in a soup with dried osmanthus flowers added for aroma. Either dumplings or rice balls can warm up the body.

在冬至這一天，中國北方人習慣吃餃子，南方人則吃或鹹或甜的湯圓，並且常在湯中加桂花以憑添香味。餃子和湯圓都能暖身。

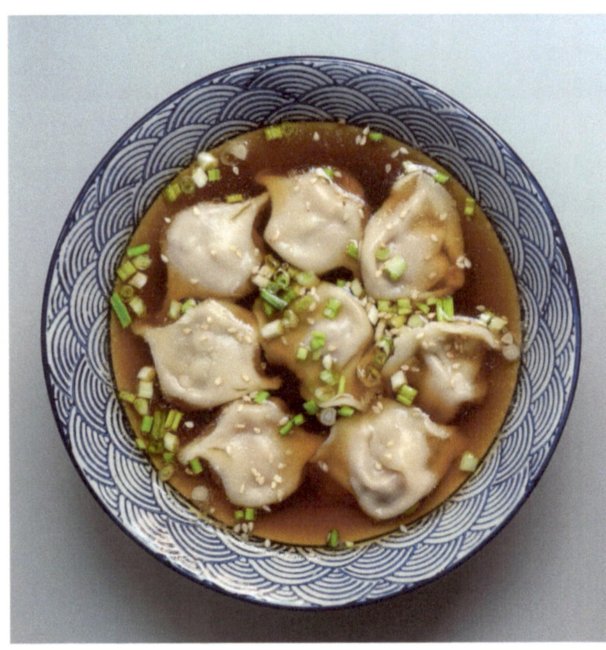

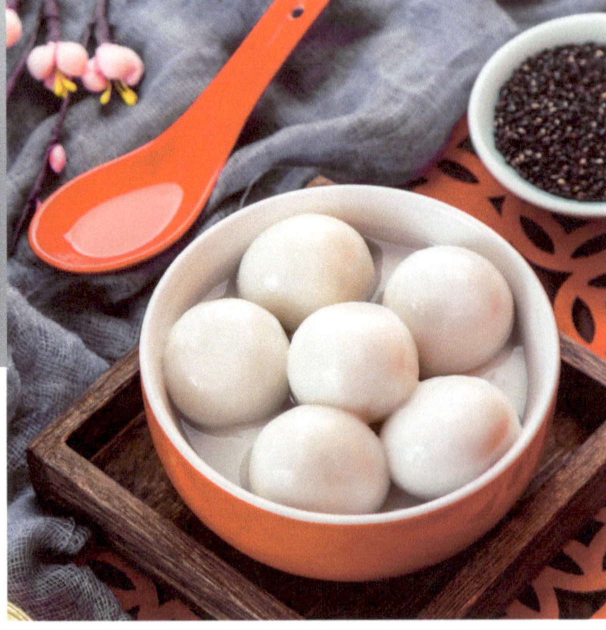

The winter solstice occurs when the sun reaches 270 degrees of the ecliptic drawn by ancient Chinese astronomers, or when the Earth arrives at 270 degrees of the celestial orbit redrawn by modern Chinese scientists to present the 24 solar terms. This day may be Dec 21, Dec 22, or Dec 23.

冬至日是太陽到達黃經二百七十度的日子，亦即現代科學家按照地球繞太陽軌道所重畫的橢圓形二十四節氣圖表上，地球運轉到二百七十度之時。這一天可能是陽曆十二月二十一、二十二，或二十三日。

Starting from this day, there is a 15-or-16-day solar term also named Dongzhi. Like the other 23 solar terms, this one can be divided into three parts. Each part is five or six days long. The first part of the solar term beginning with the winter solstice is when earthworms coil themselves. The second part is when moose shed their antlers. The third part is when hot springs start flowing.

始於冬至日的十五天或十六天節氣也名叫冬至。如同另外二十三個節氣，冬至節氣可分為三候，每一候五或六天。冬至一候蚯蚓結；二候麋角解；三候水泉動。

Despite the cold weather, nature actually begins to revive right after the winter solstice. No wonder the winter solstice has been celebrated universally for thousands of years. It is notable that daylight will get longer and longer after the longest night of the year. That explains why the ancient Chinese regarded the winter solstice as the beginning of *yang*.

儘管天氣寒冷，大自然從冬至日過後就開始復甦。難怪冬至日在世界各地廣受慶祝，已有數千年歷史。值得注意的是，冬至日過後，白晝就會開始變長。因此，中國古人認為冬至一陽生。

The *yin-yang* theory originated in China, allegedly created by a scholar named Zhou Yan (324 - 250 BC).[1] It is a hypothesis that *yin* and *yang* are the driving forces of the universe. As already explained in Chapter 4, while *yin* generates everything cold, dark, wet, passive, receptive, and female, *yang* propels everything warm, bright, dry, active, penetrating, and male.

陰陽學說發源於中國，據說是一位名叫鄒衍的學者所創立。此一學說假設陰陽是宇宙的動力。如同本書第四章所述，陽推動世間所有溫暖、明亮、乾燥、主動、衝刺、雄性的一切。陰則衍生世間所有寒冷、黑暗、潮溼、被動、容納、雌性的一切。

Yin and *yang* drive the seasonal cycle as well. The winter solstice with the longest night of the year marks the peak of *yin*, but then *yin* will decline and give rise to *yang*.

陰陽也推動季節循環。冬至是陰的頂點，但從此陰走下坡，讓陽走上坡。

At the end of this chapter is a classical Chinese poem that clearly indicates the connection between the *yin-yang* theory and the winter solstice.

下一頁的絕句就清楚顯示了陰陽與冬至之間的關聯。

---

1 Zheng, Kai. "Zou Yan" (Chinese edition). China's Great Encyclopedia, July 20, 2023. https://www.zgbk.com/ecph/words?SiteID=1&ID=697690&SubID=240755

記異 Recording a Phenomenon

Author：Pang, Ji 龐籍 (988-1063)
Translator：Crystal Tai

冬至子時陽已生　The first hour of the winter solstice is when *yang* begins reviving.
道隨陽長物將萌　Nature grows with *yang* to make every plant start sprouting.
星辰賜告銘心骨　I will ingrain what the stars are telling me in my heart,
願以寬章輔至平　Vowing to promote tolerance and bring peace to everything.

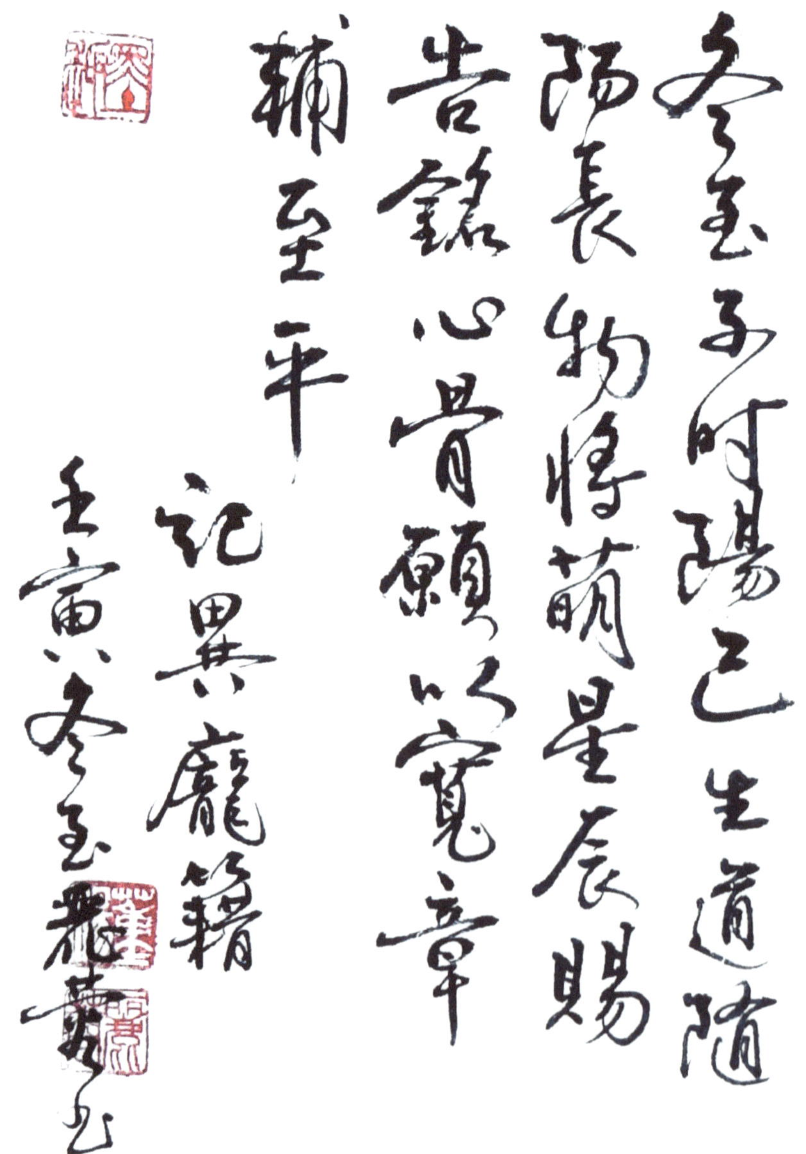

Chapter 23
Nippy Weather

There is a tree species called ume or winter plum, which unusually blooms in winter. It comes into bloom in early January.

梅樹有兩個常見的英文名字，其中之一是從日文音譯的名稱，另一個則是道地的英文名字，意指冬天的李樹。梅樹很不尋常在冬天開花。梅花通常從陽曆一月上旬開始綻放。

With winter plum blossoms comes a 15-or-16-day Chinese solar term named Xiaohan in Chinese, in which *xiao* means "small" and *han* indicates "cold." However, Xiaohan doesn't mean "just a little cold," because the weather actually gets very cold in early to mid January in the temperate zone of the Northern Hemisphere. What Xiaohan really represents is when the weather is getting colder little by little. The best English translation is probably nippy weather, because a nip is smaller than a bite and therefore quite close to the literal meaning of the *xiao* in Xiaohan.

梅花始開於小寒節氣。小寒的意思並非只有一丁點冷，因為陽曆一月上旬到中旬在北半球溫帶其實很冷。小寒真正的寓意在於冷度一點一點逐漸加強，變得越來越冷。用英文來解釋時，最好說是帶有嚙咬性的一種寒冷，因為嚙咬是小口的咬，較能配合小寒的小字。

This solar term in early to mid January usually includes a traditional Chinese holiday that marks the anniversary of Buddha's enlightenment on the eighth of the 12th lunar month. On this day, Chinese people will customarily eat porridge made of eight different ingredients in honor of Buddha.

小寒節氣既然在陽曆一月上旬到中旬，陰曆十二月初八的臘八就常在小寒時節。臘八是佛祖悟道成佛的紀念日。華人會在這一天吃臘八粥，以示尊崇。

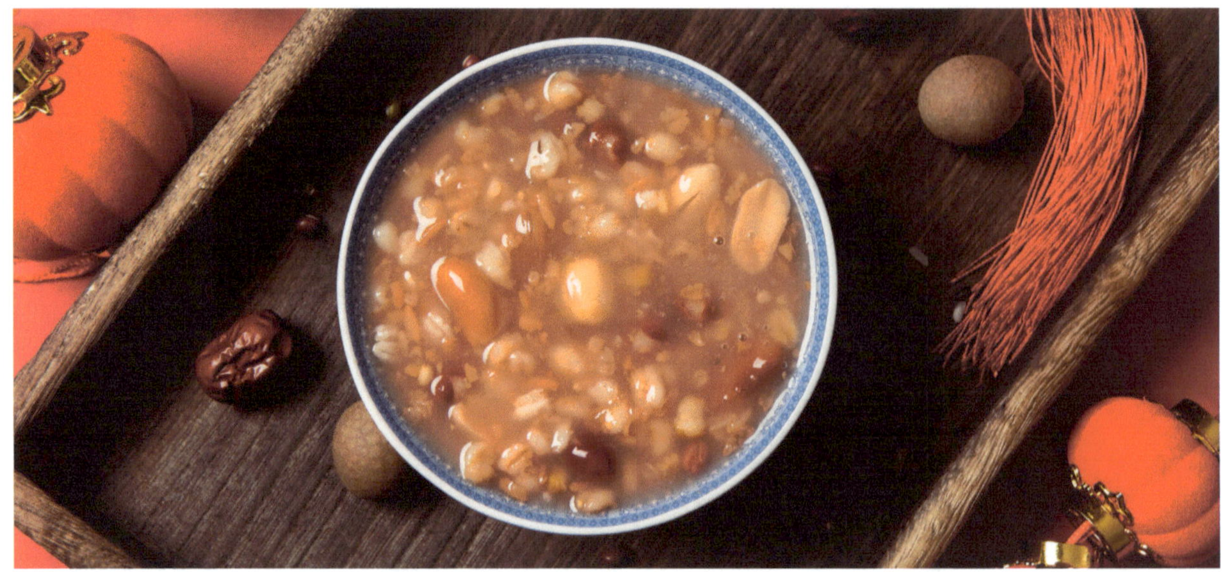

Actually, warm porridge is good for the entire solar term from early to mid January, which begins when the sun reaches 285 degrees of the ecliptic drawn by ancient Chinese astronomers, or when the Earth arrives at 285 degrees of the celestial orbit redrawn by modern Chinese scientists to present the 24 solar terms. It may be Jan 5, Jan 6, or Jan 7.

其實，溫暖的臘八粥很適合在整個小寒時節食用。小寒始於太陽到達黃經二百八十五度的日子，亦即現代科學家按照地球繞太陽軌道所重畫的橢圓形二十四節氣圖表上，地球運轉到二百八十五度之時。這一天可能是陽曆一月五日、一月六日，或一月七日。

Like the other 23 solar terms, this one can be divided into three parts. Each part is five or six days long. The first part of the solar term in early to mid January is when wild geese migrate north. The second part is when magpies begin to build their nests. The third part is when pheasants start to sing.

如同另外二十三個節氣，小寒節氣可分為三候，每一候五或六天。一候雁北鄉，二候鵲始巢，三候雉始雊。

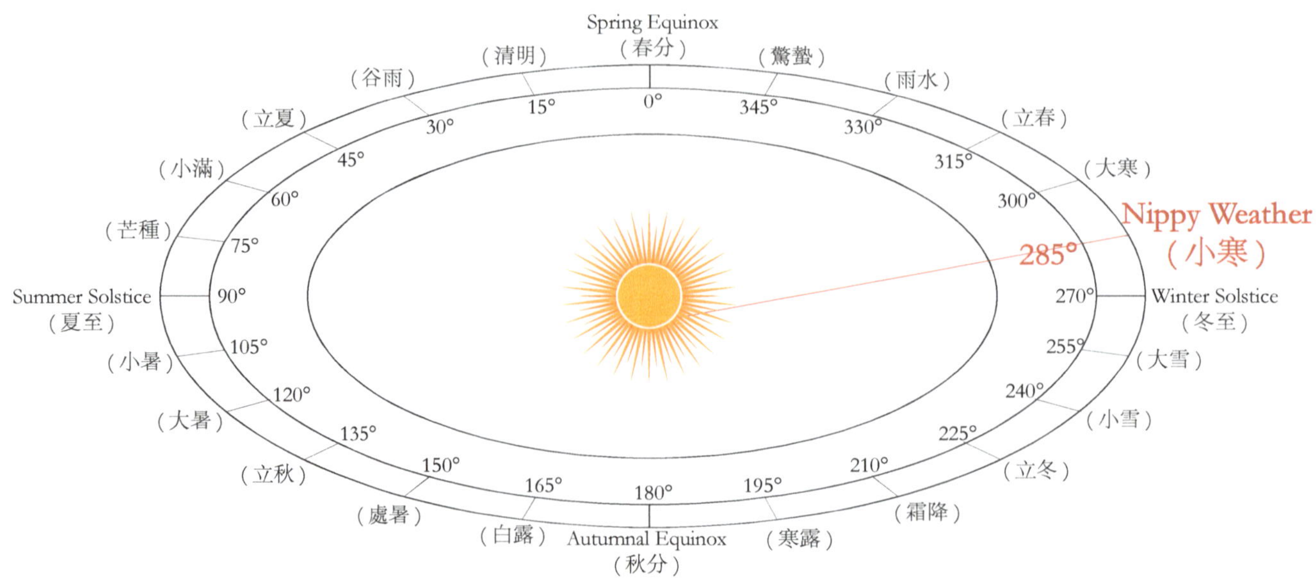

Surprisingly, nature is already reviving during this time of year despite the cold weather. Following winter plum blossoms are camellia flowers and paperwhite narcissus, also known as Chinese sacred lilies.

驚人的是，大自然已在如此寒冷的時節復甦了！不止梅花開放，山茶花和水仙花也隨之吐蕊。

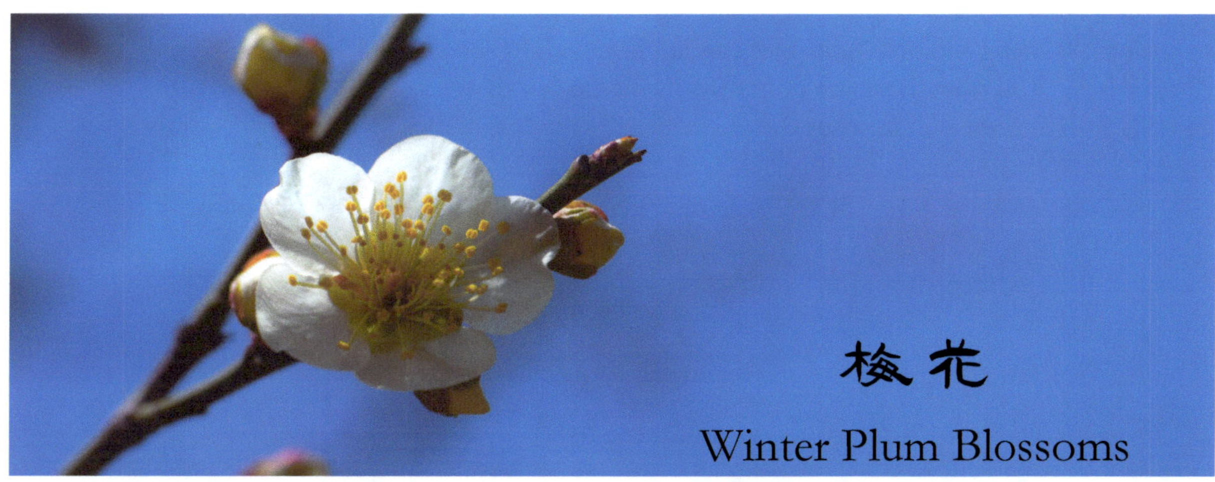

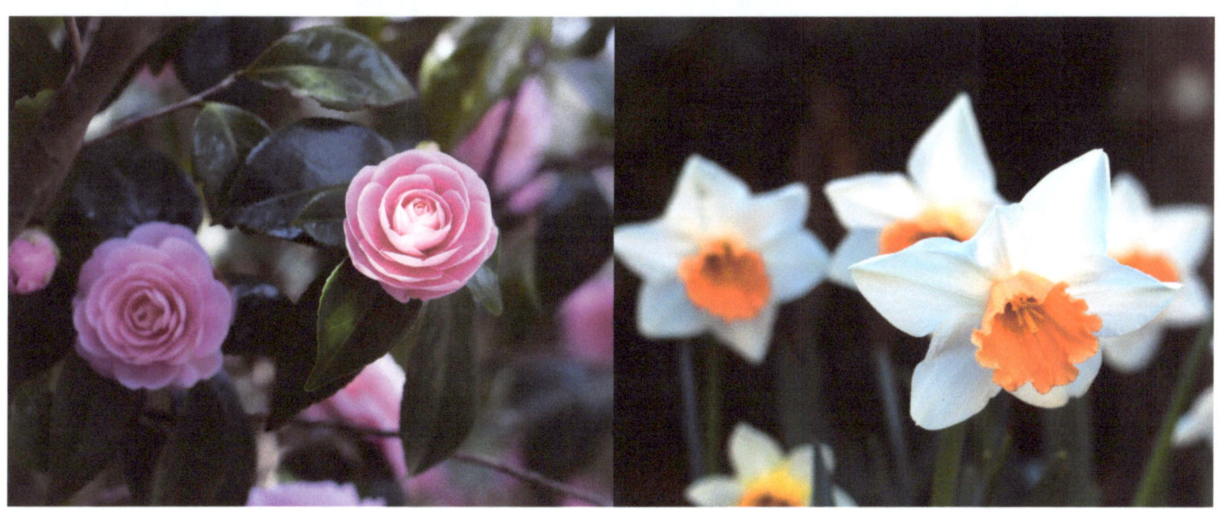

山 茶 花

Camellias

水 仙 花

Paperwhite Narcissus

Since ancient Chinese saw winter plum as the first flower species that comes into bloom after the winter solstice, winter plum trees have always been highly praised in Chinese culture for their resilience against cold weather. Many Chinese poets have written countless poems about winter plum blossoms.

由於梅花在冬至之後率先開放，中國文化一直高度讚揚梅樹耐寒的精神。許多中國詩人為梅花寫下了無數詩篇。

At the end of this chapter is a classical Chinese poem that fantastically features winter plum blossoms:

下一頁就在展示一首表現手法極佳的詠梅絕句：

梅花 Winter Plum Blossoms

Author: Wang, Anshi 王安石 (1021-1086)
Translator：Crystal Tai

牆角數枝梅 A few winter plum branches stretch from the corner,
凌寒獨自開 Being the only ones blossoming in the chilly air.
遙知不是雪 We know those are not snow flakes from a distance
為有暗香來 For the subtle scent they bear.

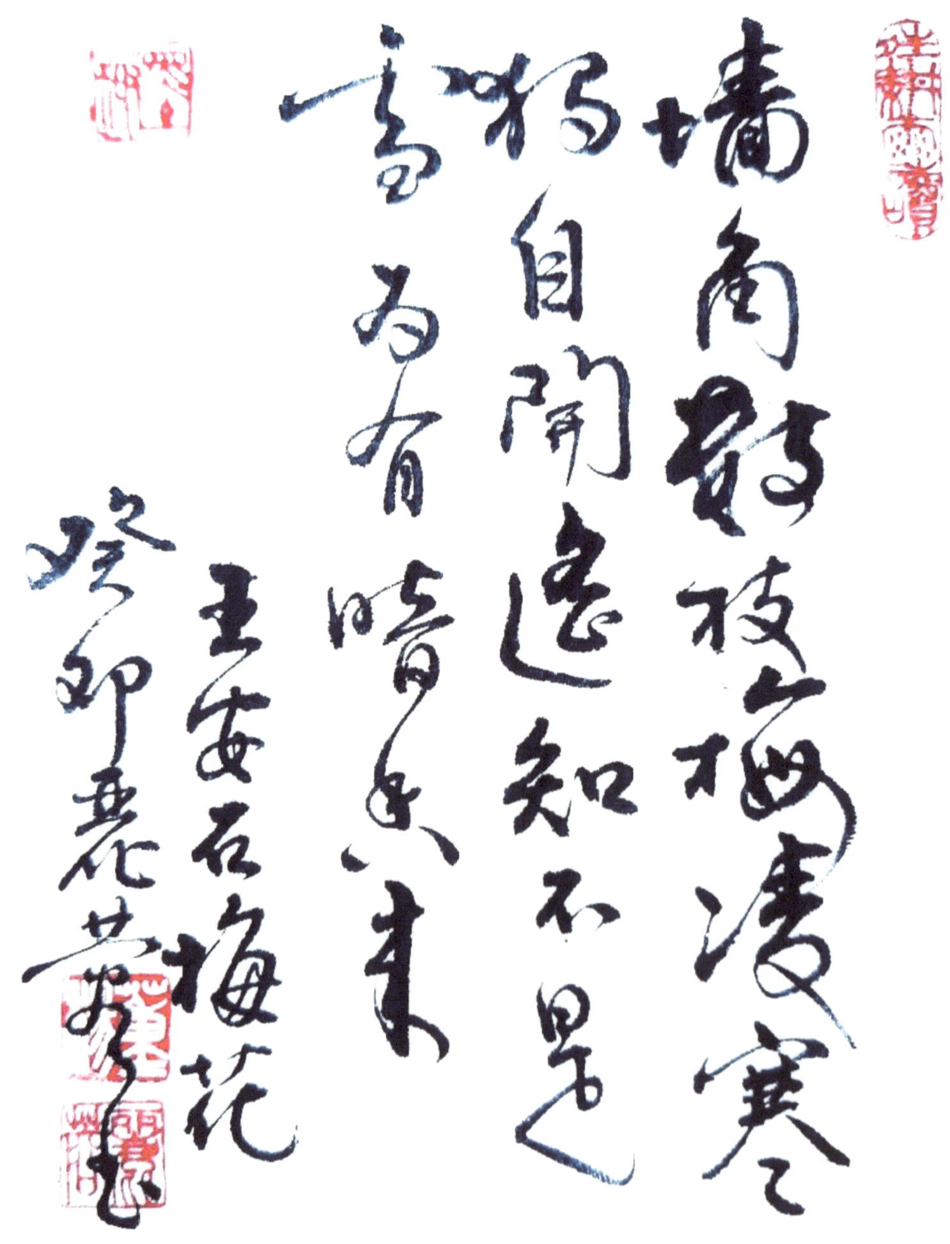

Chapter 24
Extreme Cold

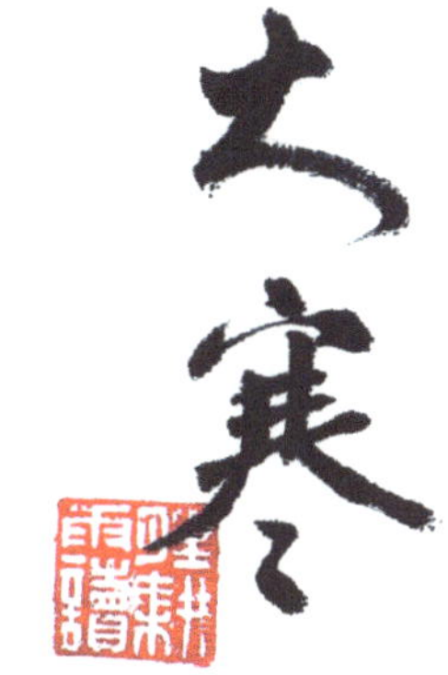

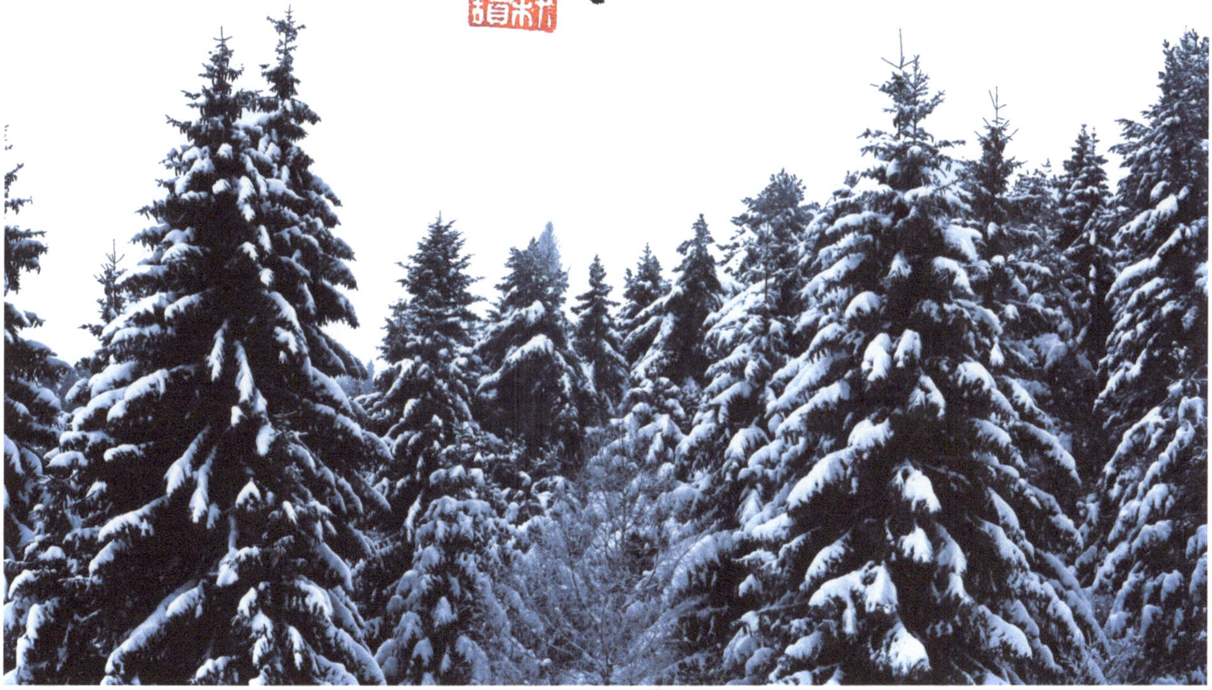

The coldest time of year is usually late January in most places of East Asia, because this is when cold fronts from Siberia arrive. No wonder a 15-or-16-day solar term starting in late January is called Dahan in Chinese, which means "extreme cold."

在東亞大多數地區。一年內最冷的時節常常是陽曆一月下旬，因為西伯利亞寒流每年此時南下。難怪陽曆一月下旬起始的節氣稱為大寒。

This solar term starts when the sun reaches 300 degrees of the ecliptic drawn by ancient Chinese astronomers, or when the Earth arrives at 300 degrees of the celestial orbit redrawn by modern Chinese scientists to present the 24 solar terms. This day may be Jan 20 or Jan 21.

大寒節氣始於太陽到達黃經三百度的日子，亦即現代科學家按照地球繞太陽軌道所重畫的橢圓形二十四節氣圖表上，地球運轉到三百度之時。這一天可能是陽曆一月二十日或二十一日。

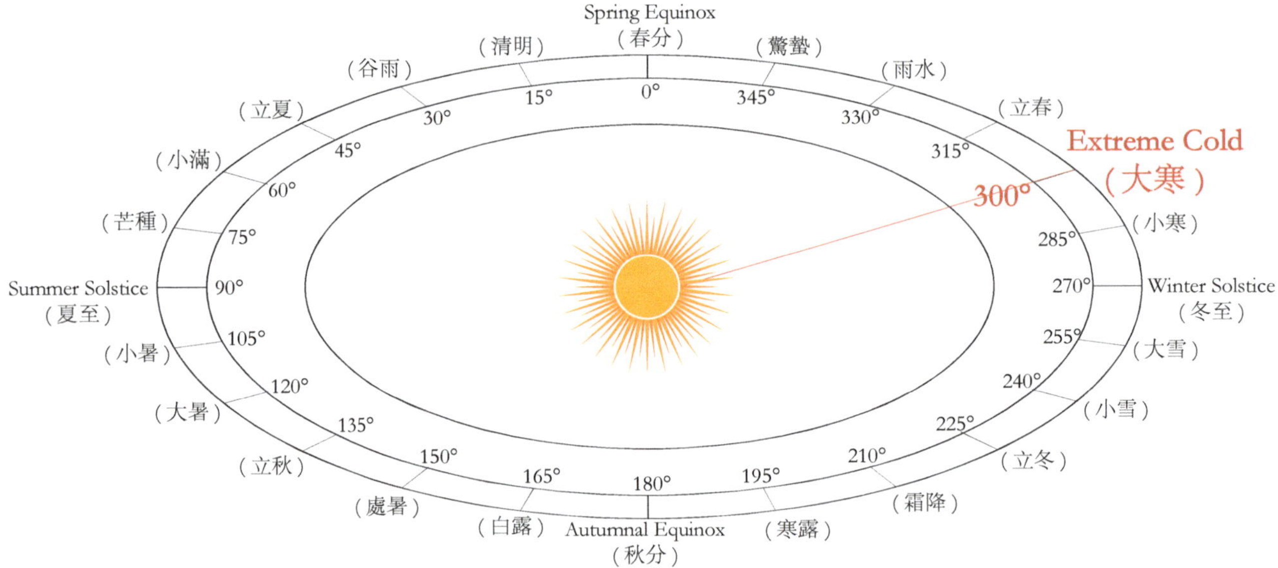

This is the last solar term of winter. Like the other 23 solar terms of the year, it can be divided into three parts. Each part is five or six days long. The first part of the solar term with extremely cold weather is when chickens begin to breed. The second part is when predatory birds become aggressive. The third part is when freshwater bodies are solidly frozen.

大寒是冬天最後一個節氣。如同另外二十三個節氣，大寒可分為三候，每一候五到六天。大寒一候雞始乳，二候徵鳥厲疾，三候水澤腹堅。

Most notably, this solar term either comes right before or overlaps with Lunar New Year, which begins with the new moon between Jan 21 and February 20. Lunar New Year's Day moves within this range on the Gregorian calendar from year to year.

最值得注意的是，陰曆新年既然都從陽曆一月二十一日到二月二十日之間的新月開始，大寒就有時候在陰曆新年之前，有時候在陰曆新年期間。

On the next page is a classical Chinese poem that sentimentally associates the last solar term of winter with the end of the lunar year:

下一頁就在展示一首悵然感嘆節氣大寒與年關將至的古詩：

歲暮 Toward the End of the Lunar Year

Author：Xie, Lingyun 謝靈運 (385-433)
Translator：Crystal Tai

殷憂不能寐 Too worried to fall asleep past midnight,
苦此夜難頹 I lament upon the never-ending night.
明月照積雪 The bright moonlight shines upon the piling snow;
朔風勁且哀 The north winds blow strongly to bite.
運往無淹物 The passage of time leaves nothing behind;
年逝覺已催 I find this year ending too quickly in fright.

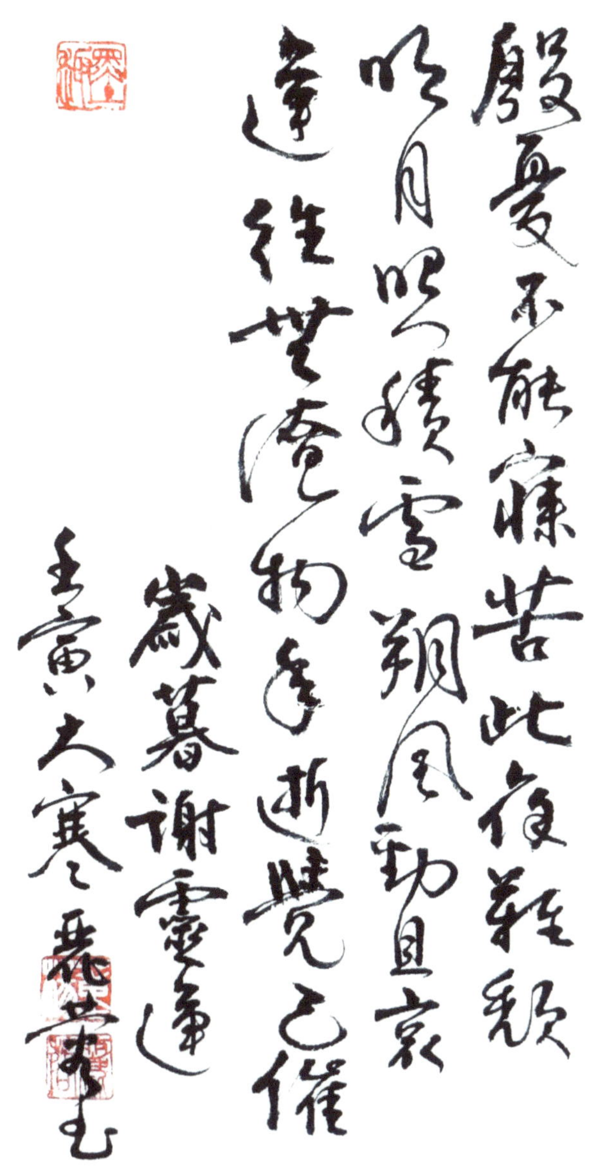

On Lunar New Year's Eve, every Chinese family will have a feast, which will definitely include a fish dish, because the Chinese word for fish sounds the same as the Chinese word for surplus. In the meantime, northern Chinese people customarily eat dumplings, which look similar to ancient Chinese gold nuggets.

在陰曆年除夕，華人家庭年夜飯總會有一道魚，象徵年年有餘。北方人還會吃餃子，稱為元寶。

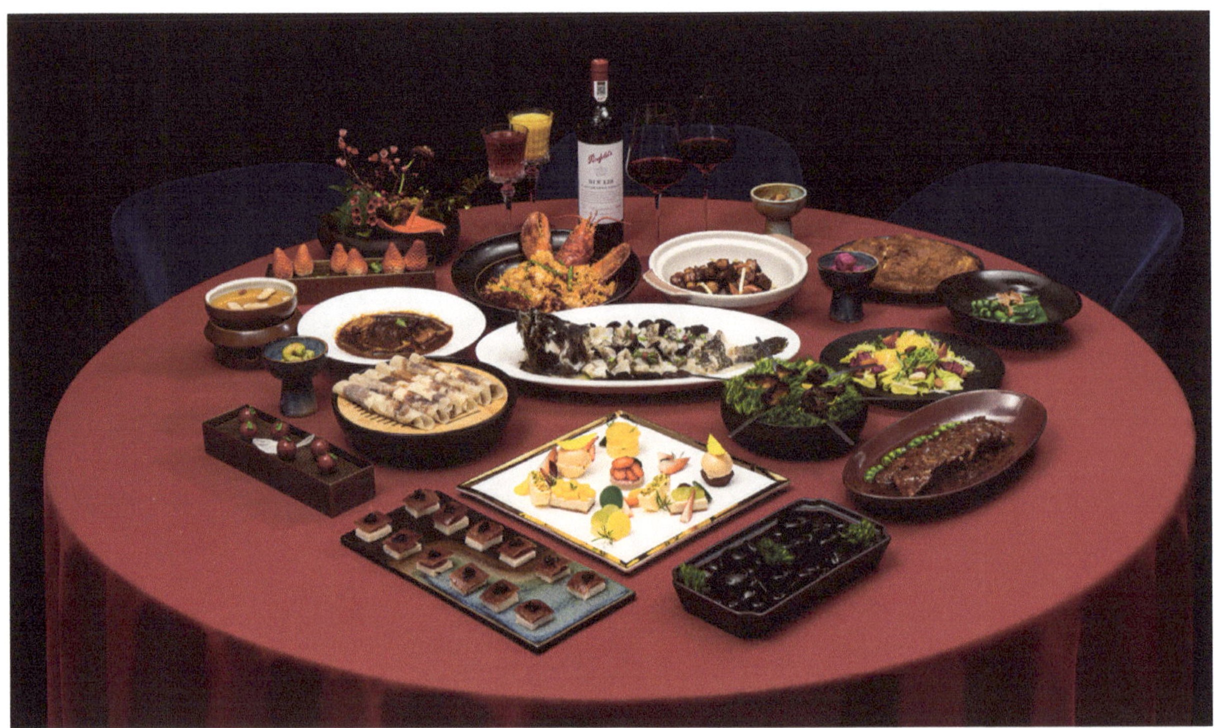

Another must-have is New Year's rice cake, or *niangao* in Chinese, in which the Chinese word for cake, *gao*, sounds exactly the same as the Chinese word for height. In Chinese culture, eating savory or sweet rice cake symbolizes reaching new heights in the new year.

另一樣必備食品是有鹹有甜的年糕，因為糕與高同音，而象徵新年新高度。

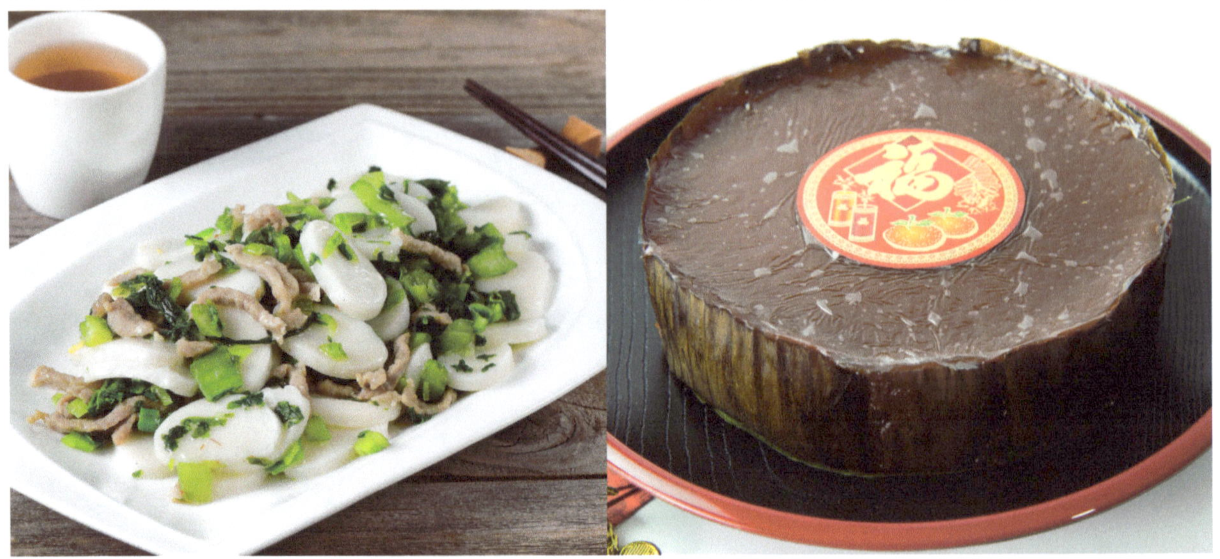

Savory Rice Cake   Sweet Rice Cake

During the Lunar New Year, many living rooms are decorated with potted orchid flowers. Orchids are among the three types of flowers that come into bloom during the solar term with extreme cold. They follow daphne and precede symplocos.

在陰曆新年期間，很多人的客廳都有蘭花盆景點綴。蘭花是大寒時節初開的三種花之中一種。另外兩種是稍早的瑞香和稍晚的山礬。

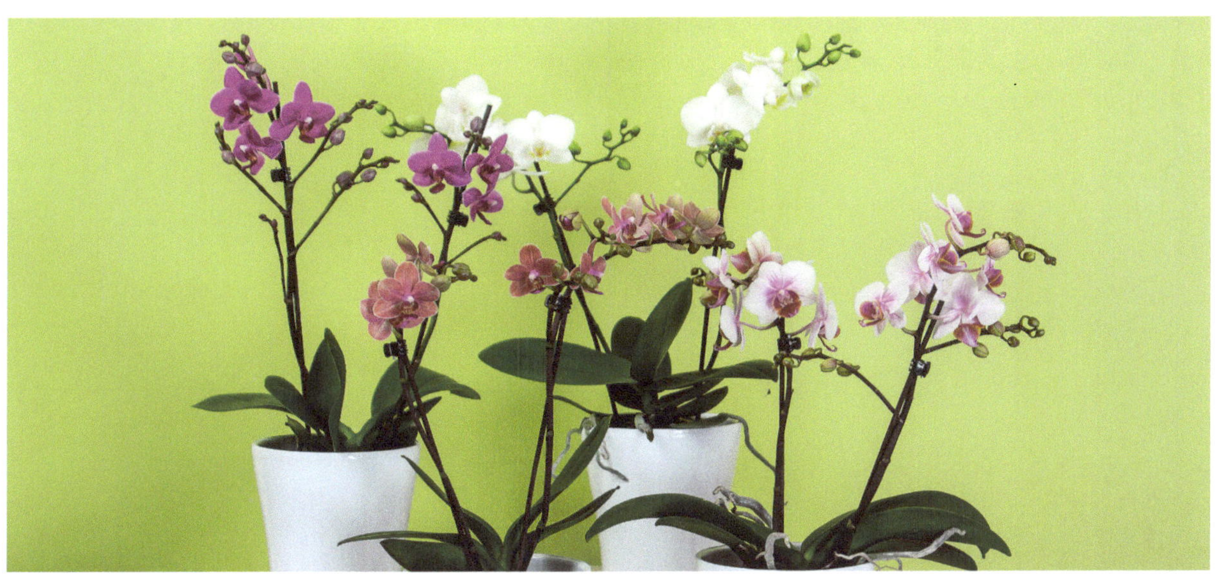

These fragrant flowers seem to agree with a Chinese proverb that goes, "Everything reaching the extreme will turn around." When the weather is extremely cold, it is the lowest point from which the temperature is bound to rise. After the coldest solar term of the year, the first signs of spring will appear. The 24 solar terms form an eternal cycle, summarized in this book, which hopefully will make the reader more aware of nature's beauty and bounty.

這些香花似乎同意一句名言：“物極必反。”當天氣極冷時，氣溫必將從最低點上升。大寒過後，立春必然來臨。二十四節氣是永恒的循環，本書予以簡述，盼望能讓讀者更加體會大自然的豐美與豐盈。

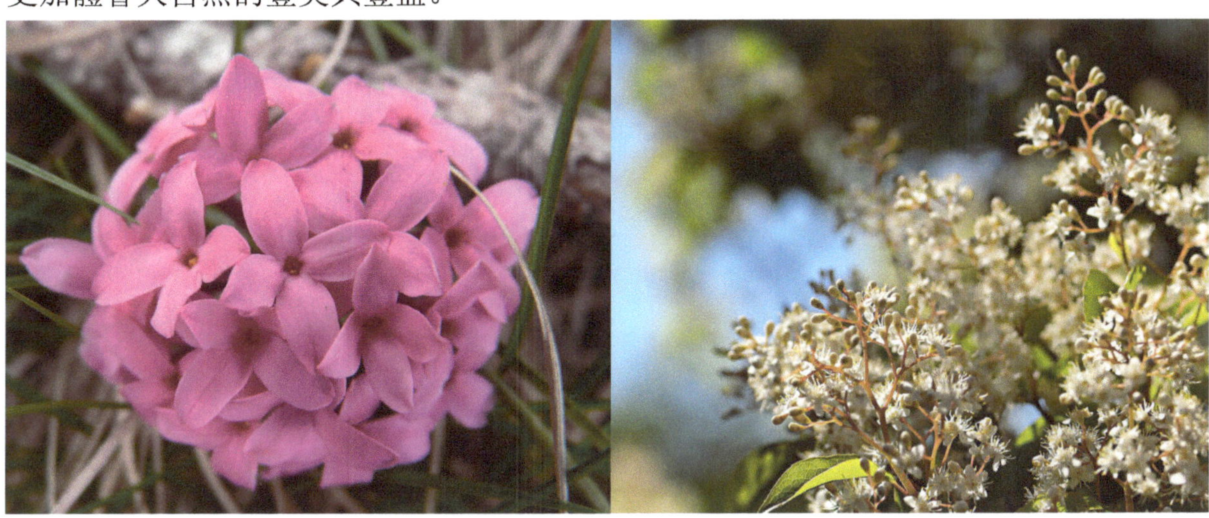

瑞香

Daphne

山礬

Symplocos

This book concludes with a famous quote from an untitled poem written in 1229 by a monk named Huikai:
本書引用南宋僧人慧開在西元 1229 年所寫的一首無題偈詩頭四句為結語：

春有百花秋有月 Spring has hundreds of flowers and autumn makes the moon so clear;
夏有涼風冬有雪 There are cool breezes in summer and splendid snow in winter here.
若無閑事掛心頭 As long as there are no worries about mundane matters,
便是人間好時節 Any time of year is a good time of year.

Happy all year round!
祝福讀者們時時寫意、年年如意！

詩意節氣

大寒

Acknowledgments
銘謝 — 代後記

This book contains artworks by two amazing artists. One of them, my maternal grandfather, did the paintings of spring scenery in Chapters 4 and 5, plus the calligraphy piece about chrysanthemums in Chapter 17. The rest of the calligraphy pieces in the book are contributions from a renowned calligrapher, Ms. Lillian Don.

本書含有兩位優秀藝術家的作品。其中，本書作者的外公有兩幅春景圖在第四章和第五章，一幅詠菊詩書法在第十七章。此外所有書法作品皆來自於書法名家楊麗蓉大師。

Unlike Ms. Don, my granddad Mr. Yu-Ting Chi was not a professional artist. With artistic talent, he studied law. He was the youngest district attorney in Suzhou, a city near Shanghai, after World War II, and a lawyer in Taipei from 1949 to 1986. About eight years later, in the summer of 1994, he sold his house with a gorgeous garden he had designed in Taipei for moving to San Francisco, where he created numerous artworks as a retiree. In 2005, he wrote his memoirs with a Chinese calligraphy brush.

本書作者的外公紀毓鼎先生並不像楊大師是專業藝術家。外公雖有藝術天賦，卻攻讀法律，曾是抗戰勝利後蘇州最年輕的檢察官，從 1949 年到 1986 年則在台北當律師。他退休大約八年後，於 1994 年夏天為了移民美國，而賣掉了曾在台北自行設計美麗花園的舒適住宅，然後在舊金山的退休生涯中寄情書畫。後來，他在 2005 年採用毛筆寫下了回憶錄。

Let me share a photo taken on one of his birthdays (coinciding with the Asian Moon Festival) celebrated in San Francisco, with my grandma, my mom, and me as well as many other family members, plus Granddad's friends.

在此分享一張某一年中秋節外公在舊金山過生日的照片。當天親友歡聚一堂，而外婆、母親，以及彼時尚是少女的本書作者都在外公身邊。

Granddad's autobiography, *Nine Memorable Decades*, is a bilingual book with my English translation, published on his birthday in 2015, regretfully after his passing. It has been accepted into the collections of the Hoover Institution Archives and the East Asian Library of Stanford University for containing first-hand information on crucial events of 20th-century Chinese history.

外公的自傳《九十春秋》很遺憾到他身後才於 2015 年在他的冥誕出版，內容經由本書作者打字、英譯。外公的雙語傳記獲選為胡佛研究院和斯坦福大學東亞圖書館藏書，因為含有二十世紀某些重大歷史事件的第一手資料。

Thanks to Granddad, I have always been interested in traditional Chinese culture despite living in the United States since my teens. I would not have been inspired to do research on the 24 solar terms without reading what Granddad had written about them.

都要感謝外公，少時移居美國的本書作者才一直對傳統中國文化深感興趣。假如沒有在外公的文字之中讀到二十四節氣，本書作者不會想到要研究節氣。

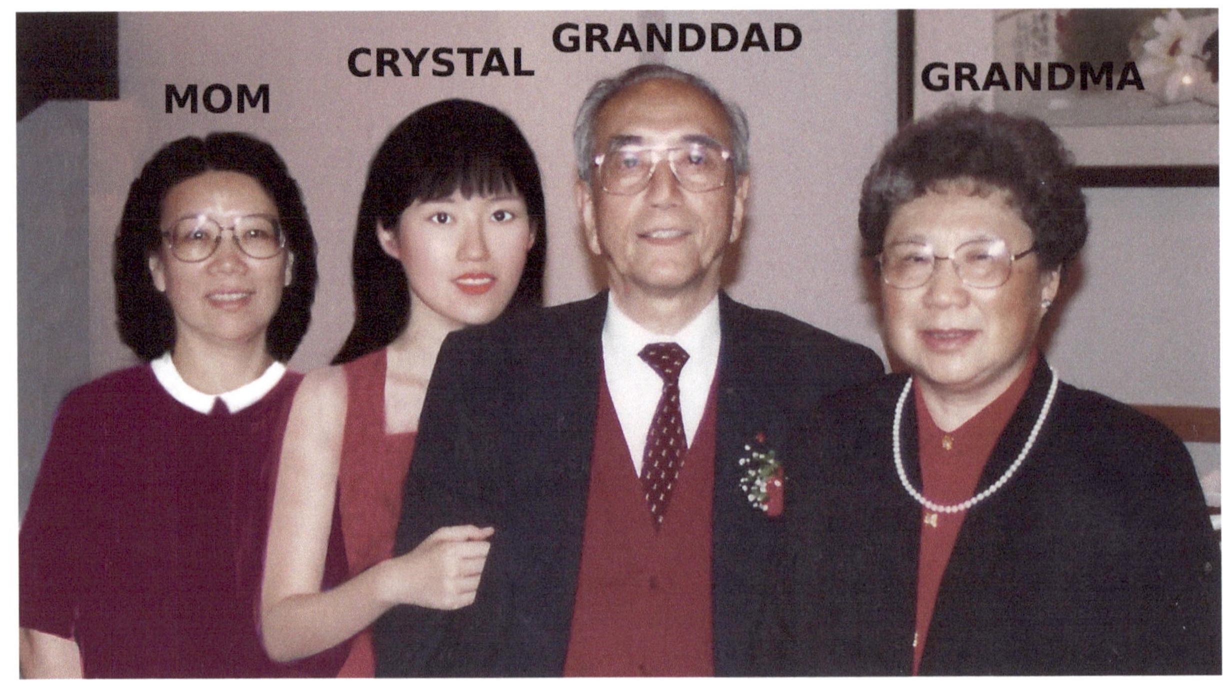

I produced a series of Youtube videos about the 24 solar terms in 2021, but I never thought I could turn a collection of the video scripts into a book, until meeting Ms. Phoenix Huan, US Bureau chief of iCultures Publications. I would like to express my deepest gratitude to Ms. Huan and the graphic designer of this book, Mr. Qi Li.

本書作者曾於 2021 年製作了一系列二十四節氣視頻，但從未想過可將那些視頻旁白結集出書，直到有幸遇見了美國文化橋出版社的美國分社長郇桓，才得以化講稿為書稿。特此對郇分社長以及本書美編李豈先生表達最深的謝意！

Last but not least, many thanks to every reader who is willing to help spread the eco-friendly messages of this book.

最後，也要多謝讀完本書，而從此願意發揚書中環保信息的每一位讀者。

About the Author
本書雙語作者簡介

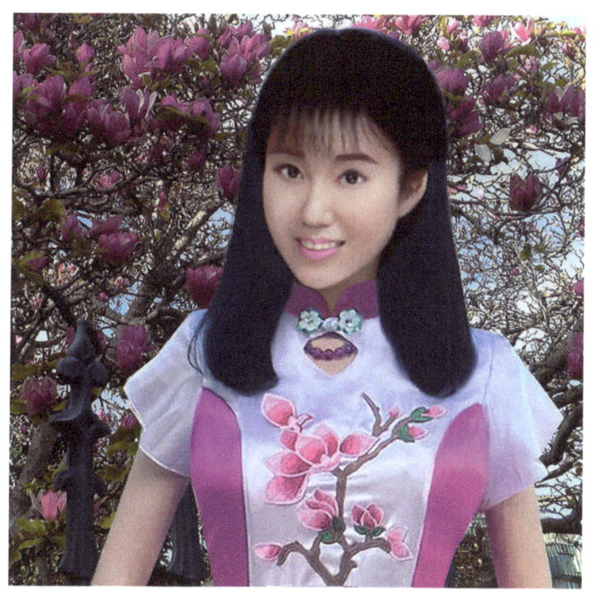

Crystal Tai was born in Taipei in the first Chinese solar term of spring. Her grandparents on both sides were from Jiangsu Province of China. Her parents were raised in Taiwan. Her family moved to San Francisco when she was in her teens. She majored in English literature in college, and later earned a Master's degree in Education Policy with coursework in Journalism from Stanford University in 2007. Since then, she has worked as a local news reporter, a communications specialist in the high tech sector, a community event emcee, a YouTuber (via Crystal Blue Sky), and an interpreter/translator. One of the books she translated, *Beijing: A Symmetrical City*, won two major awards in the United States in 2020. She also translated her own maternal grandfather's memoir book, *Nine Memorable Decades*, which is in the collections of the Hoover Institution.

盧琪綺是立春時節生於台北的外省第三代，祖父祖母是江蘇淮安人，外公外婆是江蘇泰州人。她年少時隨家人移民美國舊金山，大學時代主修英國文學，後來在 2007 年獲得斯坦福大學碩士學位，主修教育行政，副修新聞。畢業後曾任英文媒體地方新聞記者、高科技公司公關，也常應邀擔任社區活動英語或雙語主持人，並為 YouTube 頻道 Crystal Blue Sky 製作影片，亦從事口譯與筆譯。所譯《北京：中軸線上的城市》2020 年贏得美國圖書界兩項大獎。另外，她的外公自傳《九十春秋》經由她英譯，已成為胡佛研究院的藏書。

Even more impressive as a writer than as a translator, Crystal has creatively succeeded in both fiction and non-fiction. Her historical novel, *Marco Polo in Love*, has been selected by the Indie Author Project to get into the collections of public libraries all over California. As for non-fiction, Crystal has authored a few books that introduce traditional Chinese culture to Westerners. One of them is just this book, *Seasonal Living with Splendid Poetry*, the electronic version of which is also available at public libraries all over California.

她在創作方面比在翻譯方面更有成就，無論小說或非小說類文體皆擅長。她描寫馬可波羅愛情故事的英文歷史小說《傾城傾心》獲選為加州所有公立圖書館的電子版藏書。至於非小說類，她著有好幾本介紹傳統中華文化的英文作品。其中之一就是本書《詩意節氣》。本書電子版亦可在加州各大公立圖書館借閱。

Among Crystal's other non-fiction books, *A Poetic Portal to Chinese Culture* has brought her a certificate of commendation from California's Santa Clara County government. *Insights into Suzhou Gardens* unprecedentedly analyzes all the fascinating features Suzhou-style classical gardens have in common. *Yangzhou* portrays a scenic waterfront city with more than 2,500 years of history and superb local cuisine. *Chinese Couplets* is the first-ever book that presents Chinese couplets as an art form with bilateral symmetry.

此外，她的非小說類英文原創作品包括曾獲居住地縣政府頒獎表揚的《中華詩詞文化入門》，還有題材空前創新的《蘇州園林深意》、《揚州》，以及《歷久彌新的對聯藝術》。

About the Calligrapher
為本書古典詩篇揮毫的書法家簡介

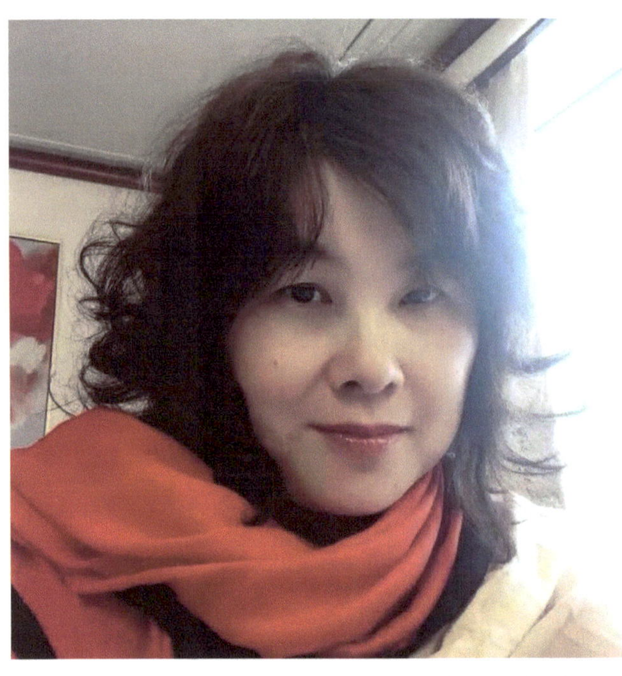

Lillian Don was born in Taiwan. In her childhood, she acquired calligraphy skills from her parents, both excellent calligraphers. Later on, she took lessons from a renowned calligraphy teacher, Jian-Lun Wu. Although she was a finance major in college, she has kept pursuing her artistic interests.

楊麗蓉生於台灣，父母皆精通書法，家學淵源，從小耳濡目染並師從書法名師吳健倫。儘管求學時代主修財經，但在書法藝術方面一直精進。

She immigrated to California after getting married and co-founded FIT Bearings with her husband Yi-Lee Don in 1988. The company for which she worked as vice president gained recognition from the United Nations World Intellectual Property Organization in 2007 as a famous enterprise. Her business experience has brought the artist in her more sophisticated wisdom. Since reducing her workload in 2017, she has been posting calligraphy pieces and Chinese articles on Facebook, attracting countless fans who have searched for her posts. Now she has over 10 million followers on Facebook. She often posts her uniquely insightful comments on current events, to which many readers resonate. She is now an influential Chinese column writer and famous calligrapher on social media. She is also a great singer who often gets invited to perform at community events and receives thunderous applause.

婚後移民美國加州，1988 年與夫君董以禮聯合創辦菲立蒙機電公司，並擔任副總裁。該公司於 2007 年贏得聯合國世界知識產權組織認可為聲譽卓著的企業。職場的歷練讓她藝術家的性格更添加圓融的智慧。自從 2017 年起，在臉書發表書法作品與散文，吸粉無數，成為網路熱搜對象，追蹤她頁面的讀者數已高達一千多萬人。除了致力於發揚光大中國書法藝術與傳統文化以外，她以獨到的視角與深刻的洞察力偶爾評論時事，引起許多讀者共鳴，已成為社群媒體極具影響力的專欄作家以及著名書法家。此外她也擅長歌唱，經常應邀在社區活動即席演唱，深獲好評。

Appendix
In-Depth Knowledge of the 24 Solar Terms
By

William Kao

The 24 solar terms, based on the sun's position in the zodiac, were collectively created by farmers in ancient China to guide the agricultural affairs and farming activities. The 24 solar terms reflect the changes in climate, natural phenomena, agricultural production, and other aspects of human life, including clothing, food, housing, and transportation. The 24 solar terms play important roles and have greatly influenced people's basic needs in life, and they still have an important function nowadays.

The 24 solar terms embody a complete circle of the Earth's revolution around the sun and divide the circle into 24 segments, with each segment being about half a month long. The start date of each solar term is basically fixed with minor differences of within one or two days. Each month has two solar terms.

A solar term (節氣) is any of the 24 periods in traditional Chinese lunisolar calendars that matches a particular astronomical event or signifies some natural phenomena. The transitional points are spaced 15 degrees apart along the ecliptic and are used in the Chinese lunisolar calendar to stay synchronized with the seasons, making them crucial for agrarian societies.

Because the speed of the movement along the ecliptic varies depending on the Earth-sun distance, the number of days it takes between each pair of solar terms changes slightly throughout the year, but it is always between 15 and 16 days. Each solar term is divided into three pentads (候 ;hòu), so there are 72 pentads in a year. Each pentad consists of five, rarely six, days, and are mostly named after phenological (biological or botanical) phenomena corresponding to the pentad.

The Origin of the Solar Terms

As early as the Spring and Autumn Period (770–476 BC), ancient Chinese already established two major solar terms, namely *ri nan zhi* (日南至) and *ri bei zhi* (日北至), indicating the southernmost and northernmost positions of the sun, respectively.

As of the end of the Warring States Period (475–221 BC), eight key solar terms (First Signs of Spring, Vernal Equinox, First Signs of Summer, Summer Solstice, First Signs of Autumn, Autumnal Equinox, First Signs of Winter and Winter Solstice) were established to mark the four seasons, according to the different positions of the sun observed by ancient Chinese astronomers as well as seasonal changes they saw.

The rest of the solar terms were initiated in the Western Han Dynasty (206 BC–24 AD). Hence most of the solar terms are based on the climate of Xi'an, the capital of the Han Dynasty. According to *The Book of Documents*, one of the Five Classics of ancient Chinese literature, the first determined solar term was Dongzhi (Winter Solstice) by Dan, also known as the Duke of Zhou, while he was trying to locate the geological center of the Western Zhou dynasty (1046-771 BC), by measuring the length of the sun's shadow on an ancient type of sundial called tǔguī (土 圭). Then four solar terms were set, which soon evolved into eight solar terms. Eventually, in 104 BC, all the 24 solar terms were officially included in the Taichu calendar. It has become an essential component of the Chinese calendar ever since.

The Significance of the 24 Solar Terms

From the names of the 24 solar terms, we can see that the division of the solar terms has fully incorporated the variations of natural phenomena, especially in relation to climate as well as plant and animal life. Therefore, the 24 solar terms can be divided into three groups.

Group I comprises eight solar terms, all of which reflect seasonal transitions. The solar terms that feature initial signs of spring, summer, autumn, and winter, respectively, are meant to reflect the transition from one season to the next, dividing the year into four seasons, each of which is exactly three months long.

The other four solar terms in Group I are the Vernal Equinox, the Summer Solstice, the Autumnal Equinox, and the Winter Solstice. They represent an astronomical aspect and reflect the turning point of the variation of the altitude of the sun.

Group II reflect the year's weather changes: Transition from Snow to Rain, Clear and Bright View, Rain for Crops, White Dew, Cold Dew, the Appearance of Frost, Light Snow, and Heavy Snow are all about precipitation. They indicate the timing and intensity of rainfall, snowfall, dew, and frost.

In addition, Mild Summer Heat, Fierce Summer Heat, Last Remnant of Summer Heat, Nippy Weather, and Extreme Cold reflect the changes of temperature in different times of year.

Group III embodies natural phenomena: Maturing Crops and Awned Ears of Grain represent the maturity and harvest time of crops, while Awakening of Hibernating Creatures manifests insects' activities that have been observed.

Last but not least, the beginning of every two solar terms either coincides with the start date of a Western zodiac sign or comes very close, generally within two days. That shows a universal aspect of the 24 solar terms, definitely worth of Westerners' attention.

About the Contributor

Dr. William Kao received his BSEE, MSEE and PhD from the University of Illinois Urbana-Champaign. He has worked in the Semiconductor and Electronic Design Automation industries for 30 years holding senior and executive (Director, VP) engineering management positions at Texas Instruments, Xerox Corporation, and Cadence Design Systems. He has authored more than 40 technical papers and holds several software and IC patents.

Dr. Kao currently teaches Renewable Energy and Clean Technology courses at UC Santa Cruz Silicon Valley Extension, and at the Silicon Valley Technical Institute in San Jose. He is also on the Technical Advisory Board for Sigma Quest on the topics of Energy and Environment, and Quality Control, and is a consultant for several Clean Tech companies.

In the nonprofit sector, Dr. Kao is President and Founder of CARES (Chinese American Renewable Energy Society).

Bibliography
參考文獻

Barstone, Tong, and Chou Ping, ed. The Anchor Book of Chinese Poetry: from Ancient o Contemporary, the full 3,000-Year Tradition. New York: Random House, 2005.

Cao, Xueqin. Dream of the Red Chamber (Chinese edition – 紅樓夢）, c 1791. Northwest International Press, 2013.

Chi, Yu-Ting. Nine Memorable Decades (bilingual edition). San Francisco: Createspace Publishing, 2015.

Cheng, Rongjing. Everything about the Taichu Calendar（漢太初曆考）. Shanghai: Shanghai Bookstore publishing, 1994.

Encyclopaedia Britannica. "Ecliptic." https://www.britannica.com/science/equinox-astronomy

Gleason, Carrie. Chinese New Year. New York: Crabtree Publishing Company, 2009.

Hao, Zhixin, ed. The 24 Solar Terms Hidden in the Map (Chinese edition – 藏在地圖裡的二十四節氣）. Beijing: Beijing Books Company, 2019.

O'Connor, Rachael. "Today Marks the First Day of Spring on the Gaelic Calendar." Irish Times, Feb 1, 2021.

Stevenson, TJ, et al. "Disrupted Seasonal Biology Impacts Health, Food Security, and Ecosystems." Proceedings of the Royal Society B. Oct 22, 2015.

Wang, Mingqiang. Traditional Chinese Solar Terms (Chinese edition - 中國傳統二十四節氣）. Nanjing: Phoenix Science & Technology Publishing, 2016.

Wikipedia. "Solar Terms." Wikipedia Foundation. https://en.wikipedia.org/wiki/Solar_term

Yu, Shicun. A Book of Time: Yu Shicun Talking about the 24 Solar Terms (Chinese edition – 時間之書：余世存說二十四節氣）. Beijing: China Friendship Publishing Company, 2016.